LADY CLEMENTINE

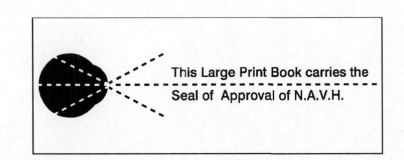

This Large Print Book carries the
Seal of Approval of N.A.V.H.

LADY CLEMENTINE

MARIE BENEDICT

THORNDIKE PRESS
A part of Gale, a Cengage Company

Copyright © 2020 by Marie Benedict.
Thorndike Press, a part of Gale, a Cengage Company.

ALL RIGHTS RESERVED
The characters and events portrayed in this book are fictitious or are used fictitiously. Apart from well-known historical figures, any similarity to real persons, living or dead, is purely coincidental and not intended by the author.
Thorndike Press® Large Print Core
The text of this Large Print edition is unabridged.
Other aspects of the book may vary from the original edition.
Set in 16 pt. Plantin.

LIBRARY OF CONGRESS CIP DATA ON FILE.
CATALOGUING IN PUBLICATION FOR THIS BOOK
IS AVAILABLE FROM THE LIBRARY OF CONGRESS

ISBN-13: 978-1-4328-7277-9 (hardcover alk. paper)

Published in 2019 by arrangement with Sourcebooks, Inc.

Printed in Mexico
Print Number: 01   Print Year: 2020

LADY CLEMENTINE

I

CHAPTER ONE

September 12, 1908
London, England

I always feel different. No matter the sphere I inhabit, I always feel set apart. Even today. Especially today.

The weak, early September sun strains to break through the darkness of the cold morning. The pallid rays illuminate the cavernous bedroom assigned to me by my benefactress, Lady St. Helier. They hit the white satin dress hanging on the mannequin, reminding me that the gown waits for me.

As I finger the delicately embroidered, square-cut bodice, its sleek Venetian fabric finer than any I've ever worn, I am seized by a sensation fiercer than the usual isolation that often besets me. I crave connection.

I hunt for the clothes the maids unpacked from my trunk and placed into the dresser drawers and mirrored armoire when I arrived at 52 Portland Place a fortnight ago. But I find nothing other than the corset and undergarments meant to be worn under the white gown today. Only then do I realize that the maids must have packed my belongings back into my trunk for my journey afterward. The mere thought of afterward sends a shiver through me.

Tying my gray silk dressing gown tightly around my waist, I tiptoe down the grand staircase of Lady St. Helier's mansion. At first, I don't know precisely what I am seeking, but I have an epiphany when I spot a housemaid working in the parlor. She's kneeling before the fireplace grate.

The sound of my footfalls startles the poor girl, and she jumps. "Morning, Miss Hozier. May I help you with anythin'?" she says, wiping her blackened fingers on the cloth dangling from her apron.

I hesitate. Will I endanger the girl if I enlist her help? Surely Lady St. Helier will forgive any protocol breach I cause today.

"As a matter of fact, I could use your assistance. If it is not too much trouble, that is." The apology is heavy in my voice.

After I explain my predicament to the girl, whose age must match my own, she races away down the back hallway toward the kitchen. At first, I think she may have misunderstood my request or thought me mad. But I follow her, and when she scurries across the rough wooden kitchen floor toward the servants' staircase, I understand.

Wincing at the loud clatter of her work boots stomping up the stairway and down the hallway of the attic where the servants' bedrooms are, I wait. I silently pray that her racket does not rouse the rest of the staff. I fear that if they appear for their morning chores and find me in the kitchen, one of them will alert Lady St. Helier. When the girl returns with a bundle in hand — without any additional servants in tow — I sigh in relief.

"What is your name?" I ask, reaching for the bundle.

"Mary, miss," she answers with a minuscule curtsy.

"I shall be forever in your debt, Mary."

"It's my pleasure, Miss Hozier." She gives me a conspiratorial smile, and I realize that she is enjoying her part in this unorthodox plan. It may be the only deviation in the sameness of her days.

As I pivot and walk back toward the grand staircase, Mary whispers, "Why don't you change in the pantry, miss? Less chance of being found out than if you head back up them stairs. I'll make sure your clothes are returned to your bedroom before anyone notices them."

The girl is right. Every step I take up that creaky grand staircase is one step closer to waking the lady of the house and her servants. Taking her advice, I enter the jar-lined pantry and close the door only partially to ensure some light will reach the enclosed space. I let my dressing gown and robe slide down and puddle on the floor, and I unwrap the bundle. Pulling out a surprisingly sweet floral dress, I shimmy into its floor-grazing cotton and then lace up the black boots Mary thoughtfully included.

"Fits you right well, Miss Hozier," the girl says when I step back into the kitchen. As she hands me her coat off the peg on the wall, she says, "Godspeed to you."

I hurry out the servants' door at the rear of the house and make my way down an alleyway that runs behind the row of luxurious Georgian homes lining Portland Place. I pass by kitchen windows beginning to glow with lamps lit by servants readying the house for their masters. A bustling world lies behind the mansions of Lady St. Helier and her friends, but because I always enter through the front doors, I've never witnessed the province at the back.

The alley lets out onto Weymouth Street, where a motor bus stops. It's heading west to Kensington, and I know the route fairly well as I've taken it the other direction toward Lady St. Helier's on several occasions. Mary's wool coat is too thin for the brisk morning, and as I wait for the bus, I wrap it tightly around me in the vain hope of extracting a bit more warmth from its meager fibers. I wonder how Mary makes it through the winter in such a coat.

The unadorned hat that Mary leant me bears only a small brim, and consequently, the working girl disguise does nothing to mask my face. When I step onto the bus, the driver recognizes me from the photographs that have run in the newspapers in recent days. He stares at me but says nothing at first. Finally, he sputters, "Surely you're in the wrong place, Miss" — he drops his voice to a whisper, realizing that he shouldn't reveal my identity — "Hozier."

"I am precisely where I mean to be, sir," I answer in a tone that I hope is kind yet firm. His eyes never leave my face as he takes the fare Mary had given me from her savings — which I plan to replace multifold — but he doesn't say another word.

I keep my gaze lowered to shield my face from the curious onlookers who have been

13

alerted to the oddness of my presence by the driver's reaction. I hop off the bus the moment it nears Abingdon Villas, and I feel lighter the closer I come to the cream-colored stucco house bearing the number 51. By the time I reach up to lift the heavy brass knocker, the tightness in my chest begins to loosen, and I breathe with ease. No one answers the door immediately, but I am not surprised. Here, no bevy of servants lies in wait in the kitchen, ever ready to answer the knock of a front door or the ring of a master's bell. Here, one servant does the work of many, and the household inhabitants do the rest.

I wait, and after several long minutes, my patience is rewarded with an open door. The face of my beloved sister Nellie, still creased with sleep, appears. She rushes in for an embrace before the shock of seeing me registers and she freezes.

"What on earth are you doing here, Clementine? And in *those* clothes?" she asks. Her expression is quizzical. "Today is your wedding day."

CHAPTER TWO

The comforting smell of steeping tea rises to my nostrils, and I allow the steam to warm my face and hands. Nellie has not pressed me to answer her question, not yet. I know she will soon insist on an explanation for my unexpected visit, but for now, I indulge in the temporary quiet of the parlor. These silent moments alone with my sister, here at home, may be enough to carry me through the day.

"You are not thinking of calling off the wedding, Clemmie?" Nellie interrupts the silence with a tremulous whisper. Neither of us wishes to waken a single member of the sleeping household — least of all Mother.

"No, no, Nellie," I whisper back, reaching for her hand. My knuckles brush across the table where my sister and I used to spend

15

hours doing needlework for our cousin Lena Whyte's dressmaking business, a necessity to help with household expenses.

Relief softens her features. I hadn't realized how fearful the very idea that I might cancel *this* wedding made her. It had been cruel of me not to justify my appearance from the beginning. "Nothing like that, dearest. I simply needed the familiarity of home for a moment. To calm my nerves, as it were."

"Nerves over what? The wedding ceremony itself? Or the man you are marrying?" Nellie, my little sister and the twin to my only brother, surprises me with her astuteness. For too long, I'd considered her youthful and inexperienced, not at all the confidante that my indomitable elder sister Kitty would have been had she lived beyond sixteen, had my beautiful, fearless sister not succumbed to typhoid. I should not have underestimated Nellie.

Her question awakens a memory of the first time I met my intended. It was an evening at Lady St. Helier's mansion, the very place from which I'd just fled. I had initially resisted my benefactress's invitation to dinner on that cool March night. My suitable gowns were in need of mending, and I had no clean white gloves, I'd lamented to Mother. In truth, my long afternoon tutoring French had exhausted me, but I didn't dare speak plainly, as Mother loathed any reminder that we girls needed to contribute to the household upkeep. She preferred to believe her title and aristocratic heritage would magically provide funds for housing, food, and servants, a strange contradiction with her decidedly bohemian views on the malleability of the marital vow and her clear focus on her extramarital relationships and little else, certainly not us children. She would brook no excuse to turn down an invitation by my generous, wealthy patroness, who was Mother's aunt and adored helping the young make their way into proper society. So Mother loaned me her own gloves and Nellie's simple white satin princess dress, and off I dutifully went, if a bit past schedule.

But late as I was, the dinner guest to my right still had not materialized by the time the staff served the second of five courses. I'd begun to despair of any conversation other than the boring weather reports recounted by the elderly gentleman to my left when the dining room door swung open with a slam. Before the butler could announce the tardy guest, a round-faced man with a sheepish half grin marched in, offering his apologies to Lady St. Helier before settling into the ornately carved chair next to me. As the chair's feet scraped loudly against the wooden floor, drowning out the butler's announcement of his name, my attention was drawn to the man. His cheeks had the softness of boyhood, but on his forehead, I saw the deep grooves of adult worries.

Who was this gentleman? He looked familiar, although I could not place his face. Had I met him at another social occasion? There had been so many.

"Miss, I regret any inconvenience my delinquency caused you. An empty seat at a formal dinner is no easy matter. Please excuse me," he said, meeting my gaze with unsettling directness.

Unaccustomed as I was to such candor, my surprise precipitated a blunt response. "It is no inconvenience at all, sir. I arrived only moments before you, my work having delayed my own arrival." I immediately regretted my words, as girls of my class were not meant to have employment.

He looked startled. "You have a position?"

"Yes," I answered, a bit on the defensive. "I am an instructor of French." I didn't dare mention the income-generating needlework that Nellie and I also undertook.

His eyes shimmered with enthusiasm. "That . . . that is wondrous, miss. To know something of work and the world is invaluable."

Did he mean it? Or was this a bit of mockery? I didn't know how to respond, so I decided to thread the needle with an innocuous response.

"If you say so, sir."

"I do indeed. It is refreshing. And your regular immersion in French and its culture, ah . . . of that, I am jealous. I have always held a healthy appreciation for the cultural and political contributions France has made to Europe."

He seemed in earnest, and his views matched my own. I took a chance and responded in kind. "I agree wholeheartedly, sir. I even considered studying French, its culture, and its politics at university. In fact, my headmistress encouraged me to do so."

"Indeed?" Again, he seemed surprised, and I wondered if I'd been too honest about my youthful ambitions. I did not know this man or his views.

I softened my aspirations with gentle humor. "Yes. Although, in the end, I had to settle for a winter in Paris, where I attended lectures at the Sorbonne, visited art galleries, and dined with the artist Camille Pissarro."

"No small solace," he offered with a smile, his eyes lingering on mine. Did I imagine a glimmer of respect in his light-blue eyes? In the low candlelight, their color shifted from pale aquamarine to the color of the dawn sky.

We grew quiet for a moment, and it seemed as though the rest of the guests — an illustrious mix of political figures, journalists, and the odd American heiress — had reached a lull in their conversations as well. Or perhaps they had been listening quietly to us all along. I realized that I'd been so engrossed in discussion with my tablemate that I'd quite forgotten the other diners.

The gentleman stammered for a moment, and to avoid embarrassment, I returned to the chicken on my plate, now grown quite cold. I felt his eyes on me but didn't turn. Our exchange had been unusually personal for a first meeting, and I didn't know what to say next.

"Please forgive me, miss." His words were unexpected.

"For what, sir?"

"For my unforgivable lapse in manners."

"I do not know what you mean."

"A woman like yourself deserves every courtesy. I realize now that I have not offered even the bare minimum — an introduction beyond the butler's announcement. This is particularly inexcusable given that I arrived too late for the usual formalities. Will you allow me to introduce myself?"

I gave him a small nod, wondering what he meant by "a woman like yourself." What sort of woman did he think I was?

"My name is Winston Churchill."

Ah, I thought with a start. The familiarity of his appearance was explained. While I believed I'd met him in passing several years earlier, I knew his face not from that earlier social occasion but from the newspapers. The gentleman sitting next to me was a prominent member of Parliament and rumored to soon become the next president of the Board of Trade, which would make him one of the most important members of the government. His rise through the leadership ranks had been riddled with controversy, as he'd changed parties from Conservative to Liberal a few years before, favoring free trade and a more active government with legislation protecting the welfare of its citizens. This led to constant coverage in the dailies, including a lengthy interview in the *Daily Chronicle* by the *Dracula* author,

Bram Stoker, a few months ago.

If I recalled correctly, some years before, this Mr. Churchill had actually voted in favor of the female suffrage bill, an issue quite dear to me. During my school years at Berkhamsted School for Girls, my headmistress, Beatrice Harris, had instilled in me a taste for female independence. Her lectures on suffragism had fallen upon keen ears, because, having grown up with a mother who professed nonconformist beliefs but actually relied upon her aristocratic status and many liaisons for sustenance, I wanted to pursue a path of purpose and, if possible, independence. And now, sitting before me was one of the few politicians who had publicly backed an early effort for the women's vote. I suddenly felt quite nervous but exhilarated at the same time.

The rest of the table had grown quiet, but my dinner partner didn't seem to notice, because he cleared his throat loudly and continued. "I hope the mere name Winston Churchill doesn't scare you off. I'm quite the pariah these days in most households."

A fierce heat spread across my usually pale cheeks, not from his words but from my worry that my ignorance of his identity might have led me into some kind of gaffe. *Had I said anything inappropriate?* I wondered as I quickly reviewed our exchange. I did not think so. If Kitty had been in my place, she would have managed this interaction with aplomb and humor instead of with my awkward pauses and nerves.

I settled upon a response. "No, sir, not at all. I find your views quite in line with my own, and I am delighted to make your acquaintance."

"Not delighted enough to share your name, it seems."

My cheeks flamed even hotter. "I am Miss Clementine Hozier."

"It is *my* pleasure, Miss Hozier."

I smile at the memory now. Before I can answer Nellie, her twin, Bill, bounds into the room. Bill is my younger brother and still schoolboy gangly despite his position as an officer in the Royal Navy. He is midbite into an enormous apple that promptly drops to the floor when he sees me. "What in the devil are you doing here? Not skipping out on another commitment, I hope?"

Leaping to my feet, I jab his arm for the reference to my not one but two jilted fiancés — Sidney Cornwallis Peel, grandson of the former prime minister Sir Robert Peel, and Lionel Earle, men with lofty titles or positions and the promise of financial security but with whom I foresaw a life of staid decorum and scant hope of purpose. While I eschew the unconventional life led by my mother, I found that I could not commit to either of these fine gentlemen solely for the sake of propriety when I longed for a life of meaning and — dare I think it — emotion, even though decorousness was a powerful lure.

Nellie, Bill, and I burst into laughter, and I feel impossibly light. The heavy sense of isolation I felt in the long hours before dawn fades away, and in the presence of my siblings, the aisle-long march to my new life no longer seems an insurmountable journey. Until Mother walks into the room.

For the first time in memory, Mother is speechless. No judgmental lectures on her pet topics, no public redressing for perceived slights, no under-the-breath yet audible remarks about bourgeois acquaintances. And most incredibly, it is me — the least favored and often ignored of her children — who has rendered mute the outspoken Lady Blanche Hozier.

Nellie, the favorite, leaps in to defend me. "Clemmie is here only for tea and a quick visit, Mama."

Mother rises up to her full height and finds her voice. In a shrill, mocking tone, she says, "A visit? At dawn? On the morning of her wedding?"

No one answers. Such questions are not meant to be answered.

With her blond hair in disheveled strands around her still-beautiful face, she stares at each of us in turn, making yet another criticism dressed up as a rhetorical question. "Can any of you think of anything *less* appropriate?"

I almost snort with laughter at our bohemian mother, never one to follow the strictures of society, church, or family, doubting the *appropriateness* of her children's behavior. She, whose own behavior has long flouted the traditions of marriage and child-rearing through multiple simultaneous affairs and long absences. And we, who cling to convention as a life raft in the sea of our mother's tempestuousness.

Glancing at Nellie and Bill, I recognize the cowed expressions beginning to form on their faces, and I remind myself what today means. For me, for our family. Instead of submitting to Mother's irritation and hoping a remorseful look will dissipate her foul humor, I assemble my own features into an air of amusement. Today, I will assume a powerful mantle, and this is my first effort at making plain that the balance has shifted.

"Surely you don't begrudge your daughter a brief trip across town to see her family on the morning of her wedding, Mama?" I ask with a smile. I'm trying to sound like Grandmother, also called Lady Blanche, who, as a Stanley of Alderley inhabiting Airlie Castle, embodies all the strong and assertive qualities the Stanley matriarchs are known for, including female education. Not that Mother follows suit in her own beliefs; she is unorthodox in every view except on the subject of female education. I cannot understand it, but I suppose it's that Mother's focus lies on her relationships with men, most of whom find female education distasteful.

Mother doesn't answer at first, unused to being challenged. Finally, she speaks, in a forced and deliberate manner. "Of course not, Clementine. But I will arrange for a brougham to pick you up and take you back to prepare at Lady St. Helier's within the hour. After all, there will be over a thousand people watching you arrive at St. Margaret's church to walk down the aisle."

CHAPTER THREE

September 12, 1908
London, England

An hour passes on the mantelpiece clock, and I am still submitting to the ministrations of Lady St. Helier's personal maid. As she tends to my hair, coaxing its heavy chestnut strands into an elaborate pompadour, I examine my face in the mirror. My almond-shaped eyes and profile, often described by others as Roman or well chiseled, whatever that means, appear the same as they do every day. Yet this day is unlike any other.

I watch the minutes tick by on the clock, almost incredulous that most women of my acquaintance spend a significant portion of their days in some version of this process. They waste hours while their maids assist them in changing from one outfit into another, from one coiffure to another, as they move from one social occasion to the next. Mother's peripatetic, often penurious, lifestyle meant that I'd performed all the maids' chores myself on those instances when I was invited to an event requiring intricate updos and formal attire, but more often than not, I wore a simple tie-and-shirt-collar blouson, a skirt, and a basic hairstyle. I know now that even if my future life as Mrs. Winston Churchill allows for an abundance of personal maids, I do not want my time spent in this frivolous manner.

A glint of sunlight reflects off the large ruby at the center of my engagement ring. I wiggle my fingers, making the light catch and dance on the facets of the ruby and the diamonds that flank it, and recollect Winston's proposal. In the mirror, I see a smile curving on my lips at the memory.

By midsummer, the invitations to visit Winston at Blenheim Palace, one of England's largest houses and the only nonroyal home to have the designation of palace, began pouring into our home in Abingdon Villas. Blenheim was owned by Winston's cousin and close friend, the Duke of Marlborough, who went by the name "Sunny" after one of his titles, the Earl of Sunderland, and Winston was spending part of the summer there. I demurred at first, not out of reluctance to see him but out of despair that I did not own the proper gowns required for such a grand occasion.

His invitations continued until I could not refuse without rebuffing the man to whom I'd grown unexpectedly attached. Letters and visits with Winston over the preceding four months had revealed him to be wonderful company, not at all the brusque pundit that the newspapers labeled him. In the long missives he penned to me during a trip undertaken with my mother to Germany to fetch Nellie back from a tuberculosis cure, he brimmed with the sort of enthusiasm and idealism that I, too, had about politics, history, and culture. In his company, I felt drawn into the thick of things, as if I was becoming an essential cog in the core of England.

I felt another kinship with him as well, a sense of aloneness in the world. We had both been raised by unconventional, unaffectionate mothers: mine, who'd entered into an unhappy union with Colonel Henry Hozier before engaging in perhaps happier affairs with several men who fathered her four children before their divorce, leaving the caretaking of us to servants; and his, the exquisite American-born heiress Lady Randolph Churchill, née Jennie Jerome, whose number of affairs rivaled that of Mother and who'd left the raising of Winston and his younger brother to their beloved Nanny Everest. Our fathers, if indeed my mother's former husband could be called my father, given his uncertain parentage and our very few encounters in the years after the divorce, played even lesser roles than our mothers; it seems that Lord Randolph, in particular, actively disliked his elder son and, during their limited time together, would spend it critiquing him. Winston and I had been left in an uncertain state about our place in society and in relationships. But, to our delight and surprise, that sensation disappeared when we were together.

My nervousness about visiting Blenheim grew as my train passed through the verdant countryside with its undulating hills and approached the palace, long rumored to be one of the most luxurious outside of those estates owned by the royal family. What would I face at the great house? Winston had given me no details about the weekend plans, other than to mention that his cousin would be present, although not his wife, Consuelo, as they were divorcing, as would his mother, Lady Randolph, who, Mother had reminded me, I had met briefly on several social occasions. I was excited to see

Winston but uncertain about the rest of his party.

A brougham retrieved me from the station, and after we'd traveled a fair distance, the driver called back to me, "We'll be passin' through Ditchley Gate in a moment, miss."

Glancing out of the window, I noticed an ornate wrought-iron gate, flanked by an enormous stone gateway, looming before us. When a gatekeeper emerged from a lodge to open this imposing entryway, I glimpsed a long drive, bordered by rows of lime trees, traversing a vast plateau. *Surely, I thought, this must be the drive to the palace.* Yet as we set out, we continued over a bridge that crossed a meandering lake and passed several other large buildings, none of which seemed to be our destination. *When will we reach Blenheim Palace?* I wondered. My nerves were stretched near to snapping.

The driver called back again. "We'll be at the central gate in a jiffy, miss."

Ah, I thought, *thank goodness. We are very nearly there.* I straightened my skirt and patted my hair and hat to ensure that everything was in its place. The drive surface changed, and I welcomed the crunch of the wheels on the stones as a signal that we'd finally reached the palace. The brougham passed through a small archway carved into a limestone wall, and as the carriage lurched forward to a stop, I readied myself.

When I finally descended from the brougham, I stepped out onto a great court that faced the grandest house I'd ever encountered. A wide, pillared portico stood at the center, lined with statues and carvings of warlike figures, and two vast wings stretched out in my direction from either side. From nowhere, four servants appeared and rushed toward me, taking my bags and guiding me up the stairs to the imposing front doors of Blenheim.

I climbed the steep steps, my heart racing both from the effort and the anticipation, and the doors to the great hall magically opened as I approached. As soon as I stepped inside, I saw that Winston stood in a row of friends and family — or at least I presumed they were friends and family, as Lady Randolph stood comfortably among them — under the enormous archway at the far reaches of the seemingly endless hall, all waiting to greet me. The only family members missing were Winston's beloved brother, Jack, and his new wife, Lady Gwendeline Bertie, affectionately known as Goonie, who had recently married and were away on their honeymoon. What on earth did Winston have planned?

My heels clattered across the vast expanse of black and white marble tiles as I began to walk toward my hosts. I winced as the sound echoed under the sixty-foot, fresco-adorned ceiling and around the massive pillars supporting the round-topped archways lining the hall. Winston's broad smile never faltered, and my gaze locked upon his beaming face instead of the intimidating artwork and sculptures and ancient weaponry I passed, all part of Winston's family history.

He stepped up and placed a firm, calming hand on mine as he made the introductions to those I did not know, his cousin Sunny, his close personal and political friend F. E. Smith and his wife, and a secretary from the Board of Trade among them. Then he insisted that I retire to my room to get ready for dinner, with two of his mother's maids in tow. My cheeks flushed as I realized that someone in his group must have recognized that I didn't have a maid of my own and rushed to address my gaffe.

As the maids unpacked my bags, I sauntered around the impossibly high-ceilinged bedroom suite complete with a japanned four-poster bed, astonished to find a fire roaring in the fireplace despite the warm

August weather, an unnecessary indulgence. In mere moments, the maids descended upon me with brushes, combs, and pins ready to create a fashionable confection out of my simple chignon. Perhaps they concentrated their efforts on my hair when they realized precious little could be done about my limited wardrobe.

From the moment I crossed the threshold into the gold-adorned state dining room, past the long murals and tapestries celebrating the Marlborough military accomplishments and family portraits by such luminaries as Sir Joshua Reynolds, John Singer Sargent, and Thomas Gainsborough, I could not summon the poised, talkative young woman I'd been with Winston these past few months. I felt like a fraud in his world. I felt intimidated by the pervasive reminders of the Churchills' historical importance and the comfortable banter between Winston, his mother, and Sunny, and I allowed myself to retreat into the background. It was an old habit from the days when Kitty was still alive and I'd watch from the shadows as my beautiful sister held a room captive with her wit and charm.

As the women and men parted ways after the meal, Winston approached me. I worried that he'd express concern, even disappointment, about my quiet throughout the meal, but instead he begged my pardon. "My dear Clementine, can you forgive me for monopolizing the dinner conversation? I talked so much with Mother and Sunny, you could not have gotten a word in edgewise."

I tried to recall the exact nature of their extended discussion, as I'd been somewhat distracted by the furnishings and frescoes of the dining room. The talk had focused on the impending meeting between King Edward and Kaiser Wilhelm about the increasing size of Germany's navy, and I hunted around for an appropriate comment. "Please, Winston, there is absolutely no need for apologies. I was intrigued by your remarks about naval expansion and Germany's efforts to rival England as a maritime force. I quite agree that our country must maintain its dominance and not allow Germany to challenge us."

A broad smile engulfed his full face. "That's one of the things I love about you, Clementine. Unlike most young women whose eyes would be glazing over at such talk, you listen, understand, and engage with the important issues of our day. Your intellect is very appealing. As is the nobility of your thoughts."

While I understood and appreciated that he'd just given me several compliments, my thoughts fixed upon one word. *Love.* Had he just said *love?* Neither of us had ever used that word before. I did not — could not — answer, except to nod and look at him through eyes downcast.

"I say," he said in his version of a whisper, which wasn't altogether quiet, "let's you and I take a walk through the Blenheim rose gardens tomorrow morning to see if you think they justify their reputation. I can also promise vistas of the lake."

"I'd like that," I answered.

"Wonderful," he said, reaching out to caress my hand gently. "Shall we say ten o'clock in the breakfast room?"

I nodded my assent, and we bid each other good evening. My steps felt light and my mood a bit giddy as I joined Lady Randolph and Mrs. Smith for dessert, hoping to rectify the lackluster impression I'd made on them earlier.

The next morning, ten o'clock came and went, and eleven was fast approaching without an appearance by Winston or any-one else, for that matter. Where on earth was he? Hadn't we agreed to tour the rose gardens by this time? I had already partaken of the lavish food on offer, selecting poached eggs, late summer strawberries and cream, and strong tea, and was standing before the row of windows, peering out over Blenheim's manicured gardens, when someone finally entered the breakfast room.

Turning at the sound of footsteps, I expected to see a sheepish Winston. Instead, a shocked Sunny stood in the archway of the breakfast room, and his expression told me all I needed to know about Winston's whereabouts, as he'd already confessed to me his habit of working until the first light of dawn and then resting until late morning. Winston was still sleeping. I was furious at him for placing me in this awkward position. I started walking out of the room without a word, never mind that I stood before the Duke of Marlborough.

"Miss Hozier, I've been sent to invite you for a drive around the estate," Sunny called out, covering for his dear friend and cousin. "Winston has been unavoidably detained. Work, you know." My face must have registered my disbelief, but Sunny plowed ahead. "He was hoping you could meet him at one o'clock instead. He should be finished with his work by then, and it's a better time to view the roses in any event."

The gulf between how I wanted to react and how I should react widened. Although

I felt humiliated, I was a guest of the esteemed man standing before me, and I cared deeply for the one still asleep. I decided to answer cordially but to make my expectations clear. "That would be lovely. But may I presume that I will see Winston in the great hall *precisely* at one?"

Sunny stared me directly in the eyes in a look that seemed like appreciation. With an emphatic nod, he said, "I can promise you that."

When I descended the grand marble staircase adjacent to the great hall at one minute past one o'clock, Winston was waiting, his face bearing that sheepish expression I'd anticipated hours before. As I approached him, I summoned up my full five feet seven inches, making me the slightest bit taller than Winston. I wanted him to understand that I expected respect and consideration from him.

He clasped my hands in his, saying, "I feel I am always apologizing to you."

"Occasionally, you do so when there is no need," I answered, wanting him to understand with my emphasis on *occasionally* that this was *not* one of those times.

"Yet my behavior requires that I make amends," he half announced, half asked.

"Yes," I said, pausing to let him await my

verdict. "But I forgive you."

His sigh of relief was audible. "Shall we venture out to the gardens?"

I smiled to indicate the incident was behind us, and we walked to the rear of the palace and exited through a nondescript door leading to a rolling hill. My hand in the crook of his arm, we stepped out into the golden light of the summer afternoon. As we strolled down its expanse toward a well-delineated path, Winston shared a bit about the creation of the Blenheim Palace and its grounds, which were given by Queen Anne to the First Duke of Marlborough in 1704 for leading the English victory over the French.

"Family lore has it that, at the invitation of the Fourth Duke of Marlborough, the landscape architect Capability Brown signed on to the job of fashioning the park at Blenheim in 1763, fully expecting the project to last only a couple of years. He stayed for ten."

"Capability? What a name."

"Poor chap. His actual name was Lancelot, although I can't figure why choosing to be called Capability was any better."

I laughed, a hearty outburst that Nellie and Bill often told me was a guffaw. Mother loathed my laugh and often cautioned me to stifle it in public. But Winston laughed along with me, and I sensed that he actually enjoyed my rather indelicate roar.

He continued. "By the time poor Capability had finished" — we start giggling again at the reference to Capability, and once he gains his composure, Winston continues — "he'd planted thousands of trees, making a veritable forest that seems perfectly natural but is actually an artful contrivance. With clever use of dams, he also constructed the Great Lake that you can see to your right and the Grand Cascade, one of the most exquisite waterfalls I've ever seen. We must explore that another day."

"That would be marvelous. The grounds are breathtaking, Winston," I said with a squeeze of his arm. "And they are in remarkable shape given that they were created in the 1700s."

"Well," he said, clearing his throat, "you can credit Sunny with the restoration of the Blenheim grounds. They were in sorry shape until he got his hands upon them."

With Consuelo's money, I thought to myself. I'd heard rumors, of course, about the unraveling of Sunny's marriage to the American heiress Consuelo Vanderbilt, who'd married Sunny in 1895 at the insistence of her mother. Neither had particularly cared for the other, and by 1906, the demise of their bond was inevitable. But while the newspapers published catty reports about their separation, Sunny seemed an affable fellow to me, and Winston simply adored him.

We ambled down the path in comfortable silence. Winston pointed out an area of the lake where he'd caught his first fish with his beloved Nanny Everest helping him. Although Blenheim belonged to Sunny, not Winston, his attachment to the property was unmistakable. His personal history was intertwined with the estate. He had been born in the house, after all.

No house held such hold on me. From time to time, an aspect of one house or another might remind me of one of our London rentals or the townhouse in Dieppe we inhabited for nearly a year. But these were houses, not homes, temporary residences to be discarded when Mother wanted to sojourn. Or when a new relationship required a change of scenery.

A shock of fuchsia and crimson appeared as we rounded a bend in the path. I released my hand from Winston's arm and walked over to a rosebush robust with full blooms. Leaning down to inhale the powerful, fragrant scent, I felt Winston's arm slide around my corseted waist, and I shivered with pleasure. He had never touched me anywhere but my hand and arm, unless we were dancing. And then, of course, it was in full view of society.

Standing, I turned to face him. His cheeks were flushed, more so than when we were walking. "Clem, Clem —" he stammered, a habit that surfaced when he was nervous.

Without warning, without even a shadow cast by darkening clouds, a crack of thunder sounded. We both looked up. A formidable black mass had formed to the north and was threatening to blanket the sky.

He grabbed my hand. "We best move quickly back to the house. These summer storms can be fierce."

Hand in hand, we started walking briskly toward Blenheim on the path we'd meandered down only moments before. What had Winston been about to say? He'd seemed on the brink of something momentous, judging from the flush of his cheeks and the stutter of my name. Was it possible that he'd planned on discussing his intention? *Surely it is too soon for a proposal,* I thought. We had only known each other for five months, a courtship of the written words of letters interspersed with several visits, always in the company of others and often interrupted by trips, mine to Germany and his to locations much farther afield, demanded by work.

The rain trickled down gently from the clouds at first and then became a torrent. We ran down the path until Winston tugged my hand and we veered toward a small structure. I realized that it was a little Greek temple, with four Ionic columns holding aloft a triangular pediment. There was a marble bench within, and Winston motioned for me to sit upon it.

"The Temple of Diana," he explained with a swooping hand gesture around the interior of the small structure, decorated with stone plaques depicting the goddess, as he sat down next to me. "I understand it was built as a folly in the late eighteenth century as a nod to the Roman goddess of the moon, the hunt, and, and" — his stammer took hold briefly before he blurted out — "chastity."

Winston handed me a handkerchief, and we giggled as we wiped our faces dry. The rain pelted the temple's roof, and we relaxed in the shelter of its walls. The temple afforded a fine view of the Great Lake through the trees, but rather than commenting, I stayed silent. I hoped Winston would return to his earlier, interrupted topic.

A spider crawled across the leaf-strewn temple floor, and I focused on its nonlinear path as a means of calming my nerves. Through my peripheral vision, I noted that Winston's cheeks were flushed again, but I resolved to keep quiet and wait for him to speak first.

Finally, he cleared his throat. "Clementine."

I glanced up from the floor and met his gaze. "Yes," I said with a warm smile and encouraging nod.

"Since I was a young boy, I've had the unerring sense that my future and that of Great Britain were inextricably intertwined. That I'd be called upon to help our country in terrible times." His cheeks turned a deeper red. "You probably think I'm harboring some grandiose delusion and want to run for the hills."

I hastened to reassure him, careful not to reveal my disappointment at what surely couldn't be a prelude to a proposal. "Not at all, Winston. I admire your commitment to our country." I barely allowed myself to think what a thrill it would be, if we ever did marry, to engage in this great endeavor with him. I deeply desired the purposefulness of a traditional, stable marriage to this man, so different from the emptiness of

Mother's bohemian life with its constant changes in locale, finances, and attention due to the vagaries of her ever-varying roster of relationships. Not to mention how meaningful life with Winston would be compared to the other gentlemen to whom I'd been engaged.

The red of his cheeks faded, returning to its usual fairness. "Oh, Clementine, I'm so relieved you understand. I hope you also understand my need to have a strong, noble woman at my side," he said with an expectant gaze at me.

He seemed to be awaiting a response, but I couldn't fathom what to say. I'd guessed that he was building to some sort of proclamation; I'd even dared to hope he might propose. But declaring a need for a "strong, noble woman" was hardly tantamount to asking for one's hand. Still, I didn't want to discourage him should a proposal be hidden in there somewhere, so I gave him another encouraging nod and waited silently.

He cleared his throat again and began speaking. "I have grown very fond of you over these past months. More than that, much more. I daresay I've fallen quite in love with you, Clementine." He paused, then with eyes shimmering, asked, "Might

45

you feel the same way?"

He had finally uttered the words I'd been longing to hear. I examined this man, over a decade my senior and an important, if controversial, member of Parliament, and saw the sensitive person who lay beneath the blunderbuss of his exterior, one who understood and shared my sense of being different. In that moment, I knew with utter certainty that I could make a life with him. It would not be an easy life — no, it would be one of striving and ambition — but it could be an important and purposeful one.

"I do, Winston," I answered, sensing my own cheeks blush with a surge of emotion. Throughout my two prior failed engagements, I had never once professed my love for those gentlemen, as I'd never felt a surge of emotion for either one. What I felt for Winston was utterly different and much more powerful.

"Oh, Clementine, you cannot know how happy that makes me." He enveloped my hands in his and took a deep breath. "I know our courtship has been brief, but I wonder if you'd do me the honor of becoming my wife. It will not be an ordinary marriage, but it will be a very great one."

Without breaking his intense gaze, I

answered without hesitation. "I will become
your wife, Winston Churchill."

answered without hesitation. "I will become
your wife, Winston Churchill."

CHAPTER FOUR

September 12, 1908
London, England

The bells of St. Margaret's chime a soft melody that matches the gentle beauty of the sixteenth-century, white Portland stone church nestled between Westminster Abbey and the Houses of Parliament. The music soothes my nerves until the jarring, masculine clang of the bell of Big Ben begins to sound out the hour. The noise drowns out St. Margaret's subtle song, and for a moment, I am lost in the cacophony of the competing bells and their lingering reverberations. And then, it is suddenly, unexpectedly quiet, and a strange pause hangs in the air.

"It's time, Clemmie," Bill whispers.

I look over at my little brother, resplendent in his naval uniform, the only man I'd ever want to walk me down the aisle, even if my alleged father had still been alive, as I'd hardly known him in life. The tall, composed gentleman sitting beside me is hardly recognizable from the young boy, always the last of the Hozier siblings to trail in Mother's wake as we moved back and forth between England and France. While Mother sought freedom from societal restraint and creditors as we journeyed from place to place, we siblings hunted for stability and order in each new home. Bill finally found it in the navy, and I wonder whether I will finally find it today, with Winston.

My brother is correct, of course. The bells have finished pealing, and we must step out of the carriage through the throngs of people, photographers, and journalists gathered around St. Margaret's. All this attention, which began with our wedding announcement, was terribly unwanted initially. At first, I worried that the attention would be of an unsavory sort, highlighting the differences between our family and other aristocratic families. Differences in funds. Differences in servants. Differences in neighborhoods and homes. Differences in fathers. Differences in mothers. I'd been terrified as to what a close and watchful eye might divulge on close scrutiny. But as the days passed and the articles and pictures grew in number, I began to realize that the general public saw me through an entirely different lens than the one through which my peers looked. To the world at large, I was beautiful and aristocratic, stemming from a long and ancient line of nobles. No one seemed aware that I'd once lived in an apartment above a fishmonger in Dieppe or that my true paternity had long been in question. The journalists and people standing outside St. Margaret's only want to catch a glimpse of the bride on what has been hailed as the biggest wedding of the year. But in this moment, that bride seems to be someone other than me, and I find myself unable to move.

"Clemmie, did you hear me?" Bill says, a bit louder.

Slowly, as if I'm peering at him through a haze, I nod.

"All right, then. I'll climb out first, and then I'll turn back to help you step out of the carriage." He shoots me his winningest smile as he opens the carriage door. "Can't have the beautiful bride stumbling in front of all these cameras, can we?"

The gentle ribbing is meant to cajole me out of my frozen state. But his quip preys upon an actual fear, and I almost swat Bill as if he were still a small boy. Instead, I reach for his arm as I alight from the carriage, squinting into the sunlight of the early autumn afternoon and the bright flashes of countless cameras.

Once I land on the steady, cobblestoned ground facing the entryway to St. Margaret's, I glance to my right to ensure my bridesmaids have disembarked from their carriages as well. Relief flows through me when I see the smiling face of Nellie. I doubt I could face a single minute of today without Nellie and Bill by my side.

Behind Nellie stand my four other bridesmaids — Winston's cousin Clare Frewen, my cousins Venetia Stanley and Madeline Whyte, and my dear friend Horatia Seymour, whose father had been Prime Minister William Gladstone's private secretary. In their gowns of amber satin, black hats wrapped in roses and camellias, and bouquets of pink roses, the girls look like identical parts of a whole.

My stomach lurches at the sight of my cousin Venetia. I adore Venetia, but her presence reminds me of the drama surrounding her best friend, Violet Asquith, the twenty-one-year-old daughter of Winston's superior, the new Liberal prime minister Herbert Henry Asquith. In the year before Winston and I met, Winston had befriended Violet, who became enthralled with

51

Winston's intellect and political savvy. Two days before our wedding, Violet, who grew hysterical at the news of our engagement and sent a letter to Venetia excoriating me, wandered off at dusk on a path that bordered a cliff with a sixty-foot drop near Slains Castle, which the Asquiths had rented for their summer holiday. When she failed to reappear by nightfall, her father organized a search party of houseguests, servants, and villagers for his missing daughter. After four hours of hunting on the moonless night, Violet was found uninjured on a flat stretch of lawn near the castle, ready with an explanation of how she'd slipped and fallen unconscious on the sharp, cliffside rocks. Since news of this incident reached London, society has been aflutter with speculation as to whether Violet's "fall" constituted a suicide attempt, an accident, or an intentional ploy. Regardless, the presence of Violet looms at our wedding, which, I believe, was her aim all along.

Nellie breaks away from the bridesmaids' ranks and walks to my side. I assume she's seen the troubled expression on my face and believe she's about to give me a reassuring hug and wish me well. Instead, she reaches up toward my tulle veil and coronet of orange blossoms to adjust them. She gives me a small kiss on my cheek, just as "Lead Us, Heavenly Father, Lead Us" begins to play on St. Margaret's organ. It is my cue.

Clutching my white tuberoses almost as firmly as I clutch Bill's arm, he and I walk through the doors of St. Margaret's. Every pew in the vast church, bedecked in white flowers as I'd requested, is packed to capacity with guests. When Winston had set our wedding for a month from our engagement, I'd half thought he had insisted on the date — a time when many aristocrats and members of Parliament were traditionally away on holiday — so his naysayers, still smarting from his political party change, wouldn't have the chance to snub the invitation outright. From the crowd in St. Margaret's, however, few seem to have declined. All that matters to me is that Violet has refused the invitation. I didn't think I could keep a steady gait down the long aisle with her jealous, angry eyes upon me.

As I step into the nave, the guests crane their necks and face us. I try to keep my gaze fixed on the stained-glass window behind the gilt alter at the church's east end — such a masterpiece — as Bill and I progress down the long aisle. We pass the first of the many white Gothic arches lining

53

the aisle without incident until I recognize the esteemed chancellor of the exchequer, David Lloyd George, in the crowd. I hesitate.

"Breathe, Clemmie, breathe," Bill whispers in my ear.

When my breathing doesn't deepen and my step doesn't quicken, he whispers again, in an approximation of our grandmother's slight Scottish lilt, "If you don't, I'll box your ears."

His words are so unexpected and inappropriate, I begin to giggle. My shoulders begin to quake in the familiar beginnings of an enormous guffaw, but before it escapes, Bill pinches my arm. "Don't you dare, Clemmie," he whispers.

Thanks to my sibling, my composure returns. I continue down the aisle, nodding occasionally to guests I recognize. As we near the first row of pews, I see the gaze of Winston's mother fixed on me. Her new husband, George Cornwallis-West, nearly the same age as Winston and conspicuously not present at my engagement weekend at Blenheim, has not bothered to turn his head in my direction. By contrast, I receive warm grins from Winston's brother, Jack, handsome with his bushy mustache, and his new wife, Goonie, her pretty, delicate features framed by her shiny dark-brown hair. My relatives, few compared to Winston's, are beaming as they watch my progress, including my august grandmother, whose demeanor is usually imbued with Scottish stoicism, and Lady St. Helier, who grins at me, delighted in the role she played here. Even Mother, lovely in a plum silk gown trimmed in white fur, is smiling, although I soon identify a more likely source for her delight than her daughter. She has rearranged church seating so that next to her, in a place of utmost prominence, is Algernon Bertram Freeman-Mitford, the First Baron Redesdale; he is my mother's sister's husband and the man long rumored to be my actual father.

Bill squeezes my arm, understanding my reaction without a single word. *I will not allow Mama to spoil my day,* I think to myself as we reach the altar. And I turn to face Winston.

Through the cloud of my veil, I study my intended. Standing next to his best man, the heavily mustachioed Lord Hugh Cecil, Winston looks stout rather than tall as he does in my imagination, but no matter. The twinkle in his eye and his half smile are for me alone. And with his nimble mind, passionate ideals, and the solace we find in each other, he is my home. The one for which I have searched my entire life.

We grin at one another like greedy children, and all the anxiousness of the day fades away. For a few passing seconds, it is just us two.

Our silent exchange — indeed the quiet of the entire church — is interrupted when the marriage officiant, Bishop Welldon, pointedly clears his throat. As Winston's former headmaster at Harrow, the bishop knows Winston well and launches into a lengthy speech about my husband-to-be and the sanctity of marriage. I despair that I may not even be mentioned in this discourse, on my wedding day no less, when I finally hear my name and the word *wife,* but only in the context of the little known impact a wife can have on her politician husband.

Winston and I wait until the conclusion of Bishop Welldon's lengthy speech, more like a monologue than a sermon, to exchange our vows. When Winston repeats his pledge with a tender voice, I see tears well up in the corner of his eyes, and I have to stop myself from tearing up as well. The ceremony concludes with a brief kiss that leaves Winston and I blushing and beaming at each other. Until the bishop interrupts us, that is, having decided that the altar of our wedding day is the appropriate time for a chat with his old student.

As I politely wait for their inopportune discussion to finish, I stare down the nave, over the heads of our guests to the stained-glass window at the west end of St. Margaret's. A brilliantly colored portrait of Queen Elizabeth I peers back at me with an unflinching gaze. England's longest reigning monarch would have never tolerated being kept waiting like this, and I feel almost as if she's taking me to task for allowing the bishop to detract from my moment.

I think about the bishop's description of my future — as a hidden force for good upon my important husband. Is that all anyone expects my life to be? I may be only twenty-three years old to Winston's thirty-four, without the education, accomplishments, or nobility of my intended, but my life will not serve solely as the invisible prop for my husband.

CHAPTER FIVE

October 14, 1908
London, England

As our Pullman car approaches Victoria station, I tick off the buildings we pass, expecting to be comforted by their familiarity. Instead, the city appears gray and misty after weeks of searing Italian sun. This dark return to London signals the conclusion of our honeymoon, and I feel a wave of sadness that our languorous days and nights must end.

I recall sitting with Winston on the balcony of our suite at the Lido Palace Hotel on the banks of Lake Maggiore, Italy. We'd been admiring the views of the sapphire-blue lake and the surrounding mountains, still snow-capped in places. A peaceful quiet had settled upon us, and we entwined our fingers and tipped our faces toward the afternoon sun. As chunky rays of sunshine warmed us through our white linen clothes,

58

I experienced a transcendent sensation of peace and belonging — and love — such as I'd never felt before. It is this moment that I wish to preserve upon our return.

The weeks of our honeymoon, spent exclusively in each other's company, were our true courtship. In the first week, we explored the splendors of Blenheim Palace without Sunny or any other family member in residence, and I began to understand the full impact of Winston's childhood neglect and the resulting fervent adoration of his larger Churchill ancestry. Eight days at Baron Arnold de Forest's Moravian castle in Eichhorn, Austria, followed, where we wandered through the ancient, emerald woods and started to untangle ourselves from our carefully fashioned public personas. A frenzy of six days in Venice, indulging in Renaissance Madonnas, palazzos, and sleek black gondolas helped shed the remainder of our facades, but it wasn't until the final, splendid week at the Lido that we peeled away the last layer of our worldly shells and surrendered ourselves. There, we stood before each other, vulnerable and exposed, and became true husband and wife. I made a silent vow that I would protect our union. But as we return to foggy London with all its demands and social constructs, I worry who we will become. How can I safeguard this fusion of selves that we've managed to fashion?

"Cat?" Winston whispers, awakening me from my reverie.

"Yes, my Pug?" I answer my nickname with his own.

We had enjoyed the physical love of our honeymoon, the first time for each of us. During those intimate moments, a certain bashfulness had arisen between us, and we'd taken to calling each other by pet names, perhaps as an oblique reference to our more animalistic natures.

A lopsided grin appears on Winston's lips, and perhaps inspired by his own honeymoon memories, he reaches for my hand. I touch my ungloved fingers to his one by one before sliding my hand into his. He pulls me toward him until I perch on his lap, fully enveloped in his arms. We kiss, and I feel the heat surge within me. As I briefly break away to catch my breath, I realize that we have pulled into Victoria station and slowed down next to a full, waiting train car, all of whose passengers are staring at us.

We erupt into laughter, our extravagant happiness making us unembarrassed by their gazes. Our giggles linger as I tug down the dove-gray wool jacket of my Frederick

Bosworth traveling suit, and we step off the train into the carriage waiting to take us and our trunks back to Winston's bachelor home. The roll and lurch of the carriage over the city streets, bumpy with their mixture of wood, macadam, granite, and the occasional cobblestones, makes me unexpectedly nauseous, and the merriment fades. Only when we approach 12 Bolton Street and I look into my husband's shining eyes does the discomfort disappear, and I realize that, for the first time in my life, I am home.

"Shall I carry you over the threshold?" he offers with arms outstretched as we stand before the imposing front door.

A smile reappears on my face at the notion, but I shake my head in mock protest. "That seems rather barbaric, doesn't it? After all, it's not as if you've stolen me from my village and I'm arriving back at your hut kicking and screaming. We have chosen each other quite willingly."

"We have indeed," Winston whispers in my ear.

Then he kisses me again and laughs. Without speaking, we link hands, wordlessly choosing to cross over the threshold together.

We step into the spacious entry hall of his

narrow but tall building, which contains, as he'd told me, four floors with a basement. As we stroll through the ground-floor dining room and morning room and then upstairs to the drawing room and library, I am pleased with the simple ivory woodwork, subtle paint on the walls, and accents of mahogany in the staircases, ornate mantelpieces, and dining room furniture, all aglow with electric lights. But then I notice that all the table surfaces in the library are cluttered with miniature versions of war — metal soldiers, cannons, horses, and artillery, as if we've interrupted a battle — and that every chair has heaping piles of books teetering. The masculine library, in particular, decorated in leather and bold nautical colors, resembles nothing so much as a boy's bedroom, and I wonder how we will ever entertain guests in these spaces. Clearly, Winston undertook his socializing at others' homes or his club. I wish protocol had allowed for me to visit his home before we married, as I could have addressed some of this decor.

He gestures around the library, saying, "It's been waiting for a womanly touch, as you can see."

His expression is sheepish and somewhat apologetic, and I reassure him with a kiss.

"It's wonderful. And we will make this our home. Just you wait and see, Pug."

"It's been waiting for *you* all this time. As have I."

Our kissing continues in earnest until we hear a throat clearing. We jump apart, and I wonder who would dare interrupt us. Any reasonable servant would understand how to silently absent himself from this private moment.

Only then do I see her. Standing in the doorway to the library is Winston's mother, resplendent in a boldly striped peacock-green gown cut in the latest fashion. She is smiling beatifically, as if her very presence should infuse us with joy.

"Mama?" Winston calls out, his tone a mixture of shock and pleasure.

"Lady Randolph?" I exclaim, astonished by her presence.

"You are family now, Clementine. Please feel free to call me Jennie," she says with another serene smile.

No wonder the smile of Lady Randolph — Jennie, I mean — has that Madonna-esque quality, I think. She's grown to expect delight from her son simply because she is present. Even in inopportune moments.

"Did I hear someone say 'waiting for a womanly touch'?" she announces, clearly pleased with herself. I sense no contrition for her intrusion upon our intimacy.

"What have you been about, Mama?" Winston asks with a wag of his finger as if his mother were a naughty schoolgirl.

After a brief interlude with kisses and greetings for us both, she announces, "I have a surprise for the newlyweds. I've been busy while you were gallivanting across Europe."

I am leery. Over the course of our honeymoon, Winston told me many stories about his lonely upbringing, and while he would never describe his beloved mother in pejorative terms, I'd heard about the many letters he wrote to her, pleading for her attention while she traveled the world in the company of her lovers. She neither responded to his pleas nor defended him against the railings about his lisp or weak constitution by his father, whose preference for Winston's younger brother was unabashed and undisguised. Only when Winston had become an adult and made a name for himself had she begun to show him the slightest bit of affection, and even then, only when she could benefit from the association. I easily identified her self-serving behaviors, having recognized them in my own mother.

"Whatever have you done?" Winston's

pleased tone holds none of the mixed emotions I'm feeling. Having waited so long for her notice, he would never do anything to jeopardize or critique it. From him, I sense only satisfaction at the attention she is paying us.

"Come, let me show you."

She leads us up the steep stairs to a door at the end of the third-floor hallway. The door is slightly ajar, and she pushes it open with a light tap. From a quick survey of the room, I discern that it is the master bedroom, and I spin around toward Winston, wondering what his reaction will be that his mother — not he — would be the first to introduce me to the room holding our marital bed.

While his expression shows astonishment, I quickly learn that the decor is what shocks him. "Mama, what a surprise!"

A wide smile forming on her rosebud-shaped lips, she stares into Winston's face. "Do you like it, darling? The master bedroom needed redecorating, with a dash of that 'womanly touch' you mentioned. You couldn't have welcomed Clementine home to the tired nautical theme that pervaded your old bedroom."

No one asks me my opinions on the decor. This slight would have normally upset me

— it is the room that Winston and I will share as husband and wife, after all — but not on this occasion. I know that if I *had* been asked, I could not have stifled my horror at the overabundance of frills and sateen bows and ruffles and flowered fabric muslin covers. It resembles a room in a house of ill repute. Or what I imagine one would look like anyway.

I feel as if I cannot breathe in this cloying environment, but mercifully, a housemaid interrupts us with a knock on the open bedroom door. Winston turns, raising an eyebrow at her. "Yes?" he inquires, his tone unexpectedly sharp.

An expression of apology crosses her features, and I feel badly for the girl. She's only doing her duty.

"I am sorry, sir, but a messenger delivered letters from Parliament. He said they were urgent."

Winston's eyes light up; no hint of disappointment appears on his face. "Ah, duty and all that."

With her son's attention diverted, Jennie turns her calculating gaze upon me. I meet her eyes, seeing this woman for who she truly is. This makeover of our bedroom telegraphs the extent of her willingness to insert herself into our lives, even into our most intimate moments. I realize now that she championed our marriage because she believed I would be a timid mouse, staying in the background while she manipulated Winston for her own ends. On our honeymoon, Winston and I had created a circle of trust, and I need to reinforce that circle in this moment. If I do not, then it will only be a matter of time before Jennie will attempt to mold not only our home and Winston's career but also our marriage and even me.

That circle encompasses politics. During our courtship, Winston had written to me that his life centered on politics, but I hadn't understood how fully until our honeymoon. I know now that if I want to play a meaningful part in his life, I must become involved in his political world, building a walled fortress around us. And it's a natural fit for me, as I'm deeply interested in the rights and treatment of men and women alike.

I leave Jennie behind and slip my hand through the crook of Winston's elbow. "Come, Winston. Let's review the letters together. If the work beckons you, it beckons me."

II

CHAPTER SIX

November 15, 1909
Bristol, England

My step feels light. With each movement forward, the confinement of pregnancy, the birth itself, and the long, sometimes lonely, recovery afterward are shed, like an unwanted skin. These trials, of course, I had heard other women describe, but until I suffered through them myself, I could not imagine how metamorphic they would be. Now I know. And with each step, I leave them in my wake. I rejoin Winston in the work we undertake together as part of our unique marriage.

As I walk down the aisle and closer to the stairs descending from the train into the station where we will meet with local politicians, I summon myself into the wife and person that Winston requires of me. I am determined to return to the unit we had become since our marriage, at home and at work. Until my pregnancy intervened anyway. I remember the words of his August letter, which I'd received during my convalescence at the Blunts' estate in Sussex after Diana's July birth: *Recover, my Cat, as I will need you to assist me in the approaching election. I have a key role in mind for you.* His words reinforced my purpose, spurring along my recovery, and they push me forward now.

This moment feels long in coming. After Diana's birth, I'd taken some time alone for recuperation, first to Sussex at Wilfrid Scawen Blunt's Newbuildings estate and then to my Stanley cousins' estate Alderley Park in Cheshire, leaving the baby in London under the care of a nurse and the supervision of Winston. After I returned, I'd assumed that I would step back immediately into the part of Winston's political confidante and social companion. In fact, I'd prepared for this role during my convalescence by keeping abreast of current affairs and studying the dozens of political books Winston had assigned me — including the indecipherable *The Life of the Bee.* But when I returned to our new house on Eccleston Square in late August, I discovered that Jennie had insinuated herself into every facet of the daily life of our household, as well as the routines of both Winston and Diana — from the daily menus to the servants' cleaning regimens to the decor of our new home to Diana's napping schedule to Winston's wardrobe and social agenda. Untangling her imprint — and finally her — from our home took weeks, and even then, I only achieved my goal because her husband, George Cornwallis-West, summoned her.

But then, Jennie's departure coincided with Winston's. Kaiser Wilhelm II of Germany summoned my husband for an extended trip to inspect the military and to visit the country's labor exchanges. Immediately upon his return from the continent, his constituency demanded his presence in Dundee. When he came back to London after his trips, long-neglected parliamentary matters consumed him, and I soon heard rumors that Violet Asquith had begun to accompany her father to meetings in the hopes of encountering Winston. While I was powerless to stop Violet's efforts, I knew I had to reclaim my role at my husband's side.

London had been stiflingly hot — too hot for the baby — so I made a proposal: I would decamp to the Crest Hotel in Sussex with Diana and the nurse, and he would give us his undivided attention on weekends. The picturesque landscape surrounding the hotel, reminiscent of Scotland, provided an inviting backdrop for nights of affection between Cat and Pug and days discussing political issues, just us two.

As president of the Board of Trade, Winston had succeeded David Lloyd George, both in title and purpose. Winston and I were in full accord that Lloyd George's Liberal welfare programs should be continued. We reviewed plans to improve working conditions and provide labor exchanges and pensions for workers, and when Winston protested that the only way to fund these programs was to tax luxuries and land to the detriment of his aristocratic friends and family members, I encouraged him to stay true to his convictions. We agreed that everyone must pay their share.

Our only note of political dissension on these long Sussex evenings stemmed from the impact that the suffragettes' recent campaigns had on Winston's public support for the women's vote. Their militant actions, spurred on by the Women's Social and Political Union, included the smashing of government and shop windows, burning of homes, assault of governmental figures, and even bombing of public buildings. While I did not condone the suffragettes' activities, my support for the women's vote did not waver, and Winston worried that he disappointed me in this regard. I understood that, in his mind, a support for the suffragettes was a support for their tactics, so I extricated a promise to reconsider the women's vote when they had backed down from their current maneuvers.

But when I returned full-time to London with Diana and the nanny in the autumn, the long stretches when Winston was traveling or doing the work of Parliament seemed interminable. I was left alone with the tasks of finalizing our new home on Eccleston Square while fending off Jennie's interference and minding Diana alongside the nanny or Goonie, who'd recently had a little boy, and I felt simultaneously overwhelmed with my responsibilities and isolated from Winston and the hub of political work. Finally, I understood Mother's need to keep her children at bay, even to maintain a separate house for us and our governess, nearby but distinctly apart. I began to wonder why no one had told me that the maternal state didn't come naturally to all women. Not that I didn't love Diana. I did, but the actual caretaking of the infant left me empty. When Winston finally summoned me for a specific role in helping with his Parliamentary reelection in early November, it felt like a reprieve.

Before I disembark from the train, Winston tugs on my hand from behind. The stiff navy skirt of my traveling suit rustles against the floor, and I turn toward my husband's familiar half smile. He pulls me close for a private kiss, whispering, "This trip is the first time we've been *truly* alone since Italy." I giggle at his reference to the fact that I became pregnant during our Italian honeymoon, and thus, we were three by the time we returned to England.

I breathe into his neck. "How I long to return."

"If only important affairs did not require our attention," he answers. While his voice contains a note of wistfulness, I know that he actually thrives on "important affairs" and longs to always be in the center of the nation's activities. "But since they do, I am honored to have you at my side. You will be a great help, Cat, in securing the votes. It will be the first of our political triumphs."

Hand in hand, we step off the train onto the platform of the Bristol Temple Meads railway station. The interior of the station bears none of the stately Tudor beauty of its exterior, which we had spotted as our train arrived. The busy station, which held fifteen tracks, eight of which serviced passengers, pulsates with people hurrying to and fro. From across the throngs, a group of men waves to us.

"Ah, look there. They must be the representatives from the Anchor Society, here to take us to Colston Hall," Winston speculates. We weave through the crowd toward the constituents who will transport us to the auditorium for Winston's speech and my first public talk, for which I'd prepared extensively. A general election in the upcoming months means that Winston's parliamentary seat is in jeopardy, and he plans to unveil me as part of his campaign at this event. I am to bolster not only his parliamentarian claim but also the plans of Lloyd George's government, particularly the much-disputed People's Budget.

I nod, and together, we walk toward the gentlemen. With my hand looped through Winston's arm, I feel proud to be at his side and part of the important work of the nation. *Imagine,* I think, caught short for a moment. My husband, summoned by kings and kaisers alike for his advice, seeks *my* counsel and relies upon *me* in his campaigning and policy making. I worry less and less about Violet's claim on his attention, even when she sidles up to him at social occasions, as it is me — not her — he turns to for guidance.

Winston and the men exchange introductions, and after a conversational lull, I say, "I have tremendous respect for the work your society undertakes to assist the poor and elderly in the Bristol area."

Winston nods approvingly, but the men appear surprised. Is it the words I've chosen or the simple fact that I spoke? Political wives are seldom seen and rarely heard. The ones I've encountered seem to cultivate invisibility, preferring the company of their social peers to the political creatures with whom their husbands work. But I long for a more substantial part than my predecessors and contemporaries have modeled, and Winston encourages me — no, he demands — that I assume a significant mantle, no matter how unusual.

What sort of political spouse will I become after today's launch? As I muse on the possibilities while the men talk logistics, I see a young woman striding purposefully across the platform. Dressed in the suffragette uniform of white shirtwaist, tie, and black skirt — an outfit I once sported myself while at Berkhamsted and working as a French tutor — she does not seem headed toward a particular train but toward us. She has some kind of long, sinuous object in her right hand.

What on earth is she doing? Surely she doesn't mean to approach us but is rushing to catch a train. Surely all this talk about suffragettes and their threats is making me on edge. Fear courses through me, but I do not want to appear a typical female hysteric. After all, the men do not seem flustered. They don't even seem to notice the woman, for that matter.

Before I can draw Winston's attention to the woman, she hurls herself toward him. As she releases the object in her hand into the air, her words ring out, "This is for women everywhere!"

Only then do I realize that the object in her hand is a whip. Snapping it into the air, the woman brandishes it expertly, unleashing it at Winston's chest. As she brings it back to strike him again, he stumbles backward.

Will no one help? A crowd gathers, but no one races to assist Winston. The men from the Anchor Society do not move, except for the gaping of their mouths. Shock initially renders me immobile as well, but then I see that the woman — undoubtedly a suffragette — is driving Winston back on the platform, toward the path of an oncoming train. And I realize that if I do not intervene, my husband could stumble onto the tracks and be crushed by the train's force.

Instinct takes over. I leap over a pile of luggage heaped next to me, and I insert myself between Winston and the woman. The tip of the whip, the popper, lands on the floor of the platform instead of upon Winston's flesh. The commotion unbalances him further, and the moment he begins to fall back onto the train tracks, I grab the lapel of his coat and pull him to safety.

We hold one another as the train rushes past us, its wind blowing free the loose strands of my coiffure. When I look into Winston's pale-blue eyes, I see that he is staring at me in wonder. "You saved me, Clemmie."

As I hold my husband in a grateful embrace, I see my future with Winston unspool before me. Perhaps this rescue is not meant to be my last. My husband's discerning eye perceives all but the threats standing right in front of him, and it seems that I may have to serve as the sentinel of his personal landscape and the gatekeeper of our shared ideals and our marriage.

CHAPTER SEVEN

June 22, 1911
London, England

A lone slip of paper lifts in the breeze and floats gently down onto my lap. I turn my attention from the passing crowds and study the red-edged item in my white-gloved hand. Glancing at the lettering, both typeset and handwritten, I realize that the wind caught hold of someone's hard-won Home Office pass, which allows the bearer special admittance to one of the fifty coveted viewing grandstands, this one near Admiralty Arch. *Poor soul,* I think. Instead of a bird's-eye view of the parade, this person will be jostling among the throngs of Londoners assembled to witness the coronation procession.

I look up from the ticket and back at the crowds, kept at bay by a fence of round-hatted policemen armed with bayonets. Every sort of Londoner stands behind their barrier, all hoping to catch a glimpse of King George V and Queen Mary in the Gold State Coach, a gilded confection of a carriage that has driven every British king to his coronation since the 1760s. The people have patiently watched two lengthy, separate processions — fourteen carriages for foreign royal families and five state landaus for the British royal family, each separated by horse-mounted commanders, Yeomen of the Guard, and Royal Horse Guards — before the third procession containing officers of state, our procession, even arrived. These stalwart and patriotic Londoners will have to bide their time a little longer and watch us until the twenty-fifth and final carriage appears.

As the new home secretary, the youngest to hold the nation's most important cabinet role governing the nation's affairs in a hundred years, Winston rides in an open-top carriage with me at his side. We progress down the thoroughfares of London, driven by two resplendent coachman and pulled by two impeccably groomed chestnut-haired horses, toward the great towers of the west door of Westminster Abbey where the coronation will take place. The open top affords us a view of thousands of eager Britons and they of us.

Even though we have been riding along this route for nearly an hour, I suddenly feel the eyes of the people upon me. The very notion of riding in the coronation procession makes me giddy, if a bit over-whelmed, and I squeeze my husband's hand. He smiles at me, delighted to have gifted this experience to me. When I agreed to marry Winston, I knew I'd pledged myself to an ambitious man on the rise, but I had not realized the heights for which he'd strive — and attain. Pride surges through me as I gaze at the people, many of whom have suf-fered as a result of the rapid industrial growth our nation experienced in the past century, thinking of the important work Winston is doing for them. With my encour-agement, he has secured safety standards and proper working conditions for laborers and proposed health and unemployment insurance legislation. I like to think that my insistence that we see John Galsworthy's play *Justice* nudged him toward greater social reforms than he might have sought otherwise. If only the suffragette issue could be solved as readily, we would be in perfect alignment.

The wind stirs again, rustling the plumes on my large hat. As I grasp onto the brim, Winston reaches up to secure his own cumbersome bicorn hat. After the air calms, I smooth the skirt of my pale-blue silk gown, trimmed with silver thread, and assess the state of Winston's rarely worn Royal Navy uniform, in which he looks both handsome and uncomfortable. We cannot let a single crease or muss mark our appearance on this crucial day.

How marvelous we look, I think. Yet the majesty of the day belies the reality of my daily life. To think, not three hours ago, I was in our Eccleston Square house nursing our new baby, little Randolph, or the Chumbolly as Winston and I like to call him, my hair a tumble and my gown half on. Little Diana was screaming for Nanny but had to make do with a pat on the head, because the lack of servants meant that the nanny filled many roles, one of several reasons why our nannies never stayed long. Diana had taken to calling them simply the generic Nanny. I'd given little thought to money when I agreed to marry Winston; I knew his fortunes to be greater than those upon which I'd depended in my youth, and of course, he had his connection to the Marlboroughs and Blenheim Palace, so I did not fret. Only after our wedding did I learn that Winston's noble blood carries a steady stream of connections but not funds and that, as keeper of the home, I am expected to run an upper-class home befitting the home secretary on middle-class finances. We keep ourselves afloat — but barely — on the books and articles that Winston writes to supplement our income, as neither of us has the family money that most of Winston's peers enjoy.

My body begins to shake with suppressed laughter. The chasm between my state in the early hours and the grandness of my appearance now is so vast, no one would believe it, especially those who have seen me giving speeches at Winston's side and on his behalf at political occasions. But I must not allow the undignified guffaw to escape, and I think on any number of somber topics as means of distraction.

"Whatever is it, Clemmie?" Winston whispers.

"Nothing, dearest. Nerves making an inappropriate appearance, I suppose."

His voice louder and sterner, he reminds me again, "Clementine, much depends on today. I am relying on you."

His scolding tone infuriates me, as does his use of my formal name. I am not his child. Does he really think that I will disappoint him? Has he forgotten how hard I've prepared these past three years to work alongside him? Throughout my two pregnancies and confinements, I've continued to study the stack of political tomes and daily newspapers that he assembled to fill in the patchy education I had before attending Berkhamsted. During the freer periods in between, I've chiseled away at my natural reticence — my sometimes crippling nervousness, in fact — by honing my speaking skills, first campaigning for Winston and later meeting with labor groups on his Liberal endeavors. All this while entertaining in the manner expected of the president of the Board of Trade and later the home secretary, serving the expensive Pol Roger champagne for which Winston has a penchant, no matter the strain on my tight budget, on half the income promised for these roles and a dwindling stream of royalties from Winston's books. I have smoothed his way over our dinner table countless times when his bluntness offended, and I have forged cordial connections that will serve him well. The long-faced, narrow-eyed Violet, who I now know from personal experience lacks finesse and bears a prickly manner, could never have achieved what I have in such a brief time, if ever. I've done everything in my power to create the home life of his dreams and to become the political partner of both of our dreams, and all that while bearing him two children and recovering quickly from those births.

How dare he underestimate me!

Anger flares within me only rarely, but when it does, it surges suddenly and almost uncontrollably. Even though I'm cognizant of the eyes of thousands, angry words begin to form on my lips.

Watching my face, Winston realizes his misstep and quickly reaches for my hand. "Forgive me, Cat. I know you know what today entails. What your part entails." His voice, usually so unwavering and strong, is subdued. He knows he has overstepped.

But I see that his remorse hasn't caused him to lose his command of language. He knows that the use of my pet name will soften me. I want to cling to my indignation, but we serve much grander objectives today. Still, I will not reward his harshness by using an endearment; he will get no Pug in return. "I am glad to hear it, Winston. Please do not doubt me again."

He winces at my words and the use of his formal name. While Winston appears overly confident and sometimes contentious in public, in private, he craves adoration and unconditional warmth. The absence of parental affection in his youth has left a hollow within him, in constant need of filling. But I cannot begrudge him this, as I suppose I am the same and demand the same from him.

I turn away from his beseeching stare and watch as our carriage approaches Westminster Abbey, where the coronation will take place. We draw up to the annex, designed specifically for the event to match the abbey's architecture. Along with the members of the royal family and other dignitaries, we step out of the carriage under the annex's protective archway, away from the eyes of the crowds.

Pairs of notable guests queue before us, awaiting their turn to enter the abbey. A distinctive profile catches my attention, and I take the opportunity to study the unaware Violet, who attends the coronation as her father's guest. Wearing a gown in a shade evocative of her name, her wavy, nut-brown hair is swept back into a surprisingly becoming style, far more fetching that her usual dour low chignon. As if she can feel my eyes upon her, she pivots toward me with a glare. I suppress my anger over her ongoing efforts to foist herself upon my husband and choose instead to nod pleasantly in her direction. I will never allow myself to appear ruffled by her presence in public.

I look away from her toward the guests, trying to ascertain which might be the French dignitaries with whom Winston wants me to speak. Recently, despite the domestic nature of his position, his focus has turned away from the home front, where Britain has existed in a long period of untroubled plenty, to the international scene. Tensions flared this spring between France and Germany when France, which had a treaty with Germany recognizing France's predominant interest in Morocco, deployed troops into the country's interior to Agadir, where there was a rebellion, and in response, Germany raised the specter of warfare unless it received territorial compensation. While Winston had long been concerned about Germany's rise and its imperial tendencies, this recent aggressiveness alarmed him, and he worried that the Triple Entente, a three-way alliance between France, Britain, and Russia, might not be protective enough in the face of German expansionism. Any connections we could forge with key French players could prove indispensable in bolstering that relationship, he believed, and he wanted me to put my excellent French to good use today.

The unexpected appearance of Lady St. Helier in the distance distracts me from my

CHAPTER EIGHT

November 14, 1911
London, England

I race up the back stairs, leaving the astonished kitchen maids in my wake. I have no choice but to take this unconventional route to my bedroom; the use of the front staircase is impossible. The guests have already begun to gather in the front hallway — like the rest of the house, a stultifying formal affair of yellow silk walls and rich crimson carpeting, shot through with the requisite marine blue — and I cannot allow them to see me in this state of unpreparedness.

My bedroom is located at the farthest end of the long upstairs hallway, and at the moment, it seems impossibly far away. In October, after Winston was appointed as first lord of the admiralty, a key role as the British fleet is integral to England's status as a global power, we hesitated before settling into Admiralty House, a four-story yellow brick building near Parliament that contains two thirty-foot drawing rooms for events, a library, and seven bedrooms. I held off the move, as I knew the cost of running such a house would be monumental, far exceeding the amount we spent on Eccleston Square, which already stretched our tight budget.

When we finally inhabited the house, I chose my bedroom, decorated in the omnipresent shade of marine blue with masculine furniture that some previous admiral deemed best suited for his official residence, for its distance from the nursery, where seven-month-old Randolph and two-and-a-half-year-old Diana sleep under the watchful eye of Nanny, and for its proximity to Winston's bedroom. My husband summons my opinion at all hours, a habit I encourage, but I draw the line at seeking me out after midnight. Soon after our marriage, I learned that if we shared a bedroom, his nocturnal work habits meant my sleep suffered from constant interruption. A bedroom of my own became a necessity.

But the need for separate bedrooms does not mean that we never share a bed. On many evenings, just before he readies for dinner, I leave notes for Winston on his bedroom dresser, inviting him to visit me after the meal. Occasionally, on those evenings, he never returns to his bedroom at all.

I push open the door to my bedroom, finding Helen ready with the silk ivory gown and ruby necklace, a wedding gift from Winston, I've selected for this evening's dinner. My personal maid, who came with the house, knows better than most the terrible pressure tonight's event has placed upon me. Even with the new appointment and its accompanying raise in salary, our finances are strained, and I have had to run this house on limited staff. To keep costs low, I act as housekeeper, an enormous endeavor tonight, as it is our first evening hosting at Admiralty House. Helen rushes to undress me, tighten my corset, and slip me into the dress.

As we hasten through the familiar process of dressing and I begin to arrange my hair, I hear Winston's footsteps thunder down the hallway. What on earth is he still doing upstairs? He should be in the front hallway greeting our guests, charming them in his loquacious way. Much will be asked of them in the coming days, and he will be doing the asking.

"Clemmie!" His voice booms into my bedroom before the door even opens. "Are you in there?"

I ignore him at first, hoping that he will abandon whatever has driven him to my door and return to his duty. Winston received the appointment to the lofty lord admiral position when the navy failed to provide the government with a coherent plan for British action in the event of war with Germany during the Agadir crisis. Given that he'd been warning the government about the growth in German naval power and its thirst for expansion — warnings that received only denial and resistance from naval leaders — he seemed the perfect man for the role. At least Asquith seemed to think so, and he directed Winston to prepare the navy for any eventuality with Germany.

Even though I loathed to walk away from the critical social issues around which Winston's home secretary role circled, I threw myself into becoming what *I* believed to be a perfect lord admiral's wife. Certainly, I became one like no other, as my predecessors were rarely seen or heard, like most political wives. I christened battleships, visited shipyards, practiced speeches with Winston, and, of course, attended the endless round of parties and dinners designed to secure Winston's ties to figures critical to the success of our goals. I only balked at the move into Admiralty House.

"Clemmie," Winston begged, "we must settle into the mansion posthaste. Just as a ship must be christened, so must my tenure as lord of the admiralty. The men will expect it."

"Winston," I responded firmly, "we must forestall the move for as long as possible. How will we ever afford to live in that vast, drafty old house? It will require a minimum of twelve servants, while we can only afford nine. At most. Not to mention the cost of heating that monstrosity. We could barely manage the cost of running Eccleston Square."

"But the salary will be higher, Clemmie. Surely we can afford it," he protested, always purposefully ignorant of household financial affairs.

"Not six times higher. And that's approximately how much more it will cost to run Admiralty House."

"I will limit my spending," he proclaimed.

His expression was serious, but I couldn't repress the laughter. "Oh, my sweet Pug. I don't think you know the meaning of economizing."

"I promise, Kitten." He drew close, whispering into my ear. "No more champagne.

95

No more silk underwear. I needn't always have the most choice items." His promises — which I know he is incapable of keeping — made me laugh even harder.

When I regained control of myself, I asked, "Can we not hold off the move a little longer and hold your inaugural party on the *Enchantress*?" I believed that the elegantly appointed, four-thousand-ton steam yacht accompanying the post could easily serve as the venue for the event, while incurring much less expense to ourselves. And, most importantly, putting off the move.

But even as I asked the question, I knew the answer and mentally began preparing to settle into Admiralty House. Even with Winston's efforts to limit our household spending — arranging that the large private reception rooms should be reserved only for official entertainments and thus not part of our budget — constant economy ruled my days, a topic that he has avoided assiduously.

Winston does not bother to knock. My bedroom door swings open wide with a thud, and he strides into the room, only half dressed. Helen jumps, and the hook and eye she's been painstakingly affixing comes undone. Why is he in here?

As he thunders into my room, I study him,

a whirlwind of messy red-gold hair threaded with gray, undone black necktie, and unbuttoned vest, clutching a stack of papers. My husband has no understanding of the work I've undertaken — far beyond what my contemporaries would deign to shoulder — to organize this evening, and he has no desire to know the particulars. I foster this obliviousness, intuitively understanding that if I made him privy to the details and he witnessed me toiling behind the scenes, it could jeopardize the lofty opinion in which he holds me. He might view me as a typical housewife and stop asking me to serve by his side.

"Winston, shouldn't you be downstairs greeting our guests?" I do not add "finish getting dressed" since one necessitated the other.

"They will wait fifteen minutes. Stewart is passing out champagne."

"Champagne?" I issued strict instructions to serve only wine, not the exorbitantly expensive champagne that Winston favored and that he promised to relinquish.

He ignores my question, instead making a demand of his own. "I need you to listen to my speech."

As Helen cinches me into my dress, Winston launches into his presentation, focusing on the mandate given to him by Asquith. He demands that the navy ready itself for Germany's malignant military ambitions. This directive, a departure from the prior naval guidance, will certainly unsettle the already wary leaders, who will rightly suspect that several among them will be replaced. Winston has already confided in me that, in the coming days, he will ask for the resignation of the first sea lord, Sir Arthur Wilson, and replace him with Sir Francis Bridgeman.

As I listen to him speak, I resist the urge to correct his slight speech impediment in front of Helen. He and I have worked on his pronunciations of his *s*'s — which he tends to pronounce as *sh*'s, especially when he's anxious — as it lessens the power of his words. But I must tread cautiously on that project, and certainly would never offer instructions in front of anyone else. To others, his confidence may seem unshakable, but I know only too well the silty foundation upon which it is built.

But he has no such qualms about my suggestions on the language in his speeches. Turning my focus to his verbiage, his constant use of authoritative commands catches my attention. "Pug," I begin with his nickname to soften my message, "this is the inaugural speech to your key naval officers, whose support you will need in the upcoming days. It is your first opportunity to *lead* your men into this new naval realm. All this ordering about — particularly in the context of the new mission — may be a bit too blunt for the men."

"Hmm." He considers the paper in his hand. "What do you suggest?"

I make a comment that I know he'll accept from me alone. "You have all the qualities of a great leader. Why not inspire the men to want to follow you in this course of action? If they embrace the new directive and believe that it has been a choice of their own free will, you will have an amenable navy fleet, not one that is begrudgingly following your commands."

"Sage advice, Clemmie," he says with an appreciative nod. Handing his speech to me, he asks, "What changes would you make?"

By the time we descend the grand staircase of Admiralty House to our slightly tipsy guests, we have not only altered the words of his speech, but also, once Helen left the room, rehearsed its delivery. I feel confident that Winston's pronouncements about Germany will fall upon eager ears, and that his men will see my husband for the inspirational leader he can be.

CHAPTER NINE

January 2, 1912
London, England

As I wipe the tears of laughter from my eyes, Nellie says, "Remember the time we hid our new croquet set from Grandmother in the lawn behind the gardener's cottage? So she wouldn't see us playing?"

Venetia and I burst into guffaws at the memory. When I compose myself enough to speak, I say, "Poor Mrs. Milne! She had to deal with us playing croquet in and out of the clothes drying on her line."

"All because Grandmother believed the croquet hoops would spoil the appearance of the lawn in front of Airlie Castle," Nellie adds. "Not to mention her belief that croquet was an unfitting activity for young ladies."

A maid steps into the parlor of the Stanley family London home to refresh our after-dinner drinks, the perfect ending to their sumptuous annual holiday meal for the family. We pause the conversation to hold our glasses up for refills of the Stanleys' delicious cordials. After the maid closes the door behind her, Venetia asks, "Did she ban you from riding bikes as well?"

Nellie and I shoot each other an amused glance, and Nellie answers, "Of course. Mama let us bring our bikes from Dieppe to Airlie Castle, *because* Grandmother found reprehensible the very notion of ladies riding bikes. But when we arrived, Mama decided she did not have the stomach to deal with Grandmother on the bicycle issue. So we had to take our three-mile rides to Loch of Lintrathen for fishing in secret."

"We went such distances that Grandmother thought we must be very speedy walkers," I interject, smiling at the recollection.

Venetia, draped in long strands of pearls, giggles. "We did the same thing during our summer visits to Airlie Castle from Alderley Park."

I maintain my smile, but Venetia's reference to her grand family home in the countryside of Cheshire reminds me of the great economic divide between Venetia's upbringing and our own, between the childhood of most of our acquaintances and our own.

Our merry reminiscing over summer visits to our shared family matriarch Grandmother Stanley seems a bit unfair since she isn't present to defend herself. But since she chose to spend the holidays alone again at the perpetually drafty Airlie Castle, I decide that she's made herself fair game. As I surrender to the mirth, I suddenly feel a pang of unexpected sadness. How Kitty would have reveled in this moment. Even though it's been more than ten years since she died of typhoid, I've never quite recovered from her passing, particularly since I never got to say goodbye as Mama sent me, Nellie, and Bill away as she nursed Kitty.

Our giggles subside, and I glance over at Nellie, whose severely parted chestnut hair makes her look harder than her sweet nature. A happy smile lingers on her lips, but her eyes betray a passing sadness. Has this moment made her think of Kitty too? While other family members are missing from this annual evening with the Stanleys — Bill and Mother excused themselves due to their respective work and romantic commitments — any family gathering feels bittersweet without our bold sister, who would have commanded these occasions with her wit and courage. Impossible to think that she's been gone for more than ten years. Or how different things would be with her here.

How my life has changed in that time. A marriage, two children, and countless public appearances at my husband's side and political maneuverings on his behalf. Would anyone have believed me capable of such machinations when I walked down the aisle on my wedding day? I glance sideways at Nellie and Venetia, thinking how, on the surface, their lives have remained static in the years since they served as bridesmaids at my wedding. Yet I know change has ruled their days as well.

Nellie meets my eye, and I see that hint of melancholy again, undoubtedly caused by the lingering shadow of Kitty. But we say nothing. The presence of Venetia, her gray eyes appearing steelier than usual by the hooding from her heavy eyebrows, looms oddly and prevents us from confiding in each other.

We shift into chatter over the renovations necessary for Airlie Castle's upkeep, but Randolph's screams shatter the conversation. I know Nanny will shuttle the children into the parlor momentarily, and I brace myself for Randolph's rage.

At the sight of Nellie, little Randolph pulls away from Nanny's arms and reaches for my sister. How does she connect so easily with my son, whom I find overly sensitive and mercurial?

Nanny's eyes plead with me to let them leave, and I acquiesce. "I'll ring for the carriage, Nanny. Perhaps you can take the children home and ready them for bed. I will not be far behind you."

"Thank you, ma'am." She bobs appreciatively. I understand the challenge of keeping the children quiet and well behaved outside the confines of our apartments at Admiralty House.

As she sweeps Diana and Randolph out of the room, Venetia sips her drink and asks, with a facade of innocence, "Will Winston be joining us?"

I know what she's really asking. When will the prime minister be finished meeting with my husband? Suddenly, I'm reminded that my relationship with the women sitting before me isn't a simple sister or cousin relationship but is much more complicated.

"Yes," Nellie chimes in. "Will Winston join us for dessert? It is a Sunday, after all. And I haven't see him in an age."

"How I wish he could make an appearance today. But as he is wont to remind me"

— I adopt Winston's booming voice — " 'a lord admiral's work is never done, as the sun never sets on Britain's seas.' I can only hope he will be home in time to tuck in the children. He hates to miss bedtime on Sundays. It's his only chance to read to them."

On most other evenings, no matter how harried my day, I try to read aloud a bedtime story to the children before Nanny takes them off to bed and Winston and I have dinner or attend an engagement. I adore those brief moments with my sweet-smelling, freshly scrubbed children in their pajamas. At least until Randolph's screaming and crying and pawing overtake sweet, quiet Diana and our encounter is ruined. Even at this young age, it seems Randolph is determined to take up all the space in the room.

Venetia and Nellie give a polite chuckle at my poor imitation of Winston, and then Venetia checks her wristwatch. My body stiffens. I know she's calculating the hours until the admiralty meeting is finished and she can skulk off to her clandestine rendezvous. There are rumors that my cousin is having an affair with the very married leader of our country, the prime minister, who also happens to be Winston's superior, although whether it is of physical nature or purely emotional is anyone's guess.

Nellie murmurs, "Sometimes, I fear the lord admiral's wife's work is never done either."

My sister's expression reveals concern, but I do not want to discuss this in front of Venetia. I know exactly with whom she would share this gossip, and I cannot allow such talk to reach Winston's ears. "All part of the job, Nellie."

"Sister, I worry about you. I fear the travel and entertaining — not to mention all the political work you do — are a strain on your health. You know I adore Winston, but he is demanding."

"Nonsense, Nellie. I am fit as a fiddle. I've even taken up tennis and hunting lately," I answer with a brash stare. Does she not understand that Venetia would share my complaints with her dear friend Violet Asquith as well as the prime minister himself? And that one or both of them would pass the information to Winston?

"I hear your words, but I'll be watching your physical state." She meets my stare and then breaks into an unguarded smile.

As I smile back at my kindly little sister, Venetia interjects. "It's unseemly."

Did I hear Venetia correctly? Precisely

what does she think is unseemly? A keen sportswoman herself, she couldn't mean tennis and hunting.

I turn to my cousin and ask, "What on earth are you talking about?"

She sniffs. "All this campaigning and political speech making. It is unseemly, Clemmie. Not womanly at all."

I am shocked and offended. How dare she!

"That's rich coming from you, Venetia. You are hardly the arbiter of *seemliness* these days, are you?"

She blushes, shooting a glance at Nellie. Does she really think Nellie is unaware of her relationship with Prime Minister Asquith? Half of Parliament knows that he pens her letters three times a day, even during critical meetings.

"At least no one sees me stumping for candidates. That's a man's job, Clemmie. An elected official's job. The last time I checked, no one elected you to office, and you are not a man."

Does Venetia think I will take her barbs without retaliation? Enough with tiptoeing around her illicit relationship. "That's interesting, Venetia. The last time I checked, you are not even married to an elected official, and yet the prime minister shares confidential state secrets with you in his love letters as he seeks your advice."

Nellie looks shocked. I guess she *was* oblivious to Venetia's very public affair with the prime minister after all.

"Henry calls me his guiding light, you know," Venetia says, her cheeks reddening. "And it's a relationship of the mind."

"No pet name will ever make up for the fact that your Henry — the prime minister — is a married man."

"I know your feelings on that score. You are such a prig, Clementine. Henry and Margot don't even sleep together anymore. You are the only one in our set who wouldn't consider having an extramarital relationship of any sort, even an emotional one. You and your prudish husband."

"And I have no intention that either one of us will engage in such licentious behavior. You can go tell that to your precious Henry and your best friend, Violet."

A mirthless laugh escapes from Venetia's thin lips. "Oh, no one can rein in Violet. But you have no need to fear her wiles, Clemmie. Your precious Winston is besotted with you."

I cannot bear to be in Venetia's presence a moment longer. Rising from my chair, I reach for my purse and say, "As it should be, and as I am with him."

CHAPTER TEN

March 28, 1912
London, England

I will not allow this convalescence to act as a bridle. Four weeks of ordered bed rest has forced me from Winston's side, back into the isolation of home and the screaming voices of Diana and Randolph, the latter relentless in his tantrums. No speeches, no meetings, and no social occasions, the doctor insisted, and so has Winston. Winston has sallied forth alone, or so he says.

Had the stress of the trip to Belfast caused the miscarriage and subsequent illness that confines me to this bedroom? Certainly, Nellie attributes my maladies to Belfast. The idea bothers me, but I would not change my decision to accompany Winston even with the benefit of hindsight.

While my unorthodox participation in Winston's admiralty duties raised the eyebrows not only of Venetia but also of many society ladies, the trip to Belfast sounded the alarm for my sister and sister-in-law, Goonie. Belfast, Nellie pronounced, is dangerous and far beyond wifely duty, and Goonie agreed. I knew they were correct, but they did not understand the myopic vision of my husband and his need of my guidance, particularly since rioting had been threatened over Winston's Belfast visit.

Unrest had been brewing in Ireland over home rule proposals that the country should self-govern but only under the oversight of England. The Liberal government leaders wanted Winston, in his capacity of Liberal member of Parliament, not lord admiral, to visit Belfast to speak in favor of home rule. We arrived in Belfast after a peaceful ferry ride on the Stranraer and Larne line. After stopping at the Grand Central Hotel for a lunch of local fish, we stepped briefly into the pelting rain before reentering our waiting car. As we proceeded down Royal Avenue, I pulled my fur-trimmed black cocoon coat tightly around me, and we gave each other a small smile of relief. Perhaps the worry about rioting and unionist protests, with its attendant police and army presence, had been for naught.

But when we drove closer to the Celtic football grounds where Winston was to deliver his speech, the car stopped. The street became immobilized, not with cars and carriages, but with people. A roar emerged from the crowd when they identified the vehicle holding us — their intended target.

Hands thrust through the openings in the windows, and hateful faces pressed up against the glass. The car began to vibrate as objects were thrown at it, and we felt it shake and rock as the crowds lunged against us. The front of the vehicle lifted off the ground, and our driver started to yell. Terror coursed through my body, and I wanted to scream myself. But I met Winston's eyes, and I knew we needed to maintain a strong, unflappable presence.

"Please remove your hands from the car, sir," I said loudly but respectfully, meeting the eyes of the shipyard worker hurling obscenities at Winston on the other side of my window.

He squinted his eyes, seeming to see me for the first time. "There's a woman in the car," he cried out to the men surrounding our car. The rocking ceased, and the throngs surrounding the car dispersed. Afterward, we went directly to the Celtic football grounds and gave our speeches as if nothing untoward had transpired, but inwardly,

111

I was shaking. Only later did I overhear Lord Pirrie, our host, mention the unfortunate event to Winston, whispering that if I had not faced the angry crowd with such firm but graceful insistence, he believed our car would have been upended, causing us grave harm.

A knock sounds at the door, and the distinctive tap reveals it to be Winston. I smooth my hair, spread out my silk embroidered robe, pinch my cheeks to elicit a healthy pinkness, and open the book that has been sitting on my lap. It will not do to appear inactive. Only six days remain on bed rest, and I am determined to reenter the fray immediately thereafter.

"Come in."

Winston, dressed in formal attire, peers through the crack. "Clemmie, how are you, my dearest?"

Why is he wearing evening clothes? I keep the social calendar, and I don't recall an event tonight. Perhaps he plans to stop by the club for some cards. "Quite well, Pug. Do sit down."

He perches on the very edge of my bed, as if I'm suffering from a contagious illness rather than vague womanly troubles brought about by my miscarriage.

Giving me a half smile, he pronounces, "The color has returned to your cheeks, Cat. I think you are on the mend."

"Oh, I hope so, Winston. I hate to abandon you."

"Not to worry, Kitten. Mr. Pug can take care of himself . . . although he is always happiest and most successful when his Cat is purring at his side."

His words comfort me. Leaning back into my bolster of pillows, I ask, "Are you off to the Other Club?" When Winston and his dear friend F. E. Smith were blackballed from the Club due to their perceived audaciousness and, in Winston's case, his defection to the Liberal Party, they formed their own club, the Other Club. They now count Lloyd George, twenty-four members of Parliament, and a diverse mix of distinguished society men as members.

"No, not tonight. F. E. isn't available." He looks sheepish, and I note that he has not answered my question directly.

"Where are you off to, then, dressed so beautifully?"

"The Asquiths."

If he is dressed in evening clothes and headed to the Asquiths, I know what that means. Violet.

Fury roils within me. How can he spend

the evening at the Asquiths when I am imprisoned in my bed? He knows how I feel about this, and he promised me that I'd always be at his side at social occasions with Violet. There is nothing I can do about her surprise appearances at work events. I grow quiet, unwilling to allow my anger to bubble forth. But my silence speaks volumes.

"Cat, you have no reason to worry."

"It isn't you I mistrust."

"But my prime minister has summoned me."

"Not for work, Winston."

"Work requires rapport, and that rapport can only be formed upon a solid hospitable foundation of shared experiences outside of work."

"Stay with me. Wait to socialize with the Asquiths until I am well enough to join you."

"Clemmie, you know I cannot. I am expected."

My life with Winston contains many necessary separations and absences to which I have become accustomed. But this feels different, as if I'm being purposely left behind. He kisses me on the cheek, slowly closing the door behind him. I am left alone with a toxic mixture of anger and upset.

Within a few moments, I hear tapping on

the door again, and hoping it might be an apologetic Winston, I wipe my tears away. But instead, Nanny peeks into my bedroom. I nod, and she brings Diana and Randolph to my side for a good-night kiss. Randolph is blissfully quiet for once, and I inhale their clean, warm skin.

But the children do not settle me. Images of Winston and Violet alone at Downing Street, while the prime minister busies himself with stolen moments with another guest, Venetia, torment me. Violet will agree with all of Winston's mixed views of suffrage among other things, leaving a hole into which she can insinuate herself.

On my nightstand sits a copy of the *Times*, folded to an article that I'd planned on discussing with Winston tonight, the offensive letter by eminent bacteriologist Sir Almroth Wright in which he argues that women should not be allowed to vote or to play a role in politics because of our alleged psychological and physical deficiencies. But if Winston insists on attending to the Asquiths, leaving me alone with my thoughts on this topic, then I will take my conversation to those who will listen. He will be forced to take notice of me. I may be hindered, but I will not be silenced.

CHAPTER ELEVEN

The newspaper sits between us like a third person at the table. I smooth my celadon-green gown and sip the steaming tea, my calm exterior belying my interior. My stomach churns in anticipation of Winston's reaction. He has yet to reveal a single feeling, not even about my decision to abandon bed rest five days before the doctor's orders.

He sips at his afternoon port while studying the whist cards. We have assumed this relaxed posture at our games table in an almost studied indifference to the folded copy of the *Times* sitting at the table's center for nearly half an hour. I assume he's read the paper, as it's his daily habit to review it cover to cover before leaving for Parliament. And even if, for some odd reason, he deviated from his ritual, certainly his fellow members of Parliament read it.

He clears his throat and finishes his drink. *Here it comes,* I think.

"You know you needn't have written an editorial to the *Times* to get my attention, my kitten," he says, keeping his eyes fixed on the cards. His tone is a perfect modulation of serenity, yet I sense another note in his voice. Do I hear a hint of anger? Or is it amusement? I say a silent prayer for the latter, but I don't soften my posture.

"Oh?" I ask, the picture of innocence, as I play my hand.

"Of course not." He places his cards on the table and reaches for my free hand.

"These days, one wonders," I answer, allowing my fingers to rest on his hand but not clasping back. And I do not meet his eyes.

"I know this illness has been hard on you, and I admit that I should not have gone to the Asquiths without you. But you have no cause to harbor any suspicions. My heart belongs to you utterly, and I will never love anyone but you." He lifts my fingertips to his lips and kisses them one by one. "Of that, you can be certain."

"Oh, my dear Pug, thank you for your reassurances. Sometimes, the formidable family history of infidelity — on both sides — lodges itself in my consciousness."

"You have nothing to fear with me, Cat."

Relief softens through my rigid, anxious limbs, and I am glad my missive has been received and understood. That I cannot tolerate infidelity, either physical or emotional. Winston now knows, if he did not before, that I will do my utmost to serve by his side and run our home — using sleights of hand to hide our financial state — but I will not permit him to scamper off at another woman's bidding when I am laid low. Even if that woman's father is the prime minister.

"Your piece caused quite the furor in Parliament."

I feel my eyebrow arch quizzically, and this expression prompts him to continue.

"Oh yes, Clemmie. You really know how to grab the reader from the opening lines." He relinquishes my hand and reaches for the newspaper. "I mean, it was sheer genius to reframe the question that Sir Almroth Wright poses in his preposterous article — changing it from whether women should be given the vote to whether women should exist at all due to their many deficiencies, the ones Sir Almroth Wright alleges should prevent them from voting. It really lays bare the ridiculousness of his argument."

He chuckles, and I laugh along with him.

118

Then he recites the opening lines of my *Times* salvo, and they sound ironic and powerful — not strident, as I'd worried they might seem. I wonder if the members of Parliament took the rest of the piece well.

He continues reciting from the article. Laughter escaping from him, he reads aloud from the section in which I pretend that — given the litany of faults and instabilities Sir Almroth Wright attributes to women — we should extrapolate from Wright's contentions and just eliminate women altogether.

A loud guffaw escapes from my lips, startling Winston. Had I really written that? *How bold of me,* I think. It hadn't seemed quite so audacious while I was drafting the piece, but then I'd been fueled by fury.

"Oh, Clemmie, the next bit is positively withering," Winston comments with undisguised glee and then reads aloud again, this time from the section in which I posit the question as to whether we could perpetuate the human race without women since — according to Sir Almroth Wright — women are fatally flawed. "Brilliantly scathing, Clemmie. The PM thinks so too."

"He does?" I am shocked. Asquith does not show even a smidgen of sympathy for women's rights or suffrage, and I thought Winston would suffer at his hands when he

119

learned — as everyone undoubtedly would — that the article's anonymous author "CSC" was indeed the wife of his very own admiralty lord. "I wouldn't have thought his view of suffrage extended so far."

"You don't have to be a suffragist to know that this Sir Almroth Wright fellow is a bloody fool and he is deserving of a dressing-down."

"I suppose you're right."

"Asquith went even further though, Cat. He insinuates that it was the best piece he's read on the issues surrounding women for quite some time."

"Did he indeed?"

"Oh yes. Not that it changed his position on women's suffrage, of course."

"Did he know I was the author?"

"Once I told him," he says with a mischievous gleam in his eye. I see now that Winston waited for the prime minister's reaction, then dropped his bit of news upon him.

I feel my cheeks flush, and I am suffused with pleasure. My piece, written in a fit of pique, had had an even farther-reaching impact than I'd intended. Perhaps if the prime minister finally stamps his seal of approval upon me, Violet will be forced to follow suit and abandon her overtures to Winston, once and for all. And not only Winston — but Violet — will understand that I am not to be underestimated.

CHAPTER TWELVE

May 12 and 18, 1913
HMS Enchantress *and Athens, Greece*
From my vantage point on the deck, I watch as what seems like the entire 196-man crew carries our guests' trunks onto the *Enchantress.* Had we really brought all these bags on the trains from London to Venice? It seems impossible that they would have fit on the train cars, but they must have. After all, the ladies among our guests have kept to the social convention of changing dresses four times a day throughout our time in Venice, and I swear there hasn't been a single repeat in their attire.

Shielding my eyes against the bright Venetian sky, I study the crew members' routes to the various staterooms. I'm so engrossed that I jump when I feel an arm snake around my waist, loosely corseted due to the heat. I turn to see Winston, dapper in his dark-blue lord admiral uniform, complete with white deck shoes and binoculars, smiling at me. As if intuiting my thoughts, he says, "Cat, you needn't worry that the crew will deliver the trunks to the wrong staterooms. These men are professionals through and through."

I give him a wry smile and say, "Pug, it isn't the skills of your crewmen I doubt. My concern lies with the slippery morality of our guests and its impact on room arrangements."

He chuckles. "Venetia isn't on this trip, so I don't think you need to worry about any funny business."

"True enough. I suppose vigilance has become a habit."

"One borne of necessity," he says supportively, referencing the many times that Venetia and Prime Minister Asquith have tried to camouflage their relationship — whatever it may be — using Venetia's preexisting friendship with Violet. He knows as well as I that our guests on this Mediterranean cruise to Malta via Venice and Athens have provided us with reason to be suspicious on past trips.

On this voyage of the *Enchantress,* we will be hosting Jennie; James Masterton-Smith, Winston's private secretary; and the Asquiths — the prime minister; his wife,

Margot; and, of course, his daughter, Violet. Winston's mother is in a delicate state, as she is in the process of divorcing her husband, George Cornwallis-West, on the legal grounds of desertion, although in truth, his affair provided the impetus. In the fourteen months since my *Times* article was published, my relationship with the Asquiths has turned almost friendly, and we have found ourselves playing golf and bridge together with some regularity. I remain cautious in their company, however, because although their words and glances might appear kindly and cordial to the untutored, I know them to be critical and forever looking for a misstep upon which they can pounce. Venetia always delights in informing me about the Asquiths' private opinions regarding me — namely that, while they find me attractive and eager, they believe me to be not nearly erudite and sophisticated enough for them — but she refrains from saying what is apparent to everyone. Violet continues to pine for Winston, and while I am still wary of her, her behavior as of late has given me no cause for worry.

Winston and I link arms and gaze out at the shimmering seascape. We point out the gondola route we had taken two evenings before and discuss a picnic luncheon we'd

124

taken in the Italian countryside. We compare the quality of the sunlight here with that of Lake Maggiore, where we honeymooned. I think about how these rare moments, when it is just us two, sustain me. Contented, I squeeze his arm with my free hand. On this trip, I'd left him many notes of invitation for nighttime visits, and on most occasions, we awoke the next day in each other's arms, a rarity in our usual daily lives.

My attention is diverted by the crewmen who continue to ferry items on board. They no longer carry trunks but familiar-looking crates. "What is in those boxes, Pug?" I ask, trying to keep my voice even.

He hesitates. "Drinks for the voyage."

"Pol Roger?" I ask, although I already know the answer.

"Yes," he answers sheepishly. "But not to worry, Cat. It doesn't come out of our personal budget."

How could he think our financial situation was the only thing at stake with the purchase of such lavish champagne?

"Pug, you know that our use and the cost of the *Enchantress* have been questioned by members of Parliament. Do you really think it's wise to indulge in luxuries?"

"Every pound we spend on the *Enchantress* is worth the expense." Winston sounds defensive. "Since I became lord admiral, this ship has covered nearly nineteen thousand miles and has taken me to nearly every port in the British Isles that has any connection with naval interests. From trips taken on the ship, we've inspected between sixty and seventy battleships and cruisers, as well as destroyers and submarine flotillas, and I have been present at nearly forty exercises of the fleet. And now, the *Enchantress* sails to Malta so that I can undertake critical military inspections with Field Marshal Kitchener to ensure defense of the Mediterranean. How else can I ensure that we are building the world's strongest navy?"

I almost laugh at his elaborate justification, but then I observe the expression on his face. He has complete conviction in his statements. *Winston sounds like a Tory,* I think. *Not at all like the Liberal he claims to be. What is happening to the man I married?* I wonder.

I pull away from Winston and gaze directly into his eyes. "I am not a committee of Parliament investigating the use of the *Enchantress.* I am your wife, and my only interest is in protecting us."

His furrowed brow softens, along with his voice. "Oh, Clemmie, of course you are. Your concerns are always noble."

"That may be an overestimation, Pug." I think about the children back in London, with their nannies and tutors and governesses but without their parents. Would a noble mother indulge in these lavish trips, abandoning her offspring to the care of others? Focusing on her husband and his career instead?

He reaches for my hand. "No, Cat. You are the noblest of women."

The deck clatters with the sound of ladies' shoes, and Winston says, "Ah, our guests have arrived. Are you ready?"

I pack away my worries and summon a smile. "Ready as I'll ever be."

A mischievous grin appears on his face. "As for the Pol Roger? Well, we can hardly serve the prime minister cheap champagne."

"Do we have time to see the Parthenon by moonlight?" Jennie asks, her voice thick with the wine she drank over dinner at the British legation in Athens. Since the *Enchantress*'s voyage has a military purpose, British officials have flung open their doors in welcome, and they would continue to do so along our route — Athens, Sicily, Corsica, and finally, Malta.

"We set sail in the morning, Mother," Winston answers, a note of hesitation in his voice. From our other voyages, I know he will have to meet with the captain on our return to the ship.

"Please, Winston," Jennie pleads, threading her arm through Winston's. "The moon is so bright."

We already toured the ancient temple dedicated to the goddess Athena, but our hosts at the British legation declared that "it *must* be seen by moonlight." And Jennie always must do what *must* be done.

"Oh, all right." His voice has a note of irritation, but I know he adores any opportunity to gratify his mother, particularly now. The press has taken hold of the story of Jennie's abandonment by her much younger husband — smearing her reputation as an irresistible woman — and she has been quite vocal about her suffering. Even I have been moved to empathy for my usually vain and meddlesome mother-in-law.

The Acropolis looms before us like an elusive woman. The walk there will not take long, but I wonder about the stamina of both Jennie and Margot, particularly given all the climbing and walking we've already undertaken today. I also worried about the steadiness of their step in the darkness. "Shall we have the carriages take us, Winston?" I ask.

"No need. We can manage it, can't we folks?" He calls to the rest of the group in a question that sounds much more like a command.

Asquith, arm in arm with an unusually quiet Violet, calls back, "We can indeed." No one takes any heed of Margot's grumble about the crumbling Acropolis stairs and steep hill that we must climb to reach the Parthenon.

As we walk up the Panathenaic Way at the western end of the Acropolis toward the Parthenon, I listen to Winston answer Asquith's questions about the *Enchantress.* My husband seizes any opportunity to extoll the virtues of his beloved ship, from the craftsmanship of its twin propellers to the heft of its four thousand tons to its ability to cruise at eighteen knots. He used to mention that it was built by the famous Harland & Wolff, but since the shipbuilder was also responsible for the creation of the *Titanic,* he has stopped referencing its origin.

Their conversation halts abruptly when Winston catches sight of the piles of collapsed Doric columns. "By God, look at these treasures. Terrible, really, that the Greeks have let them fall to ruins."

Asquith tsks. "Shameful."

I refrain from reciting to the gentlemen a

fact they should already know — that it is unlikely this current Greek administration is responsible for the state of the Acropolis and Parthenon. The destruction we observe was wreaked centuries before. Perhaps the government has left the evidence of past plunder and warfare intentionally intact as a warning about the vagaries of history. After all, some of the Parthenon's greatest portable treasures — its marble statues and friezes — were removed by the Earl of Elgin a hundred years ago and are housed in the British Museum.

"I say, why don't we send in a group of naval blue jackets to set the columns upright?" Winston proposes.

"Ah, Winston, who knows how the Greeks will take to that? Let's not start an international incident simply because you can't bear the sight of crumbling artifacts," Asquith answers, then begins the long ascent to the top of the Acropolis with Violet on his right arm and Jennie on his left.

Margot is left to climb the steep, uneven marble steps alone. Even though she's known for her sharp tongue and would likely scoff at our efforts to help her if we offered, Winston and I walk slowly alongside her to ensure her safety. As I do, I feel grateful that women's dress styles have recently changed from the voluminous S-shaped silhouettes to narrower, more manageable skirts. Otherwise, I would be struggling as well.

"These damnable steps," she mutters, dropping down onto a stair and pulling a fan from the tiny beaded purse at her wrist. The accessory is the only dainty element of her person. "How is any civilized person meant to climb them in this heat?"

Winston sits down next to her, removing his hat and fanning them both with it. When Margot irritably brushes it away, he sets it down on the step next to them. Picking it up, I place the hat on my own head at a rather jaunty angle and, in an attempt to lighten the mood, give them a broad grin.

Margot bestows a weak smile on me, but Winston gives me a glare of disapproval and reaches for his hat with a rough gesture. I recoil at his harshness, wounded at first and then furious. How dare he. I have served as a good wife and political asset to him for years. How can I not be allowed a bit of silliness? A moment of levity? Must every act I undertake and every statement I make be dictated by the rubric of his political success and the demands of his personal comfort?

Without a word to either of them, I stride

away, up the remaining steps to the Parthenon. I need space to separate my own thoughts and feelings from his. As I pace along the plateau at the Acropolis's peak, oblivious to both the view of Athens and the much-lauded symmetry of the Parthenon, I ponder my role and place in the world. How long has it been since I made a decision or even uttered a word without first considering Winston's reaction? His needs are like a constant noise in the background of my days.

As I step into the cella, the interior structure of the Parthenon, I hear footsteps behind me. It is Winston, lit from behind by moonlight that now appears anything but romantic.

"Are you all right? You wandered off from us without a word." He sounds simultaneously concerned and somehow innocent. How can this be? I wonder whether his tone is feigned or whether he's become so used to having my world revolve around his that he is truly ignorant.

"You don't know why I left?" I ask, gauging his reaction. It is a skill I've honed, for better or worse.

"No, I don't." He seems genuinely perplexed.

"You don't recall the expression on your

face when I put on your hat? The derision you showed to me, your wife, for being a little silly? Then your rough grab for the hat? It was not only disrespectful — of me and my efforts — but incredibly embarrassing in front of Margot."

He appears genuinely despairing. "Clemmie, I'm so sorry. I don't even remember making a face of any kind, but I would never want to disrespect you, so please accept my apologies."

He reaches for me, and I allow myself to be wrapped in his arms. Usually, Winston's embrace comforts me and puts to rest all my misgivings. But tonight, I remain unsettled. And yet I do not think that this problem is one that I can readily resolve.

I remain quiet on our return to the *Enchantress.* My silence goes unnoticed, masked by exuberant chatter over the inspiring sight of the Parthenon by moonlight. When we arrive at our dock, one by one, we cross the deck of the ship and settle into the sumptuous parlor, a wonder of gleaming brass and polished wood.

I watch as Violet sidles over to the sideboard and fills her crystal glass to the brim with ruby-red wine. Her action is curious. It is unlike her to help herself; she thrives on being served.

The sleeves of her diaphanous green gown sweep back and forth as she downs the entire glass of wine and reaches for a deck of cards. The dress defies stylistic description, and yet it suits her. After all, she herself falls into no set category.

"Shall we play bridge?" she addresses the room, holding up the cards.

Everyone but me, Winston, and Jennie decline her invitation and instead excuse themselves for the evening. I would like to join them. Exhaustion has crept up on me; the health troubles that plagued me after my miscarriage have left me without reserves of energy. But there is a gleam in Violet's eye that I dislike, and I do not want to leave Winston alone with her.

The four of us walk toward the game table, and I make certain that Winston and I sit opposite each other so we can partner. As he begins to deal the cards, Violet asks, "Shall we partner, Winston?"

He doesn't hear the innuendo in her words. But I do.

"I believe it is customary to partner with the person sitting opposite you, Violet," I say before he can answer, and I gesture to Jennie. Violet is an avid bridge player and knows the rules better than anyone on board. What game is she really playing?

"Pity," she says, her voice dripping with disappointment.

The bridge game begins. We bid or pass depending on the suit, but Violet does not become irritated with Winston's unconventional style of play, as she usually does. Instead, she seems to find every move Winston makes highly amusing and intensely wise. And she is drinking heavily.

Without lifting her eyes from her cards, Violet lifts up her empty wineglass for the crew member to refill. This is her third glass of wine since we started playing bridge, the fourth she's had if I count the drink she knocked back when we first arrived back on the *Enchantress*.

All of a sudden, Winston jumps. I glance at him and Violet, and I am just in time to see Violet's bare foot snake back to her empty shoe from underneath Winston's chair. All at once, I understand precisely the sort of game Violet is playing. I also understand why she thinks she has a chance at winning.

I stand. "Winston, I think your mother looks overtired. Would you please escort her to bed?"

Jennie sputters out her objection. "Clementine, I'm not —"

Ignoring her protests, I interject. "We

can't have any of our guests fall ill before we reach Corsica and Malta, can we?" I give Winston a pointed look.

He starts to stammer, but I cannot brook any resistance. "Please, Winston," I say in my firmest tone, the one I usually reserve for Randolph's tantrums. The timbre that smacks of my grandmother.

He acquiesces. "Come, Mother." He stands and reaches for his mother's hand.

I wait until I can no longer hear their footsteps. Then I pull Violet to her feet and speak directly in her face. "I will not stand for this, Violet."

"It's not for *you* to decide, Clementine." She speaks my name slowly and deliberately, but she is slurring her words. "It is Winston's decision."

"That is where you are wrong, Violet. I am guessing that your mother reported that a rift occurred between Winston and me tonight?"

I do not wait for Violet to answer. I can see from her eyes that I am correct.

"I suppose you imagined that you finally had an opportunity to insert yourself into my relationship with Winston." I take another step closer to Violet. I can feel the heat of her breath on my cheek and smell its sourness. "Please understand that I will

136

let nothing and no one jeopardize my marriage."

"At the risk of repeating myself" — she takes a long drink of her wine and gives me a smug smirk — "it isn't your decision."

"It is a decision that has already been made. All those years ago, when Winston had the chance to choose you, he picked me. Or have you forgotten, Violet?"

The smug smile disappears from her face, and her features fall. Tears stream down her face, and she begins sobbing. I sense that it isn't my words alone that have wounded her. Pivoting back to the entrance to the parlor, I see Winston standing in the doorway.

He walks toward me and reaches for my hand. Facing Violet, he says, "Please understand, I would pick Clemmie again and again and again."

CHAPTER THIRTEEN

July 26 and August 15, 1914
Overstrand, England

Any residual concerns over my dynamic with Winston fade as the threat of war mounts throughout Europe. Worries over the long-reaching impact of Winston's demands on my life seem petty — particularly since Winston's needs are critical to the survival of our country. As German hostility takes firm hold, Winston, wearing his hat of first lord of the admiralty, finalizes the naval preparations that will allow Britain to prevail in the war to come. And so, I surrender my apprehensions, allowing Winston and me to form an unassailable unit, one that has weathered the insidious tempest of Violet and emerged stronger than before.

War is inevitable. The June 28 gunshot that killed Archduke Franz Ferdinand, heir to the Austro-Hungarian throne, has begun a chain of cataclysmic events that, Winston has forewarned me, will undoubtedly lead to war, on the continent at least. Understanding that normal life may disappear as quickly as the single shot of that rifle, the sort of normal life I never had in my fatherless youth, I want to make a wellspring of memories from which our children can draw in the days ahead. Days when their father may be absent for long months, working in perilous circumstances. Days when he might not return at all.

We rent a beachside cottage at the Norfolk seaside, in a resort town called Overstrand. With Nanny and a maid in tow, the children and I settle into the six-bedroom Pear Tree Cottage, so named for the pear tree that is espaliered along one wall, which hugs a low, craggy cliff and stares out at the sea like a fisherman's wife. I'd arranged for Goonie and her two children to rent another property on the estate, a sweet house called Beehive Cottage that sits on the opposite end of the lawn. I know they will serve as another draw for Winston to join us whenever the political situation allows, particularly when Jack takes his military leave as well.

I am limited in my activities, because I am pregnant again. The restrictions, in truth,

139

are self-imposed. I could not bear to suffer through another miscarriage and the aftermath, so instead of my usual pace, I spend long, lazy days at the beach with my children, and I surprise myself with how much I enjoy this time. During the weekdays, I dig in the sand, point out fishing boats and gulls to the children, and insist that we dip our toes in the bracing North Sea waters. For the first time, I relish the slow minutes with my small charges and delight in their affection. But by the weekends, this celebration of the maternal wanes, and I begin to long for news and the touch of my husband.

"March on, children," Winston, pants rolled knee-high, calls back to Diana. She dutifully shoulders far more equipment than her five-year-old body should be able to carry. Three-year-old Randolph, by contrast, collapses in a fit of tears at the very suggestion that he might be responsible for his own sand pail. I wish the disparity could be explained by the difference in their ages, but I fear it is attributable to the differences in their temperaments.

I take up the rear of this busy brigade, trudging behind not only my husband and daughter but also Goonie and her children. I think about the expression on their faces when Winston arrived earlier today. When we first spotted an enormous vessel docked off the coast, its steam pipe pouring clouds of billowy gray into the otherwise cloudless azure sky, Goonie, the children, and I simply stared, marveling at the size of the ship in comparison to the fishing boats, bobbing nearby like bath toys. Only when a tiny rowboat dropped from the ship's side into the swelling sea and two men rowed its oars furiously toward the shore did we all scream with recognition and delight. The ship was the *Enchantress,* and one of the men was Winston.

I watch as my husband builds a fortress with the children. Once the castle, ramparts, towers, and moat are complete, the children scream and run in circles around the creation, assuming various warlike poses. Winston steps back to admire his handiwork and wraps his arm around my thickening waist, lightly draped with a robe over my modest bathing costume.

Rubbing his hand on my belly, he asks, "How are you faring, dear one?"

I turn into his chest. "Bearing up, Pug. But I miss you terribly. And of course, I worry."

He kisses the top of my head. His voice is thick with regret when he next speaks. "It will be some time before I can return to

Overstrand, my kitten. If at all."

"What do you mean? We rented Pear Tree Cottage for the entire summer, and you promised you'd visit every weekend that was not mission critical."

"It seems that we have reached the mission critical stage."

I pull away from him just enough to look into his eyes. "So soon? What's happening?"

I know that, for the better part of the summer, our foreign secretary has been working to prevent Britain's involvement in a war. This has required unusually tricky diplomacy, as Britain is part of the Triple Entente, and tensions have been mounting between Germany on one side and France and Russia on the other. But I'd believed that a balance had been struck and that Britain's entry into the war might be avoided for the summer.

"My kitten, I fear that the upcoming week will bring events to a head. I believe that — despite efforts to negotiate — Austria-Hungary will declare war on Serbia, which will undoubtedly lead to Russia mobilizing its army to help the Serbs, and Germany declaring war on Russia to help the Austro-Hungarians."

"No!" I exclaim.

He pulls me back into his embrace. "I'm

142

sorry, Cat, but I believe so. And it won't stop there. Germany will likely want to bring Russia's ally France into the fray by attacking via neutral Belgium. And even though the Cabinet is split on the acceptability of war with Germany, I believe that invasion will not be one we can ignore or negotiate our way around."

"Your intelligence is solid?"

"Impeccable."

I know he is right, just as surely as I know that helping France defend against Germany's invasion is the morally correct choice. If Winston's intelligence proves right and Germany does indeed attack Belgium — providing the Germans a direct route to France via the countryside and also to England through nearby ports — then our country must declare war as well. And my husband must be among those leading the charge.

My limbs begin to tremble. I try to steady the shaking, as I do not want him to think I am unable to bear the weight of this decision. Winston cannot help but feel it. He tightens his arms around me, whispering, "We will prevail, Cat. These past thirty months, I've ensured that we have the mightiest navy, well able to conquer the Germans. The fighting should be over by

Christmas."

His words don't comfort me. It matters not that Britain's fleet is fierce but that my husband will be at its center. But I know what Winston needs of me privately: unshakable faith in his ability to lead. I also know the public face he needs the lord admiral's wife to show the world: confidence. And he will get what he needs.

I press my lips together and smile at him. "I know, my love. Just as I know you will lead that fleet to victory."

He nods at me, and I see a spark of exhilaration in his eyes at the coming controversy. Does he imagine that, through this war, he'll match the military feats of his beloved ancestor, the first Duke of Marlborough? "Exactly."

"The children and I will return to London with you. As a show of our support." Despite my pregnant state and my fears, I feel mounting excitement at returning to London and becoming swept up in the wartime tide. We will be amid the making of history.

"No, my darling. You and the children must stay here. I need you to prove to the people of England that we can continue with our lives, that we need not fear." He releases me, staring into my eyes. "I must away now, Kitten. There's no need for tears.

Triumph is inevitable." Then he kisses me.

I watch as he hugs Diana and Randolph in turn, then his brother's family. We gather at the seashore, laughing and cheering as he rows back out to the *Enchantress*. Then we grow silent, understanding that this leave-taking is unlike the rest. This leave-taking could be the last.

Within days, Winston's predictions begin to prove accurate, and by August 4, Britain is at war. A desperation builds within me, and I experience an impulse to abandon the seaside and rush to Winston's side, to offer him the support and advice I know he needs during this time. Inexplicably, I also imagine London to be a bastion of safety, safer than this rather rickety seaside town, and I worry about my brother, Bill, readying for conflict on board a battleship, and Winston's brother, Jack, who is posted to the Second Division.

One restless evening, I very nearly ignore Winston's directive to stay in Overstrand and begin packing for our departure, but then our housemaid returns from her night off with curious news. A movie trailer at a local theater admonishes holiday-goers not to panic and abandon their Norfolk holidays because Mrs. Winston Churchill and her children are in the area for their holiday, and if it is safe enough for them, it should be safe enough for everyone else. I return our clothes to their armoires. How can I leave when my every move is watched as if I'm some sort of bellwether of the nation's fortunes?

While I resign myself to staying in Overstrand, despite the fact that we sit on an open coastline potentially vulnerable to attack, it feels wrong to leave Mother exposed on the French coast in Dieppe where she has retreated for the summer by herself. Since Bill is unavailable to help and I am limited by my pregnancy, Nellie agrees to extricate her from France and bring her to Pear Tree Cottage. But instead of accompanying Mother the full distance to Overstrand as she'd agreed, she drops her at a coastal train station on August 13 while she races to Buckinghamshire to help the Astors transform their mansion into a military hospital and then join a nursing corps in Belgium. I am left alone with my two anxious children and my exasperating mother while my husband directs the war from its beating heart, London.

"I swear I saw someone," Mother insists, pointing to the cliff wall below our feet. She's been here only two days and already she is setting the agenda.

She and I stand on the edge of the cliff abutting Pear Tree Cottage. Slate-gray clouds cover the sky as they have for nearly a week, and the sunny days of beachcombing and sand digging seem long gone. This weather combined with the news has left everyone on edge. My nerves become unraveled like a spilled spool of thread.

I stare at the cliff, scanning its length and studying the sandy beach that lines its base. I can imagine a fleet of German surface ships — the very sort about which Winston has been warning the government — blanketing the blue-gray sea, but I see only whitecaps and our long shadows stretching across the beach. Has Mother really spotted someone? Or has she gotten wrapped up in the spy mania spreading like a virus in coastal towns and imagined German enemies scaling the Overstrand cliffs?

"Are you certain, Mama?" My voice betrays my skepticism. I know that if the shoreline was indeed facing serious threats, Winston would recall us to London quicker than a heartbeat. Yet his letter this morning raised no such concerns, only details about his naval plans and his love.

"Absolutely. I swear I saw a figure." Her words convey strength, but her tone wavers.

147

Even if she doubts herself, she will never admit it. Mother believes in the infallibility of her own opinions.

I wonder about an enemy agent at Pear Tree Cottage. Could the children and I be a target? As the family of the lord admiral, I suppose it is possible, even though I see no evidence of a threat.

"Well, that 'figure' seems to have scuttled off without even a footprint in the sand," I decide.

She assumes an imperious pose, as if she still maintained control of my life. "How can you doubt me, Clementine? In times such as these."

Before I can answer, I feel Diana and Randolph pulling at my skirts. "What are you looking at?" my daughter asks.

"Nothing, children, only the sea. Daddy has not come by boat again," I answer, not wanting them to think that anything is amiss.

"Daddy, Daddy!" Randolph claps his hands in excitement at the possibility of his favorite playmate arriving.

I shouldn't have mentioned Daddy. I squat down to their eye level and deliver the unpleasant news. "I'm sorry, my dears. But Daddy must stay in London. The country needs him."

"But *I* need Daddy," Randolph yells and throws himself to the ground. His sobbing prompts Diana to cry, and in seconds, both children are shrieking. I reach out to comfort them, but Diana shrinks into herself, and Randolph slaps my hand away. Upon seeing my stunned reaction, he strikes again, this time intentionally.

My temples pound with the beginnings of a headache. *Where the devil is Nanny?* I think. I get back up, but my pregnant belly leaves me off balance, and I fall down on my hands and knees. Instead of helping me up, Mother scolds, "What the devil are you doing down there, Clementine?"

"Do you think I *want* to be down here, Mama?" I retort. I struggle to my feet and face my mother, my disgust plain.

Hearing our sharp exchange, the children's shrieks escalate to screams. When Nanny finally pushes open the cottage's back door and races to Diana and Randolph, I walk back toward the house without a word to her, Mother, or the children. I lurch up the stairs to my bedroom, curling into the chaise longue and resting my head against the cool wall.

I would rather be in London, facing the stresses of war, than here on the desolate seaside, dealing with Mother and the children. Why do the maneuverings of battleships and naval men seem an easier task than the managing of two small children and an elderly woman? Perhaps I am not suited to the usual work of a woman.

My breathing quickens. I rock back and forth on the chaise longue, banging my forehead on the wall in the process. I welcome the pain, as it inexplicably provides relief from the chaos within me. What is wrong with me?

Even though I know it is self-pitying — more than that, it is selfish — I want my husband. He alone understands me and gives me focus. But I do not know when I will see him next, so I reach for my pen and paper.

CHAPTER FOURTEEN

October 7, 1914
London, England
The pangs are sharp but bearable, I tell myself as I withhold a scream.

"Are you all right, ma'am?" the nurse asks, but I cannot answer. I can't catch a breath.

I nod at the doctor, midwife, and nurse lining my bedroom at Admiralty House, all assigned to ensure the safety of the lord admiral's wife and unborn child, as well as Goonie, who agreed to stay with us at Admiralty House. Strange how the self-indulgent sadness and isolation I experienced at Overstrand disappeared the moment Winston summoned the children and me back to London, which happened within weeks of his receipt of my hysterical August letter. While I suspect that many women would have preferred the remote beach location to the wartime bustle of London,

151

even with the vague threat of shoreline espionage, I delighted at plunging into the thick of things. The risks of the conflict never overwhelmed me, only the fear of marginalization.

Another contraction takes hold, and all thinking ceases. My mind can process only the pain. The body-wrenching pain and the urgent desire to push consume me.

Once it subsides like a retreating wave, the past few weeks reenter my consciousness. Have I provided my husband the help he so desperately needs to navigate the murky naval waters? Immediately upon my return to Admiralty House, I saw that Winston's brash enthusiasm for his military plans — combined with unwavering confidence in his own vision — was presenting problems with key naval staff and his ability to lead. I understood that these difficulties might hamper his ability to defeat Germany's plan of fighting on two fronts, attacking the west via France through Belgium and confronting Russia in the east. While I agreed with him that the reluctant chief of the home fleet, Admiral Sir George Callaghan, needed to be replaced, I saw that firing him with only a medal for his troubles would be a blow to the men's morale. I suggested that perhaps providing him a seat on the Admiralty Board would soothe not only his feelings but also the men's. I offered Winston a fresh lens to view his dealings with the combative secretary of state for war Lord Herbert Kitchener as well. While he would not accept disagreement from others, he accepted my proposals. But I am not at his side now, and I worry.

The waves of pain are coming quicker now, barely giving me a chance to breathe in between. The only word that slides through the agony is Antwerp. When the contraction recedes, anger rises up. Why did Winston have to be in Antwerp instead of London right now?

The German invasion of Belgium has advanced with unfortunate success to the critical port city of Antwerp, the last holdout of the Belgian military. On October 2, the very day the baby was due, Winston received word that Antwerp was on the verge of falling. Despite my begging, he offered to sail to the besieged city to assist the Belgian forces, even though no senior government official had ordered him to take the action. By October 4, he had become so swept up in war fever, he telegraphed the prime minister from Antwerp, asking to temporarily resign his lord admiral position to lead the British forces in Antwerp's port. Even though Winston was not a career military man, his request was accepted by Asquith, although I could envision the scuttlebutt characterizing it as an obvious grab for military glory.

But Winston's efforts were for naught. Even with the additional troops and fleet under his command, Antwerp fell to the Germans earlier today. The British forces were evacuated, and Winston will return to London this evening. Will the fall of Antwerp be attributed to the failure of his last-minute efforts? He will return to London on the waves of the war's first major failure.

Winston should never have raced to Antwerp. He should have left the defense of the Belgian city to a career military officer and let that man wear the stain of that fiasco. He should have stayed here, instead of leaving me alone with only the whisper, "You must stay strong, Cat."

The contractions grow closer and then blend into one ceaseless agony. I cannot stop from crying out. The pain sears like an unrelenting knife stab, rending me in two. Sweat pours from my brow, and the nurse mops my forehead in a useless gesture of comfort. I shove her hand away and howl in exhaustion and torment. The urge to push takes hold of me, and then suddenly, it ceases.

And I hear a cry.

In my peripheral vision, I see the nurse and midwife hover together. Goonie sits by my side, holding my hand, and I manage to whisper, "Is everything all right?"

No one answers me at first. Panic rises within me, but then the nurse walks toward me with a parcel swaddled in white cotton.

"You have a beautiful, healthy baby, Mrs. Churchill."

"Is it a boy?" I croak out the question.

"It is a lovely baby girl," she says as she hands me the bundle.

Goonie rises and peers into the blankets. "She's beautiful, Clemmie."

She is not a boy, as I'm sure Winston would like, but I'm relieved. Randolph is boy enough for me. She is beautiful, with her father's red hair, which will please him endlessly. I clutch at the tiny bundle, bringing my newborn daughter close to my chest.

Peeling the blanket back a bit, I gaze at her perfect rosebud lips and gently closed eyes. I smile at my daughter, who we will call Sarah. I will love her and ensure her care, but she will not hold me back.

CHAPTER FIFTEEN

January 3, 1915
London, England

I stare at the long table, set with mono-grammed china and multifaceted crystal as if an elegant dinner party were to begin instead of an unofficial war cabinet meeting. The exquisite service for twelve does not contain the usual name cards, but then the usual rules do not apply in wartime. This leaves my place at the table uncertain, however, particularly because, as usual, I am the only woman.

Unlike many of the men holding these dinners, our host, Home Secretary Reginald McKenna, seems sensitive to my situation. He gestures for Winston and me to take seats flanking Foreign Secretary Sir Edward Grey, and I gratefully settle into my chair. Servants immediately appear to ladle water-cress soup into our bowls, and as they do, the men lining the table give me sidelong glances. I know they find my presence among them distasteful; after all, they wouldn't dream of bringing their wives. But I am not here for their approval or their pleasure. I am here because I have a role to fulfill.

As I sip my soup, I listen. The men around me are tallying the latest skirmishes. Soon after the Allies began gaining ground against the Germans on both the western and eastern fronts — derailing Germany's aspirations for a quick victory — the powers that be realized that the war would likely devolve into impasse, a sort of cat-and-mouse game with each side taking turns as cat. Only an unexpected, massive victory could upend this tit for tat.

The men's tones are desultory as they discuss the machinations at the fronts, and I want to shake them into action. How can they be so lackluster about strategy and hope when over ninety thousand military men and civilians have already lost their lives? When women and children are being shelled in coastal towns? When the government has received intelligence that Germany may soon let loose its zeppelins over London to bomb our citizens from the air? Complacency cannot rule the day, but the only animation I observe stems from remarks about yesterday's appeal by Grand Duke Nicholas of Russia for assistance against the Ottomans in the Caucasus, an idea they bat about like a tennis ball. Is Winston the only one in this room with a new idea?

I take a deep breath, reminding myself that Winston has a plan and I am here to bolster him. Despite the fact that I know this is my proper place, Nellie's words from the holidays weigh on me.

Nellie came to stay with us at Admiralty House for a long stint during the holiday season after a harrowing turn at the hands of the Germans. Over the summer, Nellie received some hasty, basic training in nursing so she could be stationed at the front. Assigned to a unit in Belgium to tend to fallen British soldiers, her nursing unit was taken captive in late August when the Germans occupied the Belgian town in which she'd been working. We were worried sick about her, and Winston kept close tabs on her status. He learned that the nurses were generally treated rather well and that the Germans were keeping on her unit to treat British casualties in the area. When the nurses were commanded to treat German soldiers and refused in late November, they were repatriated. Having my little sister at home with us had been a great relief to our shared concerns about her twin, Bill, who was stationed on a naval torpedo destroyer. Winston kept us well apprised of his status, but there were so many variables at sea.

One night after dinner, she and I lolled about on the sofa in the private parlor, giggling about something Mother had mentioned over dinner just before her departure. Nellie turned to me and said, "Do you realize that this is the first time I've seen you sit down and relax in the three weeks I've been here?"

"Surely I haven't been standing at the dining table and eating my meals, Nellie," I kidded her.

"You are always running, Clemmie," Nellie commented. Her tone was half-playful and half-serious. "Even when you're sitting still."

"Winston needs me, Nellie. Our country faces the fiercest threat in its history, and he is critical to England's success," I answer defensively. "You of all people should understand. You were just a prisoner of the Germans."

"Yes, Clemmie, Winston's work is important. But you have three young children and this vast house to run." Her voice was matter-of-fact, but her eyes were pleading. "I worry that you are running yourself ragged by managing all that and attending these endless meetings and dinners with Winston."

"My assistance to my husband is singular, and Nanny can tend to the day-to-day needs of Diana, Randolph, and Sarah as well as I can. Better."

She paused. "You know *you* are not the lord admiral, don't you, Clemmie?"

I felt as though I'd been slapped. I'd grown used to whispers and japes critiquing my involvement, but not from my beloved sister. "You sound like Venetia."

"Maybe she had a point." She reached for my hand. "But only with respect to the toll it takes upon you, Clemmie. Even if you deny it."

Winston clears his throat again, and I return to the present. I recognize the sound as his attempt to wait for the other men to finish their conversation. I'd cautioned him not to launch into his plan at the beginning of the evening but to listen for an opportune opening in the men's discussions. *If you can present your scheme just after the usual lamentations about the current military state,* I told him, *your plan will be better received.* But Winston can't help himself, and his mouth begins opening to interrupt the men's talk.

I arch my brow and give him a pointed look. His mouth closes, and he bides his time.

The secretary of state for war, Earl Kitchener, murmurs, "I heard that Christmas carols sparked an impromptu truce along the trenches. A meeting of the Germans' 'Silent Night' with the British 'First Noel,' if you will."

"The same rumors reached me. After the singing, apparently, Christmas greetings flew across the trenches," McKenna adds.

"Exchanges of whiskey and cigars, in some spots," Lord Chancellor Viscount Richard Haldane concurs.

"I understand that a rousing game of football was played in no-man's-land between English and Germans in one case," Asquith says.

"Football? Surely not," Walter Runciman, the president of the Board of Trade, chimes in.

"All along the trenches in Belgium. Impromptu truces and spontaneous games of football," Asquith insists.

As the men shake their heads in incredulity, Winston sputters. He cannot keep quiet any longer. "Why does our men's desire for peace surprise you? It is bad enough that we left our men in the trenches of Belgium throughout Christmas, festering in the soggy ground with dysentery and snow and lice. They want to come home, and we must find a way other than these interminable trenches."

What about the women and children who've lost their lives? I think. But I file that notion away for another day and another argument.

"I suppose you have a proposal?" Asquith answers Winston's call to action through the puff of his pipe.

The men chortle, as if the idea of Winston *without* a bold idea is unfathomable. But in their laughter, I also hear derision. A rage begins to brew within me, but I tamp it down to allow Winston to take center stage. This is his moment, one to which we have been building in our nightly discussions.

Winston puffs on the cigar that has recently become ever-present in his mouth. "As a matter of fact, I do."

"Let's hear it then," Asquith orders with a sigh.

"We have been presented with an urgent appeal from Russia to help with the Ottomans, who are in league with the Germans. What if we showed our naval might in the Dardanelles? If we take control of the Dardanelles strait between the Turkish mainland and the Gallipoli peninsula, we could capture the Turkish capital of Constantinople. This maneuver would have two key impacts — it would weaken Germany by eliminating Turkey as one of its allies, and it would open up a sea route between our country and Russia to aid with supplies."

As he lays out the details of his plan, I gaze at the faces of the men at the table. Their brows furrow and their eyes look wary, and I even see Asquith shoot a cynical look at Kitchener. Have I erred in encouraging Winston to propose this bold course? Have I believed too much in his vision and importance to our country in this war effort? I say a silent prayer to a god I've much ignored that Winston has suggested the right path for the soldiers — both for their sake and for ours.

Chapter Sixteen

May 20, May 26, and June 3, 1915
London, England

When the final blow comes, I believe I am ready. Winston's torrent of letters has prepared me, or so I thought. Yet I hardly recognize the fallen face of my anguished husband when he finally returns from the catastrophe of the Dardanelles and walks through the front door of Admiralty House.

"I will be blamed, Clemmie," Winston whispers into my hair. We cling to each other in the foyer, ignoring the presence of servants in the background. I think but do not say that it is my fault as well. I encouraged him to pursue the Dardanelles strategy, even when it was ill received by the senior government officials.

The Dardanelles campaign had commenced with Winston's usual bullish zeal. He worked around the clock with naval and military staff to convince them of his plan

164

and to organize the onslaught. The success of the plan required both an abundance of naval forces to take the Dardanelles strait and a sizable military contingent to conquer the Gallipoli peninsula afterward. Winston set sail to much fanfare, and I followed his every movement by letter and news reports.

The naval bombardment began on February 19, but soon afterward, Winston wrote to me that Vice Admiral Carden's efforts seemed halfhearted. This suspicion was confirmed in mid-March when Carden resigned due to illness and Rear Admiral de Robeck replaced him. De Robeck had no appetite for the attack and called off the entire naval plan after one French and two British battleships were sunk by mines. Without adequate opposition from the sea, the Turkish fleet was able to restock its troops on land with ammunition, so when War Secretary Lord Kitchener and General Sir Ian Hamilton's army plan was initiated in April, their troops suffered terrible losses on land — a horrific thirty thousand British, ten thousand French, and more than thirteen thousand Australians, New Zealanders, and Indians.

In an effort to get the operation back on track and give meaning to the men's horrific sacrifice, Winston appealed for naval reinforcements first to Asquith, who deferred to the local admirals. My husband then entreated the mercurial Admiral of the Fleet Lord Fisher who, having supported the mission at the start, turned on the Dardanelles plan and blocked Winston's efforts.

If only I hadn't encouraged him in the Dardanelles plan, the terrible loss might have been averted, I think. *If only I had accepted that the government's lackluster response from the outset meant Winston would receive lackluster support throughout the course of the campaign, perhaps I could have dissuaded Winston from the idea of taking over the Dardanelles.* But I say none of this; there are others accountable as well. Others with hands on the wheel of this disaster.

"How can you be blamed, Winston? The plan was sound. If you had been given adequate naval support, the capture of the Dardanelles would have been a success, and the Turks would never have gotten supplies through to their troops. We would have secured the Gallipoli peninsula and vanquished the Turks. Maybe even shortened the war. Asquith, Hamilton, Kitchener, and" — I can scarcely say the name, but I force myself to spit it out — "Fisher refused to send the promised help. They are to blame."

"You and I know that to be true. But I was the campaign's most vocal champion, and it was the bloodiest loss in all of British military history —" His words catch, and I know he is holding back tears. "And the people quite understandably want blood in return."

"But why does it have to be *your* blood? Can the blame not be shouldered by all those involved in the affair?"

"It seems as though I have already been made the sacrificial lamb, my sweet kitten."

My heart thuds so loudly, I worry that Winston can hear it. "What do you mean?"

"Rumors are flying that Asquith was approached by the Conservative leader, Andrew Bonar Law, who threatened to undo the wartime detente between Conservatives and Liberals if a head doesn't roll for the Dardanelles. You know the Conservatives have loathed me ever since I switched parties, and Asquith knows it too. I've heard from a reputable source that in order to save his own hide, Asquith made a deal with the Conservatives to form a coalition government with the Conservatives upon my removal from office. And Lloyd George agreed."

"No!" My hand flies to my mouth.

"I wish it wasn't true, Cat. But it is." He sighs, a sound that seems to emanate from deep within him. "I am finished."

How could Asquith do this to Winston? After all his work and dedication. All his loyalty. All his brilliance.

My tears suddenly subside, only to be replaced by rage. "How dare he! This is an affront not only to you but to the people of our country! You are the only one in the cabinet who has the power and imagination to vanquish the Germans. And you would have been well on your way to accomplishing that if you had been supported by your peers," I say, seething. "By people who agreed to the plan, even if they were half-hearted in their acquiescence."

To my astonishment, my fury does not spark a flame within Winston. He only kisses my hair and whispers, "It matters not, my dearest Clementine. I have been eviscerated of power. And one can do nothing without power."

With the utterance of those words, I know my husband has surrendered to a certain fate.

We do not receive the official notification of Winston's removal for nearly a week, on

May 26. Even though I'm unaccustomed to the ritual, I find myself praying constantly, praying that Asquith does not force my husband out. I know what this will mean to Winston. But the lambasting Winston receives at the hands of the daily newspapers, combined with the abusive calls of "Dardanelles" and "Gallipoli" I get from passersby whenever I step out in public, make clear that even if Asquith hasn't made a deal with the Conservatives, Winston's ousting is inevitable.

When the notice of his dismissal arrives, we leave Admiralty House within the hour, as I'd packed our belongings earlier in the week. Our summer rental of Hoe Farm is not yet available, and we rented our house on Eccleston Square when Winston became lord admiral, so we decamp to a house on Arlington Street owned by Winston's aunt Cornelia and her son Lord Wimborne, where we spend long hours seated in wingback chairs before the fire contemplating our future, oftentimes in silence. After five days cajoling my husband into discussion, we receive an envelope from Downing Street. While Winston wonders aloud as to why Asquith would write, I stay quiet. I am wary that the missive might reference the scathing letter I'd jotted off to Asquith, unbeknownst to Winston, just before the dismissal, in which I'd extolled my husband's virtues — along with his importance to the war effort — and excoriated Asquith for even thinking of firing him. In fact, I called out the prime minister on his real motivation for firing Winston, namely ensuring the people's opinion of him.

But when a hopeful Winston slices open the envelope with the sharp sterling knife on Lord Wimborne's desk, the letter within makes no mention of my dispatch. Instead, inexplicably, the prime minister and his wife, Margot, have summoned us to Downing Street for dinner. And I am to arrive early to take late afternoon tea with Margot.

Smoothing my gown, an unadorned gray muslin that I consider somber enough for the occasion, I stand at the front door to Downing Street and ring the bell. A familiar-looking maid admits me but will not meet my gaze. Does she know something I don't? Or is she like everyone I pass on the street, standing in judgment of a catastrophe that has been unfairly attributed only to my husband.

She leads me to Margot's sitting room, a space to which I'd never been invited before. Early on, I'd attributed my exclusion from her private chamber to her ongoing disappointment that Winston had married me instead of Violet, but now, I wonder whether it stems from my familial tie to Venetia. Until very recently, the relationship between my cousin and Asquith continued apace, and I feel certain Margot knew about it all along.

How will she greet me? I wonder as we march up the three flights of stairs leading to the prime minister's private residence. Will she deride me for my harsh letter to her husband? Or will she apologize for the terrible penance they've forced my husband to pay?

When we finally reach the sitting room, Margot is waiting. Her features are sharp and her gray eyes hard, but she feigns softness. She stretches out her generous arms to wrap me in an unwanted embrace, saying, "Oh, Clementine, how I've been thinking about you. What a challenging time."

Her words — carefully chosen to approximate sympathy without admitting any guilt — enrage me. I keep my body rigid in the encasement of her arms, but when this doesn't put Margot off, I push her away from me.

"How could you?" I rail.

"Now, Clementine, shouldn't it be *me* asking *you* that question?" she answers coolly, her facade of softness turning brittle. "What on earth are you talking about, Margot? Your husband sacrificed mine over the Dardanelles. When you and I both know that the fault was not Winston's." My tone is every bit as hard as hers.

"I am talking about the letter that you sent poor Henry." She pauses, and for a moment, I wonder who she is talking about. But then I remember that she calls Asquith "Henry." "Who has already taken quite a beating over this Dardanelles mess. I forgive you for writing such hateful words, of course. Heat of the moment and all that. But I hardly think you are in a position to unleash any more anger."

"*You* forgive *me?*" I practically scream. "For speaking the truth to 'poor Henry'? I don't want your blasted forgiveness, and I've done nothing to forgive in any event."

Margot glances around the room. "Please, Clementine, take a seat and compose yourself." As I storm toward the door, she mutters, "You are foolish to act this way. You will burn whatever bridges Winston has left."

Her words cut me to the quick, but I don't turn back. Before I can reach the handle, the door pushes open. Asquith himself enters the room. "I heard voices," he com-

172

ments, clearly displeased.

I know from Winston, and to a lesser extent Venetia, that the prime minister seeks adoration from women — not challenge — and prefers his "ladies" to have a malleable morality. In the past, he has found unappetizing my rather inflexible moral positions and even went so far as to call me a bore for refusing the gift of a couture gown from King Edward VII's mistress. Now I surmise from his tone that he finds my unfeminine, raised voice disturbing to his sensitive ears.

I want to hurl myself at him, but Margot's admonitions ring in my ears. Have I indeed damaged the remnants of my husband's career? I hesitate, even though I long to berate him for his disloyalty and his carrying-on with Venetia as young soldiers are being killed by the thousands. *Although, I think with a certain glee, I suppose those shenanigans have ended now that Venetia has agreed to marry the junior minister Edwin Montagu.*

Asquith speaks before I decide upon my words. "I wish that there had been another way, Clementine. We needed to show the country was unified in its decision-making."

How dare he intimate that he'd been forced into firing Winston. I will not placate him. I say nothing, forcing him to entrench himself further in his indefensible position.

"I know it will seem small consolation at the moment, but I promise you this, Clementine. I will protect Winston as best as I can so that — in the future — he can play the role to which he was born."

While I'm pleased with Asquith's acknowledgment of Winston's potential and impending greatness — even though I doubt his promise to protect my husband — I wonder how the torpid, self-serving Asquith knew precisely how to manipulate me. I'd believed him to be utterly disconnected from anyone's feelings or motivations other than his own.

But I was wrong. He knows I will do whatever necessary to protect my husband. Even if it means temporary silence.

CHAPTER SEVENTEEN

September 22 and November 4, 1915
Surrey and London, England

Do you think you can put these to any use?"
I say, trying to keep the irritation from my
tone as I hand Winston the box of paints
and brushes from Goonie's collection,
which the children also use from time to
time. I am careful not to allow the paint to
splatter on my dress. Money is scarce these
days, and my clothes must last, even the
simple ones.

"They're utterly botching this war. For
nearly six months, I've been forced to sit
idly by with long, tedious days of unsolicited
leisure" — he gestures around to the picturesque rolling hills of Surrey surrounding us
— "while those fiends in London cast away
all chance at victory. To think of the thousands of lives lost because of their egos and
ineptitude."

"Did you hear me, Winston?" I interrupt

his vitriol with a question, my hand still outstretched. This time, I don't bother to mask my annoyance. I've heard this tirade before countless times, and while I fully agree with his point of view, I cannot countenance it anymore. Giving voice to these sentiments only serves to further enrage him.

"I did, I did," he grumbles without a word of apology. His mood has become so dark as of late. He treats his depression as if it's something separate and apart from himself. But I believe that it's his visceral reaction to being expelled from the center of power.

But Winston isn't done spewing his bitter sentiments. He practically yells, "Do you really think a daub of paint will bring back those soldiers?"

My free hand shifts to my hip, and I match his tone. "Do you really think that it's appropriate to speak to your wife in that manner? I am not one of your subordinates, Winston." I dislike the loud voice and tyrannical manner in which he's begun to speak to our staff and, when he was in office, those who reported to him, although I had no control over that realm. In *this* realm, however, I will not sit by quietly while he screams at me or the servants, no matter how frustrated he is with his current position.

His eyes widen as he realizes the impact of his words. "I am sorry, Clemmie. It's just the headlines getting under my skin." He reaches for the box of paints, saying, "Hand them over. Let me see what havoc I can wreak with them."

The mild summer days spent in the bucolic landscape surrounding Hoe Farm in Hascombe near Godalming in Surrey had served as salve for Winston's wounded pride at first, particularly with regular visits by the newly engaged Nellie and occasionally her fiancé, Bertram Romilly, a rather quiet fellow from a reputable military family. Together with Goonie and our gaggle of children, we explored the nearby woodlands by daylight and dined on favorite foods in the picturesque fifteenth-century stone manor house by night. But the comforts of Hoe Farm proved short-lived.

Within weeks, I find Winston sitting despondently at his desk instead of gallivanting with the children, who he has recently found overwhelming, particularly Randolph, who is prone to teasing and naughtiness. Even though he still sits on the Cabinet and War Council, he has been marginalized, and his new position as chancellor of the duchy of Lancaster, an empty role given to ousted politicians, has no demands, and he cannot tolerate his ostracism from the center of power at this critical moment in our nation's history. It is the worst imaginable punishment for a man who sees himself as essential. When I examine his blank stare and slack expression, I feel as though I am watching him grieve for a lost part of himself.

The brush and paint provide him with a diversion. I recruit our friend John Lavery, a talented painter of portraits and landscapes, and his wife, Hazel, who is herself a wonderful artist, to give Winston lessons and guidance in his endeavors. And when his interest seems to wane, I offer my husband further distraction in the form of trips to the National Gallery for artistic inspiration. The barrage of negative headlines about the botched military decisions by the new coalition government, however, undermines any delight he finds in his canvases, and people we thought were friends abandon us — even Violet disavows Winston once and for all and becomes engaged to Sir Maurice Bonham-Carter. I soon realize that nothing will appease my husband's pain except a return to action.

And if politics can no longer be his pathway, I will find him another.

Drinks in hand, we sit before the fire at Jack and Goonie's London home, where we've gone to stay for the time being as a necessary economy for both families. Always sensitive to the moods of others, Goonie has taken over the task of seeing the children to bed, understanding that Winston and I need time alone. His mood has been black since he returned home from Parliament today.

"I've been excluded from the newly reorganized War Council," he says, keeping his eyes fixed on the fire.

The news does not surprise me. His place on the prior war cabinet had been a holdover from his days as lord admiral, and he had power in name only. As a result, I'd perceived Winston's hopes of inclusion in the new War Council as far-fetched in light of the Dardanelles and would not indulge conversation about his efforts. Time and noteworthy acts outside the government are the only way to heal his blighted reputation, I'd come to believe. But Winston, typically impatient, does not want to play the long game.

I nod in sympathy. "That's unfortunate,

Pug. But there may be other ways to restore your position."

"Oh really, Clementine? Are you suggesting I have not thought of everything?" He speaks sharply to me, and I grow quiet, closing around myself like an oyster around its pearl. I wait for the apology I know will come, as his mounting despair has yielded many outbursts and has required many apologies.

"Kitten, I'm sorry. This damnable business of isolation is driving me mad. Please share your ideas with me," he offers.

I breathe in deeply. I have an unorthodox proposal for him, which, in truth, stems from a seed that he himself planted. Until now, I have brooked no discussion about this idea, but I know that I must bury my own needs and anxieties about Winston's safety to offer him this avenue toward hope.

"Actually, it's an idea of yours about which I've finally come around."

"What idea?" His brows knit in confusion, an expression I see rarely upon his face. His mind operates so quickly that he is rarely perplexed.

"Volunteering your services for the front." I will myself to sound strong and confident. I cannot allow my voice to quiver with the fear inside me.

"Th-the front?" The stutter to which he reverts in times of great stress emerges. Is it prompted by the thought of fighting alongside soldiers in the dangerous muck of the trenches? Or is he shocked that — after eschewing the idea for months — I am now suggesting it myself?

"Yes, Pug. As usual, you were wise in your proposal." I use the word *proposal,* although his regular rants about resigning his position and enlisting in the army are hardly fully formed plans. They are closer to empty threats. But I now take him at his word. I must.

"Go to the front? Really, Clemmie?"

Is he asking the question of me or himself? I wonder.

"I've come to believe that it is the only way to salvage your reputation and restore power. Politics will not deliver you there."

"By fighting in the front line?"

"Yes," I answer without hesitation, even though the specter of injury and death looms large in my consciousness.

He stands up and paces around the room, puffing on his cigar. "It could work, Clemmie. It would show the PM and the people that if I'm prevented from commanding the war from afar, I am willing to fight alongside the men in the trenches. That my dedication to our country is unshakable."

"And that your bravery knows no bounds." I rise from my chair and stand before him.

"Yes," he says with a nod, "it demonstrates courage and self-sacrifice. A quality in short supply among most men of my class. I will write a letter to Asquith today, resigning from this ridiculous chancellor post and offering my services to the front." He wraps his arms around me, whispering, "What would I do without you, my sweet kitten?"

"You will never have to know, Pug," I whisper back.

CHAPTER EIGHTEEN

November 16, 1915, to April 6, 1916
London, England

At different points in my marriage, I believed that Winston had put me to the test. There were the long days at Admiralty House where I juggled the management of the house and our three children, the necessary social engagements, and the constant counsel my husband demanded. The weeks ordered to my bed, where I healed from my miscarriage while Winston dined with Violet, presented particular challenges. I perceived the dark months after Winston's public blame for the Dardanelles to be the worst of my married life. But I was wrong in thinking that I'd experienced trials.

From the moment Winston dons his uniform and heads to the Franco-Belgian border at Ploegsteert as a lowly major in the Oxfordshire Hussars, my responsibilities reach new heights. His constant stream of letters shows admirable optimism for the savage conditions, regular gunfire, and constant downpours, a record of only eighteen days without rain in a five-month span. But they also contain demands for a bevy of impossible-to-obtain items — sheepskin sleeping bags, a bathtub made of tin with an accompanying copper boiler, leather waistcoats, hampers of cigars and chocolate, even periscopes — for which I scrounge and then send to the front. All while managing the children and the house we share with Goonie on a tiny fraction of his old lord admiral salary.

Yet sourcing these scarce objects is an easier task than the more intangible goals he lays out for me. He wants me to fight on his behalf here in England as he fights for English liberty in France. I am to lay the groundwork for his return to power.

Anything that might repair his damaged reputation and provide opportunity upon his return from the trenches, I undertake and report back to Winston in our regular exchange of letters. I court journalists who might plant favorable nuggets about Winston in the papers. I lunch with governmental figures who could suggest him for posts. I manage urgent constituent affairs, as Winston never relinquished his parliamentary seat. I meet with Lloyd George, as we believe that he may succeed Asquith one day. I even deign to court the Asquiths, hosting them for bridge and several rounds of golf, as a hedge against our bets in the event that Lloyd George does not ultimately prevail.

But Winston does not praise me for these efforts. He pushes for further bolstering of the Churchill name. I decide to undertake my own projects, focusing on those near to my heart — women and workers. The front is in dire need of emergency gas masks, so I design a campaign enlisting housewives to make them. I join the Munition Workers' Auxiliary Committee to run nine canteens across northern London, offering meals day and night for the critical munitions workers to ensure they have adequate food, as company managers often fail to provide enough for their around-the-clock shifts. As I do, I insist that the female munitions workers — of which there are more every day — have the same rights to canteen breaks as the men.

I work nearly as many hours as the armaments laborers, much to the criticism of women of my acquaintance who find my efforts among the working class unsavory. But instead of finding the long days and physical work taxing — particularly once I give up our motor out of financial necessity and have to reach the far-flung canteens by patchwork routes of the train combined with the tube or trams — I discover that I find it exhilarating and rewarding to be in the thick of things, even as my hours with the children grow fewer. The exertion also helps stave off my constant worry about Winston's well-being.

"A letter arrived from Mr. Churchill, ma'am." The pert young maid, whose name I can never recall, hands me an envelope when I arrive home at midnight after a long evening serving munitions laborers at the canteen.

I thank her and take the letter as she slides off my coat.

Except for the rustle of my coat as the maid hangs it in the wardrobe and the tick of the grandfather clock in the front hallway, the house is silent. Under Goonie's capable supervision — much more capable than my own — the children have been served their suppers, bathed, and tucked into their beds. *How long has it been since I read Randolph, Diana, and Sarah a bedtime story?* I wonder. That ritual was once my favorite, a bright light amid the onerous darkness of children's chores. As I ponder whether the children have even noticed my absence, a troubling thought strikes me. Have I *ever* read a bedtime tale to the eighteen-month-old Sarah?

What sort of mother have I become? Is it the war and Winston that have made me so remote? Or is it an unfortunate consequence of my upbringing? A failing in my nature?

I pour myself a short brandy and sink into the settee in the study. What will today's letter from Winston contain? Detailed descriptions of the front, with its water-logged trenches and battalions of lice? Lists of obscure items I'm meant to procure despite the rationing of wartime? A detailed description of how he very nearly missed being hit by a shell, but that I was not to worry? At the very least, I will be spared the diatribe over whether he should be given a brigade or a battalion to command, now that the matter has been settled. My concern about his well-being buzzes like an insect in the back of my every thought and action, and even though I sometimes cannot restrain myself from writing that I wish he could come home, I try to stay strong and banish my fears to the back of my consciousness.

Before I read the letter, I pick up the blurry snapshot lying in the center of the table abutting the settee. Cut from the *Daily*

187

Mirror on the day he left for war, it shows Winston in his uniform. I recall the herculean effort it took for me to remain stoic that day amid the melodramatic weeping of Jennie and the wailing of the children. I knew that Winston needed my brave face, not my tears, so I waited until he left to submit to my sobs. I kiss the hazy photo; no image of him has ever made me prouder.

As I slice open the envelope, pages of Winston's scrawling handwriting spill onto the floor. As I assemble them in order, a phrase jumps out at me. *I believe it is time for my return.* Surely I have read his words out of context. After all, while his prior letters had enumerated his dissatisfaction with the governmental decisions, he had always written that he would not return unless he was wounded or could resume governmental control.

I begin with the first page. Glancing over familiar complaints about the way in which governmental decisions are playing out on the battlefield and in the trenches, I also see a description of the alternate, much preferable plans he'd pursue if given the opportunity. My eyes linger on the final line on the second-to-last page, in which he maintains that he's necessary for England's success in the war.

My stomach lurches. I flip to the final page, but I already know what words I will find there. *I believe it is time for my return.* It is the very thing for which I have been simultaneously wishing and dreading.

I place the letter down on my desk with a shaking hand. I want my husband home and safe by my side. Of course I do. I want to relinquish the worries about him that plague my waking hours. But it is not yet time. He has not even been at the front for six months, while most young soldiers have suffered there for a year or more. And none of those men are living in the relative luxury Winston enjoys, with regular hot baths, brandy and chocolate, a sheepskin sleeping bag, and a ready supply of fresh boots and clothes. I pray that he keeps these indulgences private, as he would surely annoy his fellow soldiers and undo all the messaging he's trying to telegraph to the government.

How can he even think of coming back from the front prematurely? I know from all my conversations with governmental leaders and military men, undertaken at Winston's behest, that he must stay longer to repair his reputation. He may even have to wait for the rumored Dardanelles Commission to meet and exonerate him. He needs to honor my months of laying groundwork and wait for the people and the government to beg him to return. Otherwise, his risks and our family's sacrifice will be in vain.

But how can I do what I must? How could I live with myself if something happened to him? I steel myself to undertake the necessary, but unthinkable, task.

Rising from the settee, I settle at the desk. Dipping my pen into the ink, my hand shakes as I begin to write words that will whip my impatient husband into a fury. But I also know that he will listen to me as he will no one else.

III

CHAPTER NINETEEN

January 2 and March 21, 1921
London, England, and Cairo, Egypt

As I'd hoped, Winston climbed in the days after his return from the trenches — beginning with minister of munitions, then ascending to secretary of state for war and air after Lloyd George replaced Asquith as prime minister. But with each step upward, the demands upon me grew. The end of the Great War did not bring a reprieve, because within four days of its end, our fourth child, the ginger-haired Marigold, was born, on November 15, 1918. Her birth and the end of the fighting did bring joy, and when Winston helped negotiate and witness the signing of the Treaty of Versailles in May 1919, I felt incredible pride. But my pride did not reduce my responsibilities, particularly since our peripatetic home life and insufficient funds required me to orchestrate moves from one temporary abode to another every few months until our most recent move to Sussex Square. This constant shifting of homes, too reminiscent of my unhappy, itinerant childhood, layered strain upon my already stretched nerves. I struggled along for years, desperately trying to ignore my situation, until I suddenly couldn't.

I cannot remember when my composure first snapped. I have no recollection of any particular event from which I retreated into myself. I do not think that one particular harsh outburst from Winston triggered a recoiling. I simply recall a dark hollow within me into which I crawled when the anxiety overwhelmed.

How dare I complain when others suffer far worse fates? I would tell myself. Look at my poor sister Nellie, whose husband was severely injured during the war and is forced to support her family — including two small children — on a small disability pension? How would they fare without the help we give them when we can? In comparison to them and countless others, I had no right to suffer. But suffering came whether or not I was worthy.

"We must take extreme care," Dr. Gomez says to Winston. I hear the slightest quiver in the doctor's usually commanding voice.

Better than anyone, I understand how daunting it can be to give instructions to my husband, particularly unpopular ones.

Winston chews on the end of his cigar, a nasty habit he has developed. He has been immune to my pleas to stop it. "What do you mean by 'care'?" he asks.

Dr. Gomez gives a quick glance over to the bed where I am resting. We have already rehearsed this speech. The doctor knows that he must select his words with great deliberation. I might be ill, but I have not been robbed of my senses and well-honed skill of managing Winston.

"She needs rest, Mr. Churchill," Dr. Gomez finally answers.

"Rest? You mean a vacation?" Winston stops chewing his cigar and gives it a weak puff. "I can arrange for a family trip to the Mediterranean, if you think some sunshine would do the trick. Come to think of it, we've been asked to visit Sir Ernest Cassel in Nice. Not that it will be terribly warm in France at this time of year, of course."

"That isn't exactly what I had in mind." The doctor clears his throat. "Your wife's condition is serious. She will need *complete* rest."

"Condition?" Winston asks, his brow furrowing. Has my health really escaped his notice? How can he ignore the canceled obligations and the long days I've taken to my bed? The afternoon I spent listless but for the bouts of banging my forehead against my bedroom wall? The angry notes I'd leave for him in the morning, only to send him later instructions to burn them without opening? The dinner party where I had to excuse myself during the first course, and he found me, hours later, sitting on the floor of my dressing room? Or does he wish it all untrue and so selects oblivion?

I brace myself under the layers of blankets that cover me in my bed. How will the doctor describe the utter mental and physical exhaustion I've experienced? How will he define the swings from frenetic activity — always at Winston's behest — to a tiredness so leaden and complete, I cannot leave my bedroom?

As Dr. Gomez clears his throat again before speaking, I find that my hands are clenched under my bedsheets. Will he answer as we discussed? Will he avoid the terms *breakdown* or *neurasthenia,* words laden with such heavy connotation that I fear Winston will never perceive me the same way again? While I want Winston to understand that my need for recovery is real, I never want him to think me incapable of being his full partner. The moments I spend with Winston on the nation's work are the moments I feel most alive, and yet, they drain me as well, so I walk along this tightrope.

"Mr. Churchill, your wife is suffering from nervous exhaustion. It is a very real condition that will require rest and time apart from the children, from the care of your home, and from her duties."

My body relaxes, and I exhale the breath I'd been unconsciously holding. Dr. Gomez utilized the phrase I'd begged him to use, and he avoided mentioning the most obvious cause of my stress. He did not say what everyone else thinks — that being married to Winston must be unfathomably challenging. Only Nellie will say aloud that it is Winston from whom I need time apart. *Just several weeks,* I think, *and then I can weather whatever storm Winston brews.*

"I did not realize, Dr. Gomez." Winston's voice does not bear its usual bravado. For the first time, I sense that he understands.

"She will need to be away from home for some time. Only then can she truly rest in the manner absolutely necessary."

"Of course, Dr. Gomez. Whatever my wife needs to recuperate, she shall receive."

"Wonderful. If so, I am confident of a

complete recovery."

Dr. Gomez takes his leave, and Winston ambles over to my bedside, dragging a chair with him. After he squeezes his girth into the delicate design, he reaches for my hand. "Oh, Cat, I am so terribly sorry."

"My dear Pug, whatever are you sorry for? I'm the one who'll be abandoning you and the children to your own devices." The trips I've taken in the past have always been short in duration. This will be an entirely different sort of journey.

"I fear that it is my demands that have brought you so low."

Ah, I think, *he does know.* And yet, he has never withheld his requests. I clasp his hands tightly but do not answer. While I don't want to admit to him that he's the cause of my distress, I will not lie boldly by denying the truth of his admission. It's too hard won.

"I will oversee the children and the final renovations to the house on Sussex Square. All you need to focus upon is your rest," he says.

While I appreciate his overture, in truth, three of the children will be away at school most of the time. Randolph has been boarding at Sandroyd Preparatory School for a few years, and Diana and Sarah attend Notting Hill High School as day pupils, where I long for them to have the sort of broad education I experienced at Berkhamsted. It is Marigold, just two years old and cared for by another new nanny, about whom I worry. She is prone to colds and fevers, and the nanny will need oversight.

"Even Duckadilly?" I ask him, using our pet name for her.

"Especially Duckadilly," he answers with a small smile. "I need a healthy Cat by my side. I'll need you fit for the political fights that are drawing near. Not to mention that I'll need your counsel as I assume my new post as colonial secretary."

I return his smile, but it is strained. It has not escaped my notice that, in the same breath as he urges on my recovery, he reminds me of my duties. To *him*.

Have I made the right choice to join Winston in Egypt?

The nearly two months I spent in hotels in coastal France — with only my maid, Bessie, for company — softened my nerves and mind, and by the end, when I looked at myself in a mirror, I started to see a healthy thirty-six-year-old with a certain vivacity in the eyes, not the frazzled, gray-skinned woman I'd become. I began to believe that the money we'd cobbled together for this time away was well spent.

I worried about relinquishing part of my quiet time away when Winston wrote asking me to join him in Cairo for the Middle East Conference, where matters important to British interests in the region would be discussed and postwar political issues would be settled. For a time, I didn't answer but simply considered the invitation. When I decided that I was strong enough to sally forth, I made my travel plans for Egypt. The lure of the sunlight and my curiosity about the pyramids were too great, and Winston had promised continued rest. Plus, the costs would be borne by the government, and thus the financial burden of the remainder of my "cure" would not fall upon us.

He was gentle with me from the moment we settled into the opulent Mena House Hotel, where the British delegation was staying. As our room was readied and our trunks unpacked, we sat down to tea on the veranda. Through the fronds of the palm trees that surrounded the sumptuous hotel, an oasis of greenery in the vast sandy expanse of the desert, we were greeted by a spectacular view of the Great Pyramid.

"Pug missed his Cat," Winston said quietly after we'd given the famous structure its due attention. "And so did her kittens."

"And Cat missed her Pug," I replied, softly stroking his hand. "And the kittens too," I added, although, as I said the words, I realized how little I'd actually reflected on the children during the two months away, except when I wrote their daily letters. Even Marigold had received little of my thoughts. What was wrong with me? Did I unconsciously avoid thinking about them because of the worries they prompted? Shouldn't a mother be preoccupied with her children when she is apart from them?

"I promise that this trip will be as relaxing as Dr. Gomez instructed," he said, holding my hands tightly as if shaking on an agreement. I did not know if I could trust this promise. Many times in years past, he had vowed to relent in his demands and outbursts when my nerves had been stretched so thin that even he noticed. Yet he'd never managed to keep those promises.

True to his word, however, the following days brought nothing but marvelous dinners with politicians and archaeologists and light tennis with embassy officials' wives. Winston required only my presence and no assistance, and I delighted in meeting the famous Colonel T. E. Lawrence, about whom I'd heard so much. When Winston first introduced me to Lawrence as we embarked on a visit to Sakkara, I couldn't believe that the reticent, small man standing before us was the charismatic leader who'd prevented Arab forces from aligning with Germany during the Great War. But his shyness fell away as we journeyed, and I saw his deep connection with the Arab people and his courageous conviction. *None of us are what we seem at first,* I remind myself. No one sees that my nerves are stretched near to splintering behind my own composed exterior after all.

After years of feeling weighted down by the minutiae of everyday life, I begin to feel light again and part of something larger than myself and my own worries. *The trip to Giza reinforces this sensation,* I think as I squint up at the famous sand-colored Egyptian monuments, quite unable to believe that they are real. Of course I'd seen sketches of the Great Sphinx of Giza and the Great Pyramid it guards in school and in the newspapers. But mere representations do not do justice to the reality of these limestone testaments to the prowess of the ancient Egyptian civilization.

"Makes one feel small, doesn't it, Clemmie?" Winston calls over to me.

I can barely hear him over the braying of

the camels, so he repeats himself, and I call back, "It does indeed, Winston."

He gestures for our native guide to bring his camel closer to mine, and I hold my breath, hoping he does not slide off the bony creature as he did earlier today. "Makes one's contributions feel small as well. After all, these fellows have stood for God knows how many thousands of years. I doubt any of my efforts will last anywhere near as long," he adds when he's close enough for me to hear him properly.

I know that Winston has spoken aloud his greatest fear. That his life will not have long-ranging impact for his country. He is terrified that the prescience he's felt since childhood about the crucial role he'll play in England's future will come to naught. I open my mouth to offer a reassuring word but quickly shut it when I see Lawrence approach on his camel. Winston would never want me to reveal his secret dread to him.

As I watch my husband chat with Lawrence and then Gertrude Bell, the well-known archaeologist and key political adviser, I feel an unexpected sense of calm. I haven't lost any of my newfound peace during my days with Winston in Egypt. He has gone about his work helping establish the government and boundaries of Iraq and other portions of the Middle East without demanding my help, only asking if I want to participate.

Dust flies about in the air as the other members of our traveling party gather together, and I wrap my ivory scarf around my nose and mouth. I watch as Winston, his private secretary, Archie Sinclair, Lawrence, Bell, and a cadre of English politicians and diplomats form a line with the Great Sphinx and Great Pyramid as a backdrop, and I realize that they are assembling for a photograph.

"Clemmie," Winston, red-faced from the bright sunlight, yells to me. "Come join the line! Here, to my right."

I wave him off. This is an official portrait, not the classic tourist souvenir. And none of the other politicians and diplomats have brought their wives. My presence in the image is not appropriate, as I am a mere bystander to this critical juncture in the future of the region.

"Come along, Clemmie," Winston calls out again. "We need you here. You are part of this historic moment as well."

Was I really part of this or merely a bystander to world-shaping events? History would likely only record my husband, although I've played a significant hand in his affairs. I suppose only time will tell.

As we ride back to Cairo, Lawrence informs us that a crowd of students had been protesting outside our hotel. His sources told him that the students had been invoking curses against both Winston and me for the British involvement in what they perceive to be solely Egyptian affairs, namely how the region's lands are to be ruled in the fallout of the Great War. "All safety precautions must be taken," Lawrence cautions us, but still, the anxiety that I've worked so hard to mute begins to mount.

I know that Winston will neither arrange the necessary protections nor abide by them once they are instituted. He plows through life toward his goals, without self-care or concern about his impact on others. Even though I've stayed in the background during this trip, I understand that I must step into my usual role or risk harm to ourselves and others.

"What do you recommend, Colonel Lawrence?" I ask.

As Lawrence and I review security measures, Winston chatters on with Miss Bell about the issues at stake in the conference — whether Lebanon and Syria should remain under French control and whether England should maintain Palestine and support a Jewish homeland there, among other topics. When we near the Mena House, we are intercepted by Sir Herbert Samuel, the British high commissioner for Palestine, who'd come to Cairo to warn us of a plot to murder us.

Winston and I are murder targets? My breathing becomes shallow, and my heart races. But I cannot show this; I must stay calm so that I can ensure that Winston will follow the security protocols. In situations of past danger, he's been nonchalant, even foolhardy, and if I'm not vigilant, who knows what might happen?

As I expected, Winston scoffs, "This seems much ado about nothing. There will always be talk and empty threats, especially by those who don't care for our agenda."

I am tired of his devil-may-care attitude, not only with his own well-being but with the others in our retinue. I take a deep breath and try to stop my voice from quivering. Using a tone he knows will brook no resistance, I say, "Winston, we must take Sir Samuel's warning seriously. Colonel Lawrence, can we put those precautions we discussed into immediate effect?"

"Indeed, ma'am," he answers.

Colonel Lawrence directs the car through the warren of Cairo streets so that we approach the Mena House Hotel from the back rather than the front gateway. A dense mob has assembled around the entire perimeter of the hotel, even in the back. The driver decides to plow through the throngs, but the protestors climb on the car's running boards and bang upon the windows. Seeing a number of their ranks descend upon our car, the mob moves toward us as if one entity. This scene is overly familiar, and I am terrified.

"Should we wait for the mounted police to arrive?" I ask, trying to control my breathing. This situation is very like the one we faced in Belfast, and we only narrowly escaped there.

"I don't think there is enough time," Colonel Lawrence says, turning to look behind us. "And we lost Sir Samuel's men."

"What if we send our security guards to walk alongside the car as we drive through the crowd? I don't want them to be directly in harm's way, but they aren't deterring the mob from the inside of the car," I ask.

"It's worth a try."

Lawrence instructs the security guards, and as they step out, a protester's hand slips into the car and grabs at my hat and hair. I cannot help but shriek. My hands shaking, I pry the fingers off me and shove the hand through the door. The car begins to drive slowly but steadily through the crowd until we reach the back gate to the hotel. The hotel guards gather around the car, shielding us from the protestors as we step inside the building. Once inside, I lean against the wall, eyes closed, trying to regain my composure.

Eyes alight, Winston turns to me with that half smile and says, "We made it through all right, didn't we, Clemmie?" As if the mob and the death threat and the protester's fingers in my hair were all a lark. And I realize that, despite promises to the contrary, nothing has changed.

CHAPTER TWENTY

April 13–14 and June 29, 1921
London, England, and Dieppe, France

I brace myself as the front door to our new home in Sussex Square opens, a place I hope we settle after living in countless rented London houses on weekdays and numerous temporary country cottages on weekends over the past few years. What greeting will I find within its walls? What do I even deserve after so long away from my children and duties?

"Welcome home, Mummy!" the banners declare in red and blue, written in a childish scrawl more endearing than any elegant calligraphy. They drape across the staircase and walls.

"Oh, my loves." I drop my handbag and coat on the floor, opening my arms to engulf my waiting children. Eleven-year-old Diana, nine-year-old Randolph, and six-year-old Sarah race toward me, nearly knocking me to the floor with their force. Before I left, the imbalance would have irritated me, but now I relish their embrace. It seems they forgive me my leave-taking.

I spend a moment studying the face of each child and kissing their cheeks, giving Randolph a ruffle of his hair. I do not mention how tall they seem — or how mature, as in the case of Diana — as I am wary of drawing attention to the length of my absence. The qualities I most associate with each of them — Diana's quiet, watchful manner, Randolph's sense of entitlement and desperate need for attention, and Sarah's sensitivity incongruously mixed with a dramatic flair — seem enhanced. They are more and more themselves.

Sarah's hand tentatively reaches up to touch my hair. "You wear silver thread in your hair now."

At first, I wonder what she means, and then I understand. I have changed in our time apart too. Placing my hand over hers, I say, "It seems as though I've gone a bit gray since I saw you last."

"What do you think of the place?" Winston asks, inserting himself into this moment with the children.

How can I begrudge him? I stare around the entryway to the Sussex Square house, where I glimpse a completed morning room and redesigned dining room. "Winston," I say as I turn toward him, "you've handled the renovations beautifully." Relief courses through me at the projects I needn't handle, compounded by the financial comfort provided from a recent unexpected windfall of an inheritance from a first cousin once removed, Lord Vane-Tempest. Money worries, at least for the immediate future, will not be mine to shoulder. And for once, after years of dealing with leases and rentals and overlapping of both, we might have just the right number of houses — one — instead of too many or none at all.

"Not as well as you could have, but needs must," he says, but I see that he is pleased with my compliment.

I see a shy Marigold in the arms of Nanny, standing in the back of the entryway. Slowly, I walk toward the ginger-haired, runny-nosed child, but she does not meet my eye. Does she not remember me? I suppose that the three months I've been gone constitute a significant portion of the twenty-nine months of her life. Or perhaps she's angry at me for my prolonged absence.

"Mummy is home, Duckadilly," I say to her, leaning close to her sweet-smelling face but careful to avoid the mucus.

"Mummy?" she finally asks, peering into my eyes.

"Yes, Mummy," I answer, excitement building within me at the recognition.

"No," she squeals, burrowing into Nanny's chest. She begins to cry.

I feel Winston's hand on my arm. "Not to worry, Cat. It may take a little time. Come join the rest of the kittens in the dining room." His voice drops to a whisper. "They've made a welcome home cake for you."

The next morning, I perch on the edge of my new bed, searching for my small traveling trunk. It lies hidden among the scarves and hats scattered on my bed, awaiting return to their shelves. I want to find the souvenirs I've brought back for the children from Egypt, Sicily, and Naples, where Winston and I ventured after his conference ended, and deliver them over breakfast.

I am focused on my task when I finally register the sound of someone knocking on my door. The banging is quite loud, uncharacteristically so, and by the time I open the door, a new maid has worked herself into quite a state. "There . . . there's a telegram for you, ma'am. It's marked urgent."

"Who is it from?" I ask, skeptical of this

"urgency." From time to time, Winston has sent me "urgent" telegrams from across town when he wants my immediate opinion on a matter. Never once were those communiqués actually urgent.

"I can't say, ma'am. I only know it's from France."

France can only mean one person: Mother, who had recently moved back to Dieppe. *Why on earth is she sending a telegram?* I wonder. Letter writing is her preferred means of communication, usually peppered with admonitions and judgments. Some things never change, no matter the alteration in my life station.

I take the envelope from the maid and close the door. Retrieving my letter opener from my desk, I sit down on the desk chair and slice open the envelope. I hold the telegraphed words up to the wan light from the nearby window.

BILL IS DEAD STOP COME TO
DIEPPE AT ONCE

Bill? My brother? My handsome, urbane brother — only thirty-four years old and a survivor of countless Great War naval attacks — can't possibly be dead. Images of his infectious smile at my wedding and family gatherings flash through my mind. Surely

213

in my fatigue from the travel, I misread the words. Holding the flimsy telegram up to the light again, I reread it. There is no mistake.

My body is shaking. What should I do? I'm torn between despair and action. The latter takes hold, and I sit down to write letters to both Winston and Nellie, informing them of the awful news and instructing them about the need for Nellie and I to depart for Dieppe on the morning train. I ring for the maids to repack my clothes but only the black dresses this time. My trembling has not abated when I join Diana, Randolph, and Sarah in the breakfast room — Marigold is still sleeping — although I try to hide my upset by making a show of the presentation of gifts. Yet once their delight at receiving exotic embroidered scarves and slippers abates, I have no choice but to tell them about my impending departure.

"You've only just got home," Sarah says, tears streaming down her face. Bolder than Diana, she is more apt to speak her mind.

"I know, my darlings. But Aunt Nellie and I must rush to Dieppe to see Grandmama and Uncle Bill. I received a note from Grandmama saying that Uncle Bill is ill."

"Why can't Aunt Nellie go by herself?

You've been gone for ages," Sarah continues.

I walk over to her side, kneeling next to her. "I promise to return as soon as I can. I am terribly sorry."

Glancing up at Randolph and Diana to gauge their reaction, I watch as my son's face blackens with a rage that will undoubtedly erupt at some point in the day. His temper tantrums have only increased over the years instead of diminishing as is more typical. Only Diana's expression appears unaffected. Is this simply another example of her placid nature, or has she grown so used to my absence that one more departure impacts her little? It is no more than I deserve, I know, and a reality I must face upon my return.

Nellie and I clutch each other in a tearful embrace as soon as we board the ship for Dieppe. During the boat trip, theories about what happened to our brother plague us. Bill had gone into business after he retired from his checkered naval career, but his compulsion for gambling led to financial difficulties. Winston and I periodically loaned him money to pay off gambling debts and had only three months ago extracted a promise from him to stop, but I wonder whether he'd slipped back into old habits. The sort of fellows with whom he gambled had degenerated over time, and Nellie and I speculate that perhaps they'd harmed our beloved brother.

We disembark from the boat to the familiar sounds of ship bells and seagull cries. The distance from the port to Mother's house in the center of Dieppe is short and our bags few and small, so we decide to walk. Nellie and I wind our way through the narrow alleyways, smelling strongly of saltwater and fish, until we reach the furnished house Mother rents. It is proper but modest, as her casino habit cuts deep into her finances. As does her increasingly serious drinking habit.

"Mama," I call out as the sole housemaid lets us into the house.

"In here," a small voice croaks.

Hand in hand, Nellie and I step into the parlor. There, in an armchair, sits the usually formidable Lady Blanche. Mother looks so diminished and tiny that she is hardly recognizable. I know she's in the throes of grief, so perhaps my assessment is a bit unfair, but I cannot help but think that the finale of her lifelong bohemian quest for romance and independence is terribly sad.

"He used a gun," Mother says by way of greeting, closing her eyes. "A bloody gun."

If Nellie and I hadn't comprehended the nature of Bill's death before, we do now. All our theories about violence being exacted upon Bill by some unsavory gambling characters were wrong. The harm to Bill had been done by his own hand.

Nellie sinks to the ground at Mother's side. "No," she keens, "not Bill."

Mother offhandedly pats her on the back, as if her own grief is so distracting, she cannot register that of others. Then she stares at Nellie, and as if she suddenly remembered, she says, "He was your twin."

They lean into one another, sobbing. I am left alone with my grief. I am neither mother nor twin, just the sister. I feel the loss of Kitty again. It is down to Nellie and me.

I try to understand the reasons for Bill's suicide. Was he deeply in debt from gambling and too ashamed to ask for money again? Conversations with his acquaintances yield no evidence that he'd been wagering again, and in fact, I learn that he'd just deposited ten thousand francs into his bank account. If debts hadn't prompted his terrible act, had a failed relationship of some variety led to a depression? No one seems to know anything about his personal life, least of all his family. What did I really know about my brother other than the carefully tended persona he chose to share? I feel as though I've let him down terribly.

I turn my attention to the funeral. In France, suicide is a sin, not a criminal act, but the local clergyman resists allowing Bill a proper burial. Bringing the full weight of Winston's name to bear upon the situation, I pressure the priest into capitulating, and we arrange the funeral for the Monday afternoon so Winston can attend. I allow the planning and investigating to consume me, and I don't surrender to my grief until I see my husband's concerned face enter the church for Bill's funeral. Seeing his compassion and concern for me, all the guilt and loss and devastation I'd been suppressing wells to the surface. I sink into Winston's arms and sob the tears that I've been holding back since I arrived in Dieppe.

A deep sadness follows me home from France. I try to pierce its gray veil and focus on the merry bustle created by Diana, Sarah, and Marigold, as Randolph has returned to school. But the girls sense the latent despair. Worried that my sorrow might prompt another departure, they uncomfortably cling to me at every opportunity. I fight my usual impulse to flee and leave them with the nanny, and with

Winston distracted with colonial issues and Irish problems, the girls and I settle into a regular routine. I find myself enjoying the girls and think that the worst times — my breakdown and the heartbreak of losing Bill — are behind us.

I should have kept the fleeting nature of life at the forefront of my thoughts. Every time I heard the tap of Winston's cane on the floor — the gold-topped Malacca cane that Bill had bequeathed him — I should have reminded myself that the gift of existence can be taken away at a moment's notice. If I had done so, perhaps I would have been braced for Jennie.

The sixty-seven-year-old, who still styles herself as Lady Randolph even though she is on her third marriage with the much younger civil servant Montagu Porch, had been staying at her friend Lady Horner's Mells country house in late May when she tripped on too-high heels while walking down a flight of stairs. The local doctor diagnosed a broken ankle, and Jennie returned to her Bayswater home to recover.

Because the issues of Irish governance distract again in the postwar period and preoccupy Winston and Jennie's husband is away in Africa, I visit Jennie nearly every afternoon throughout June as she convalesces. Her house is nearby ours in Sussex Square, and I develop the habit of stopping by at teatime. One-on-one, without the presence of Winston, her young husband, or the children to compete for our attention, I discover the latent animosity we'd felt for each other over the years has disappeared, replaced by a begrudging admiration. My respect for Jennie only increases when her doctor appears during one of my teatime visits and, after inspecting her ankle, informs her that her foot has developed a gangrenous infection and must be amputated. This would be a bitter pill for anyone to swallow, but I guess that Jennie, who has prized her beauty and her shapely ankles all her life, will take it especially hard. Yet she accepts the news without histrionics, and I am impressed with her grace.

Ten worrisome days after the surgery, as Jennie appears on the road to recovery, Winston and I return to our usual habits. I retire for the evening on Tuesday, June 28, after several long hours reviewing proposed policies regarding Ireland's rule with Winston, knowing he would work on some correspondence for a few hours more. When I hear an enormous crash in the hour before dawn, I assume Winston continued writing throughout the night and is finally stumbling into his bed in his room next door. Quite literally.

I roll over in my bed and attempt a return to sleep when my bedroom door flings open. Winston, in his pajamas, stands outlined in the low gaslight that lights the hallway between our bedrooms. "It's Mother."

I sit upright in my bed. "What's happened, Pug?"

"Doctor says she's begun to bleed. I'm going directly to her house." He marches off.

Standing up, I throw on my dressing gown and race after him. As he thunders down the stairs, I call out, "Winston, you are still in your pajamas. You should at least change. Or let me arrange for a carriage."

"No time to waste," he calls back, closing the door behind him as he steps into the street.

The walk to Jennie's house on Westbourne Street is short, only ten minutes or so. But Winston is in his pajamas and dressing gown, which likely means he's still in his slippers as well. I wonder whether I should go after him or send one of the servants, but the streets are pitch-black. I decide to wait instead.

I sit down in the embroidered wing chair

in the parlor. I don't dare retire to my room to change for fear of missing Winston on his return. The ticking of the grandfather clock that looms over the entryway seems deafeningly loud, but as I grow used to it, the tick-tock recedes, and I imagine I can hear the children rustle in the beds and the servants open cupboards in the kitchen.

After three quarters of an hour, dawn begins to emit the palest of light, and the front door opens. Winston steps into the entryway with none of his usual blunderbuss. Sweat beads on his brow, and his dressing gown is wide open, revealing his striped blue pajamas underneath.

"She's gone," he says in a flat voice.

"You don't mean 'gone' gone?" I ask rather stupidly. I understand the euphemism, of course, but it seems a preposterous word to use for the indomitable Jennie. Can he mean she was "gone" from her house? Perhaps rushed to the hospital?

"I do, Clemmie. She was already gone by the time I reached her bedside," he answers.

"It seems impossible." I wrap my arms around my husband. "Oh, Winston, I am so sorry."

"I feel as though a part of myself has been severed." He folds into me, and I feel his hands on my back. My shoulder is wet from his tears.

"I understand, Pug. It's how I felt with Bill. And Kitty."

We draw closer to one another, and I think how little we know of our futures. I'd believed that the strength I'd cobbled together during the time away from my family would help me weather the storm of Winston and his demands. I had no understanding that I'd desperately need that fortitude to help me survive other tempests.

CHAPTER TWENTY-ONE

August 18–23 and September 14, 1921
Broadstairs and London, England

I shake Mrs. Burden's hand as we step off the tennis courts of Eaton Hall. The American guest of my hosts, the Duke and Duchess of Westminster, has been a fierce competitor in the tennis tournament that lured me to Chester en route to our family holiday. Winston and I had planned a long stint away from London in August, with all four children spending this first two weeks lodging at a house called Overblow in Broadstairs on the Kent coast with a new French nanny, Mademoiselle Rose, and then the older three children joining us in Lochmore, Scotland, while Marigold stays on with Mademoiselle Rose in Broadstairs, as the Scottish activities are not suitable for a young child. We had hopes that the holiday would give our family some respite from the terrible losses of Bill and Jennie. And I hoped

224

to restore the internal peace I'd achieved during my time away alone.

As I share with Mrs. Burden my surprise over winning the match — after all, it had been months since I played a single game of tennis — a servant waiting on the edge of the lawn signals to me. He delivers to me an envelope on a silver tray. *Is it another letter from Winston about the death of Thomas Walden, his faithful manservant?* I wonder. Winston had been terribly upset at yet another loss, a servant who'd been devoted to him since his lonely youth when neither of his parents cared much for their son. I didn't know how to console him.

I say farewell, examining the envelope as I walk toward my guest room. The return address on the envelope is Broadstairs, which makes me think the letter must be a report from the children on their seaside boat rowing, sandcastle building, and shrimping, as well as an account of their usual sunburns. But when I look closer, I see that the handwriting doesn't belong to Mademoiselle Rose, who addresses the children's letters.

Closing the bedroom door behind me, I open the envelope. Inside is a cable from Mademoiselle Rose, informing me that Marigold was very ill with septicemia and

225

suggesting we come at once.

No, no, not septicemia, I think. Surely it's just another of her terrible sore throats and colds. Too many children we've known never recover from the infection of the bloodstream, which so often turns deadly. I let the cable flutter to the ground, and the room spins around me. I clutch the bedpost for support as I will myself to steadiness. I must get to Marigold as soon as possible.

I spring to action, instructing Bessie to pack our things. Together, we will take the train to Broadstairs, where I will race to Marigold's side and Bessie will prepare the older children for the journey to Scotland. I wire Winston, instructing him to abandon all work to meet me in Broadstairs.

By the time I reach Marigold's side that afternoon, her skin feels fiery. Her ginger hair is soaked with sweat, as is the pillow upon which her head rests, and she is listless. I tell Bessie to cable Winston to send a specialist to Broadstairs immediately.

After Bessie escorts Randolph, Diana, and Sarah from the room, I turn to Mademoiselle Rose and the landlady, who has remained in the room. "When did she become so ill?"

The nanny glances at the landlady. "She had a sore throat when she arrived, ma'am."

"I don't mean a sore throat, by God. Marigold always has a sore throat. When did she get this terrible fever?"

Mademoiselle Rose doesn't speak, and tears start rolling down her cheeks. The landlady answers instead, "About August 14, ma'am."

I cannot believe that I've heard her right. "August 14?" That was four days ago.

"Yes, ma'am," the landlady answers with downcast eyes.

"Why didn't anyone notify me until today?"

The nanny begins sobbing. "I should ha-have, but I didn't want you to be mad."

Fury surges within me, but it is quickly replaced by despair. I could have been here four days ago to help my poor baby. Four days in which I could have gotten Marigold expert medical care to keep the worst effects of septicemia at bay.

The landlady leads the nanny out of the room, and I reach for a wet cloth. I sponge my child's searing hot forehead and cheeks and then lay my cheek against hers. I should have been with her. I should never have left the care of Marigold — of any of my children — to a young, inexperienced nanny. This is all my fault.

The thud of Winston's distinctive footsteps

227

sounds in the hallway outside Marigold's room. I don't look up when I hear the door open. After all the days and months I've spent away from my children, I now cannot take my eyes off my daughter.

"Oh." A sob catches in his throat. "Poor Duckadilly."

The chair next to me creaks with Winston's weight. I dare not take my gaze off Marigold.

"How could I have been playing tennis at Eaton Hall while our daughter was suffering?" I mutter, mostly to myself.

"Cat, how were you to know?"

"A mother should know. I'm no fit mother."

The black, carved lettering looks so fresh and clear against the marble headstone. It appears not at all timeworn and faded like the nearby gravestones in this ancient cemetery of Kensal Green. Leaning down, I trace my finger along the letters of the first three words: *Here lies Marigold.* How could this possibly be the grave of my poor, precious, two-year-old daughter?

Tears trickle down my cheeks, but I brush them away. I do not want Diana, Randolph, and Sarah to see my sadness at the death of their little sister. Crying, even wailing, was acceptable at the funeral nearly three weeks ago, but one must bear up afterward. After all, everyone has suffered unimaginable losses, especially in the Great War. We are not alone.

Had my conceit over Winston's phoenix-like rise after his return from the trenches angered God? My pride in Winston's attendance at the signing of the Treaty of Versailles, the agreement that would end the Great War, was unabashed. Had we lost Marigold because of my hubris in the role I played resurrecting his reputation? Or was it simply because of my absent parenting and my self-focused indulgence in my own nervous issues? No matter the reason, the blame is mine to shoulder.

I hear Sarah humming a tune, and too late, I realize it is "I'm Forever Blowing Bubbles." Marigold's last minutes wash over me, and I feel I cannot breathe.

Winston and I hadn't left her side since morning. The London specialist had told us that nothing could be done for poor Marigold; there was no treatment for the septicemia stemming from the painful sore throat that plagued her on arrival at Broadstairs. The only course left, he told us, was to make her as comfortable as possible. And pray.

She'd been lethargic for hours when she suddenly perked up and said, "Sing me 'Bubbles.' " The popular ditty, quite wistful in its way with its comparison of the fleeting nature of bubbles and life, was her particular favorite. So I sang it in a wobbly voice.

I choked on the words and my own awful sobs, but Winston gripped my hand and prompted me along with his own voice. Together, we continued the song.

Marigold's lids opened, and her light-blue eyes fixed on us for a bright moment. For a fleeting moment, hope washed over me. Then she stretched out her little hand to ours and whispered, "Not now . . . . finish the song later." And then she stopped breathing. I don't remember anything that happened afterward, except the noise of an animal howling. Winston later told me that it was I who had made that sound.

"Mummy, where should we put Ducka-dilly's flowers?" Sarah says.

As I direct her, Diana, and Randolph to lay their bouquets around her gravestone, Sarah says, "I wish Daddy was here with us."

"Me too," Diana adds as we watch a white butterfly land upon the flowers. This is the first time she's spoken all day; in some ways, she appears to have taken Marigold's loss the hardest of her siblings.

I think, but do not say, that Winston should be here with his family. He should not have left us in Scotland for the Duke and Duchess of Sutherland's house party at their Dunrobin estate, no matter that the guest of honor was the Prince of Wales. He should have traveled with us to London, stayed with us while we mourned Marigold, and visited her grave with us today.

But I reserve the full force of my anger for myself. I should have been more cautious in guarding my child. I should not have allowed Winston to take precedence in my life. I should have heeded the warnings to care for my loved ones that began the first day we returned from our trip to Cairo.

CHAPTER TWENTY-TWO

December 23–24, 1930
Westerham, England

I turn the lock on the genie's cupboard, so dubbed by the children. As the days grow closer to Christmas, they speculate as to what delights might be tucked away in its depths, awaiting them on the magic morning. Sometimes, I wonder what they'd think of me if they knew what was hidden in my own personal genie's cupboard — the dark tangle of beliefs that, while I'm poison to my children, if I can provide order for Winston and our family, perhaps nothing bad will occur again, nothing like the loss of Marigold. But I can never let them unlock that door.

Even the nine years that have passed since Marigold's death have done nothing to soften my sense of guilt. Winston and I tried to proceed with our daily lives, but grief would raise its ugly head at the most unexpected times, and we would struggle. As would Diana, Randolph, and Sarah, as they bore witness to our sorrow and experienced sadness of their own. I now believe that, unconsciously and without openly discussing it, we both thought another child might help alleviate this despair, and in less than a year, little Mary, nicknamed "Baby Bud" almost immediately, was born. And the beautiful, serene, even-tempered Mary was indeed a balm.

But after Marigold's death, I no longer trusted myself for the children's daily care, and I no longer felt safe counting upon one of the young nursery governesses who'd streamed through our lives. I knew I had to find a steadfast, loyal soul to ensure the welfare of my children. When I learned that my first cousin, Maryott Whyte, the daughter of Mother's sister Lady Maude, had finished training as a childcare educator and nurse at the esteemed Norland College, I asked the impoverished gentlewoman — who, like me and Nellie, always knew she'd have to earn a living — to serve as a nanny to my children. Thank God she agreed, because even though she always observes her professional position, she's become much more than a governess in the years since she's been with us. She's become part of our inner circle of family and friends and, most importantly, godmother to Mary and protector to all my children. She's become our Moppet. She serves them better than I can serve them myself.

Yet even the comfort and relief that Moppet provides is not enough some days. On those occasions, when the duties overwhelm and Winston calls for my attention again and again, the need to flee — abroad or inward — takes hold. I cling to the structure I've created to prevent myself from slipping back into nervous exhaustion. I tell myself that I must stay strong, that I have the power to form a barricade against disaster. And Christmas forms a critical part of my stronghold.

The real genie's cupboard is packed tight with Christmas presents that I've been collecting since summer, now wrapped, beribboned, and ready for Christmas morning. I only have to finalize the rest of the decorations and the menus to ensure that this is the finest family holiday celebration we've ever hosted at Chartwell. It simply *must* be.

I descend the stairs in search of my trustworthy cousin Moppet, or Nana as the children sometimes call her. When I reach the bottom of the stairs, I nearly collide with the pleasant-looking, thirty-five-year-old woman. Despite her growing stoutness, she is walking quickly across the front entry in her clipped step, undoubtedly deep in thought over one of the children's needs. "Ah, Moppet. Just the person I've been looking for. Do you know if the holly and ivy are ready to hang?"

Household decorations are not in her purview, but no one knows the workings of Chartwell better than Moppet, and she enjoys being the keeper of all Chartwellian knowledge, so she doesn't mind the question. Winston had purchased Chartwell in September 1922, in the days following the birth of Mary. We'd always discussed getting a country house and had looked extensively for the perfect house and piece of land, but he bought the property without my knowledge or consent in the only act of betrayal he'd ever committed. At first, I was so furious, I refused to visit the place. Once I relented and agreed to a tour, my anger only grew. Yes, I agreed with Winston, it did have the quintessential English views over the Weald of Kent toward the South Downs and grassy slopes to the north of the house that led to a spring, the Chart Well, which feeds into a stream, but the house itself was a disaster. Its original footprint was rumored to date from the time of Henry VIII, and someone along the way had superimposed an unattractive Victorian structure on top. As we began — and now continue — renovations to make the place livable for a family of six, plus staff and the requirements of entertaining, we discovered a serious moisture problem along with dry rot, and the money and energy Chartwell has sapped from us is astonishing.

Still, despite the toll it takes upon me, I have indulged Winston in this Chartwell project with all its frustrations because I understand something about it that he does not. After herculean efforts on both our parts, Winston finally slipped from power — for what seems for good — in 1929. He had tumbled in and out of parliamentary seats beginning in 1922, until, much to my dismay, he switched back to the Conservative Party in 1924, a move that bought him several years in Parliament and the cabinet role of chancellor of the exchequer in the critical postwar years of restructuring and rebuilding not only our economy but others as well. But then, despite his party shift, his hold had been tenuous, and he fell out of favor with Conservatives and voters alike, in part because of his objection to granting dominion status to India, which would allow them to govern their own affairs in a few years. Without government power, Chartwell became the place upon which Winston could affix all his dreams about an ideal England. Now, instead of crafting domestic policies about economics, labor, and international relations, he creates walls, lakes, elaborate tree houses for the children, and even a tennis court and swimming pool. The dream is the same; only the scale and focus are different.

This exile leaves us scrambling for money, of course, as Winston no longer has a salary. So while I economize, he supports us all with his writing, since 1929 brought not only a loss in power but a loss in the inheritance and all our savings in the market crash. In truth, it is a relief to not have to stand behind him at political rallies and meetings and dinners where he's extolling the virtues of Conservative Party values that I do not support. The synergy of opinion we once shared on politics in nearly every area no longer exists. Our disagreement over the question of Indian self-governance was only one difference of opinion among many. Only our commitment to each other and our family remains.

But his demands have not diminished alongside his power, and neither have his blasts of anger and intemperate outbursts.

If anything, his need for comfort and order and *me* has increased now that his attention focuses not outward on the nation but inward on his writing and Chartwell, and I find that if his schedule is met precisely, then he is less inclined to the misbehavior that I do not want inflicted on anyone in this house, not the children, not the staff, and not me.

As a result, I focus a considerable amount of my time and energy on Winston's needs. I arrange for his long, twice-daily bath to be poured exactly at midday and seven in the evening at a temperature of 98 degrees, rising to 104. After his bath-time ritual, I ensure that his clothes are laid out with a cream shirt for morning and white for evening, his newspapers ironed, piled, and folded in a precise manner, and his six toothbrushes laid out in a row and used in strict rotation. Lunch is served at 1:15 p.m., and dinner at precisely 8:30 p.m., even if Winston doesn't appear for an hour. I co-ordinate with the cook to create menus with the hearty English fare that Winston prefers, even though I dislike it, including roast beef and Yorkshire pudding, clear soup and dover sole with chocolate éclairs, pheasant, and dressed crab. And I make myself fully available to him whenever he summons me for an afternoon game of bezique, as is his usual request, or to debate a political issue. All our fortunes and contentment rise and fall on Winston, and so I oblige, no matter the vagaries of his moods. Given his change in political views, I find it easier to focus on the minutiae of our lives, and I know I'm lucky to have the staff to help me. When my efforts are for naught and the mood becomes oppressive, I busy myself with a bit of gardening, following the advice of my cousin Venetia, herself an excellent gardener, beekeeping, or a trip elsewhere. I am determined that our family and my marriage will survive — if not always thrive — and I will not end my days like Mother, who passed away in late 1925 and suffered a sad, lonely, somewhat destitute, and often drink-fueled descent.

In answer to my question, Moppet nods. "I think I saw Grace wandering around the first floor with two gardeners and a pile of greens, Clementine."

I squeeze her arm in thanks. "I knew you'd know."

Moppet smiles warmly but hurries off. Her clear priority is the children — her young charge Mary in particular, with whom she has an extraordinary bond — and that is precisely as I wish it. The equality of our social positions means that she can jettison obsequiousness and focus upon her duties. I cannot imagine life without her.

"Grace!" I call out for the bright, efficient gardener's daughter who has become another integral part of the staff since she joined us, serving in many capacities, including secretary. Winston and the children insist on calling her a variety of nicknames, and to her credit, she never flinches or complains. Even when I do on her behalf. "Are we all set for the decorating?"

The lanky, long-nosed girl, glasses perched on her nose, strides into the entryway. "Yes, ma'am. The appropriate number of branches and strands have been laid out in the parlor, dining room, and entry hall. We are just awaiting your direction for locations."

"Ah yes." I walk into the parlor with Grace and two gardeners trailing behind me. "Let's decorate the mantle with several branches of the holly each, and wrap the ivy around the columns. Do you have the laurel and yew?"

Grace looks over at the gardeners, who nod. They are too scared to speak to me directly, or so Winston reports. "Yes, ma'am."

"Let's add the laurel to the ivy and yew to the holly. And then repeat the sequence in the dining room and entryway."

"The men will do as you wish, ma'am," Grace says. "Shall we examine the tree next?"

We stand before the evergreen, cut from the woods that border Chartwell to the rear. "It is perfectly triangular, Grace." I turn to the gardeners and say, "You have outdone yourselves this year."

They nod but still do not speak. Maybe I am as daunting as Winston tells me I am.

I continue, "Now, I think the branches will support the usual hundred candles, don't you?"

"I do, ma'am," Grace answers.

"And the men know precisely how to hang the della Robbia Christ child plaque aloft in the front hall?"

"Indeed, ma'am. They will hang it exactly the same way as last year."

"Excellent. Then I'm off to meet with the cook about the menus for Christmas Eve, Christmas Day, and Boxing Day. We will have fifteen with our six, Jack and Goonie and their children, and Nellie and her crew."

I step out of the room, but suddenly, I am overcome with the crisp scent of the Christmas tree. I inhale deeply, and for a moment,

I feel all my cares lift from my shoulders.

I turn back to Grace. "The smell of pine is glorious. I think this will be our best Christmas yet."

Through the crack in the double doors between the drawing room and the library, I stare at the quiet queue of children: our elder three, Diana, Randolph, and Sarah; Jack and Goonie's children, Johnny, Peregrine, and Clarissa; Nellie and Bertram's boys, Giles and Esmond; and, at the very end, our little Mary, of course. Astonishing, really, how they arrange themselves in approximate age order every year without the slightest instruction. Although, when I think about it, I guess that the order is probably Randolph's doing so he can enter the room near the front of the line and lord it over those who trail behind.

The children are silent, near to bursting with anticipation. I cherish this moment; it makes worthwhile all the work I put into crafting a memorable Christmastime.

"Are you ready?" I ask through the crack in the door.

"Yes," they call out in unison.

I fling open the double doors between the drawing room and the library to reveal the Christmas tree, aglow with the light of a

242

hundred white wax candles. The children step into the golden light of the room, with Winston leading the rest of our immediate family, consisting only of our siblings and their families now that our parents are gone. We watch as the children chatter excitedly about the decor and the abundance of presents underneath the tree.

"You've outdone yourself," Winston whispers. We are careful not to reveal to Mary, who, at eight years of age, still believes in Saint Nicholas, the cogs in the machinery of Christmas.

"Do you think so?" I ask.

"I do. Just look at the expressions on the children's faces."

I pause for a moment and examine our son and daughters enjoying the golden spectacle. Innocent little Mary, her eyes luminous, squeals with delight over the tree candles, but Moppet is on hand to prevent her from touching their hot, dripping wax; my cousin would choose the company of the children over her adult family every time. Womanly Diana, twenty-one years old and a student at the Royal Academy of Dramatic Arts, even though she has no real intention of becoming an actress, has shed her affected sophistication, giggling at her younger sister shaking the presents as she guesses at their contents. The stubborn, dramatic Sarah, still at North Foreland Lodge school at sixteen, has relinquished her sulkiness for a few minutes, and I can see a familiar childhood expression of wonder cross her face. Even nineteen-year-old Randolph, whose uncontrollable, sybaritic behavior at Oxford, no doubt due to Winston's overindulgence and my lack of oversight, serves as a constant source of worry, looks jovial.

"They do look happy, don't they?" I say with surprise. I am used to wariness, anxiety, or anger on their faces, a reflection, no doubt, of their feelings toward me.

"They have their noble mother to thank for their contentment," he says rather too loudly, in a manner more befitting a speech than a tender compliment.

I know I should delight in the flattering remark, but I don't. Winston wants to entomb me in my nobility, to make me part of the very structure of Chartwell, his idealized version of England in miniature. It suits him to ignore my foibles and view me as a sculpture of a perfect wife and mother, because a sculpture doesn't have needs or desires. A sculpture doesn't ask anything of him.

CHAPTER TWENTY-THREE

August 30, 1932
Blenheim and Munich, Germany
Look there, Randolph," Winston calls over to our son, eager to lure Randolph into his unquenchable adoration of his ancestor the First Duke of Marlborough. "That's the very field where your ancestor fought his greatest battle, the Battle of Blenheim, for which our family palace is named."

Randolph doesn't answer; he is doing his best to pretend he is anywhere other than a Danubian field. Why does Winston insist on trying to engage him when he's so rude in response? And why doesn't my husband give him a proper dressing-down for his behavior? Instead, he indulges Randolph incessantly — even telling august dinner guests to be quiet while Randolph drones on — even though our twenty-one-year-old Oxford dropout has no accomplishments to warrant preferential treatment. Winston's coddling of Randolph is a constant source of tension between us, perhaps even more than the divergence in our political views since Winston became a Conservative again. I know I'm not overreacting — as Winston is wont to accuse me — because I catch Lieutenant Colonel Pakenham-Walsh giving his wife an astonished look over Randolph's insouciance.

Linking my arm through Winston's, I walk him to another section of the field, away from the sulky Randolph. Normally, I would raise our son's inappropriate behavior and discuss better approaches, but with the Pakenham-Walshes present, I simply want to change the dynamics. "Can you tell me more about the role of this field in the Battle of Blenheim?" I ask, even though I've heard enough about the legendary battle to last a lifetime. At this moment, in order to drag him away from Randolph, I'd even inquire about his views on Germany's anger over the Treaty of Versailles's strictures and the impact he believes it will have on Europe for decades to come, a topic he's known to lecture on for hours to anyone who'll listen, an increasingly small number.

Along with Randolph, Sarah, Lieutenant Colonel Pakenham-Walsh, and his wife, Winston and I have been touring the Low

Countries and Germany to research battle-fields for his Marlborough biography. It has been tedious, hot work, but I wouldn't dream of allowing Winston to conduct it without me. Because of his cavalier attitude toward self-care, constant calamities befall him when he conducts research or travels alone, and in fact, just last year in late December, while on a lecture tour of the United States of America, he was struck by a car while crossing Fifth Avenue in New York City without looking, a fact that I attribute to his insistence that he visit the financier and political consultant Bernard Baruch while Diana and I stayed at the hotel. I shudder to think of how serious several of his past injuries might have been if I hadn't been present. Accompanying him is one of my many wards against familial disaster. That and keeping him to a fixed schedule as a ward against the depression that looms now that he's out of power.

When we leave the battlefield to return to Munich, we pass through a large swath of countryside. Battalions of brown-uniformed soldiers march across the flat field, practicing military maneuvers. I am surprised by the sheer number of men; I'd thought that the Treaty of Versailles prevented the Germans from gathering together large groups of soldiers.

Turning away from the window to ask Winston about this gathering, I'm taken aback by the expression on his face. "What's wrong?" I ask.

"By God, that's a lot of militia. And they are Brownshirts — Hitler's boys."

"That upstart?" While I'm quite familiar with Hitler and his Nazi party, I'd perceived his resentful rantings about the Treaty of Versailles, the economic depression, and mass unemployment, paired with his fervent national pride, to be stirrings of a mad outlier. One hears that his public speeches sound like the ravings of a lunatic. I never thought he'd catch on with the larger German populace. Now, watching this display of rabid Brownshirts, I am worried.

Suddenly leaning across me and Sarah, who sits between us, Winston draws closer to the open window.

"What on earth are you doing?" I ask.

"Shh." He places a finger across his lips. In a moment, he says, "They're singing 'Horst Wessel Lied.' "

"What's that?"

"That's the Nazi Party anthem."

The old-world European civility of the Regina Palast Hotel is a welcome respite from the fields of Blenheim and Brownshirts. The six of us sit down to afternoon tea, fanning ourselves madly in the cloying fug of the hotel restaurant. Only after a tea and a slightly stiffer drink do we relax and cool down, all except the very dramatic Sarah, who exclaims repeatedly that "she's never been this hot in her life." The Pakenham-Walshes must be terribly tired of our children by now and regretting their decision to join us on this trip.

"I say." Randolph's face appears unexpectedly animated after a long day of exaggerated boredom. "Is that Putzi over there?"

"What's that you're saying?" Winston asks, always ready to engage with his prodigal son.

Randolph waves to a blunt-featured man in a well-tailored gray suit sitting alone at the hotel bar. The man grins, waves back, and rises from his chair. As he walks over to our table, I ask, "Who is that, Randolph?"

"A fellow I met in Boston when I was on my speaking tour. He goes by Putzi, but his real name is Ernst Hanfstaengl."

"A German chap?" Winston chimes in.

"Yes, but educated at Harvard. That's what he was doing in Boston, meeting with classmates, if I recall correctly."

Randolph rises to shake the man's hand,

and he makes introductions all around. We invite Putzi, as he insists we call him, to join us for a drink and dinner if he's free. I wonder how this man, a cultured, well-spoken gentleman in his forties, came to know Randolph and what commonalities drew them together. They seem an odd pairing, unlikely to have crossed paths.

After a benign description of Winston's research and our travel to the Blenheim fields, Randolph asks, "So what are you up to these days? I'm embarrassed to admit that I don't recall."

"Well, we did have quite a few drinks that evening in Boston," Putzi says with a chortle.

Randolph laughs. "That we did." I didn't doubt it; Randolph has been overindulging in alcohol since his teenage years. Sarah looks as though she's tempted to make a scathing remark about Randolph's drinking, but I silence her with a sharp glance. The Pakenham-Walshes have suffered through enough ill behavior from the Churchill children for one day.

Putzi answers, "The family business is publishing, but for some years, I have worked in various capacities for the Nazi Party, and I'm currently the press secretary."

"Ah." Randolph blanches. "I don't think I

realized that."

Putzi's expression remains pleasant and inscrutable. "I don't think it came up in our conversation."

The waiter arrives at our table, and we all order another drink and ask for the menus. I know who will take charge of this conversation as soon as the waiter departs — Winston. The opportunity to question an intimate of the Nazi Party will be too tempting to pass up.

"Randolph tells us you're a Harvard man," Winston says with a puff of his cigar. To a stranger, this question probably seems like a simple conversation starter. But I know it's the beginning of an interrogation.

"Yes, I attended the university and actually was a member of the Hasty Pudding Club."

"Ah, good chaps at the Hasty Pudding. Did you live in America afterward?"

"Yes, in New York. I took over the American branch of my father's business, the Franz Hanfstaengl Fine Arts Publishing House, and married an American woman."

"My mother was an American woman, and I don't need to tell you what forces of nature they are," Winston says with an almost indiscernible welling of tears in the corner of his eye. He still misses Jennie terribly. She comes up frequently in our conversations, and while I do not exactly miss her, I have a certain sadness over her passing, as I'd grown fond of her in her later years.

Putzi chuckles, "No, you don't."

I dive in. I know where Winston is going, and it might help his success to vary the questioner. "When did you and your wife move to Germany?"

"We moved back to Germany about ten years ago."

"How does your wife like it? It's quite different from America," I ask, as if concerned about her shopping habits.

"She enjoys the cultural life of Germany quite a lot."

"So you weren't in Europe for the Great War?" Winston interrupts, his tone a touch more sympathetic now that he realizes that Putzi hadn't fought against him.

"No. I spent the duration in New York."

"Homesickness draw you back eventually?"

"Actually, a fellow Hasty Pudding member who worked at the U.S. embassy asked me to do him a favor when I was in town visiting family."

"Oh really?" Winston busies himself with lighting a fresh cigar, as if he is uninterested but making conversation.

"Yes, he wanted me to observe a Nazi rally and report back. I don't think he expected me to be so favorably impressed with Herr Hitler and his ability to unite and inspire the German people. So much so I moved back to Germany," Putzi answers.

"That's when you started working for the Nazi Party?"

"No, that's when I became friends with Adolf. Only after I'd known him for some time and came to believe in his ability to energize Germany with a national spirit I thought lost after the Great War did I formalize my relationship with his party."

I am simultaneously fascinated and repelled by the incongruity of this man's sophistication and his support of Hitler. It makes no sense. Even though I know that the Nazi Party made gains in the number of seats it held in the German Parliament, I'd assumed those supporters were rougher sorts to whom Hitler's rabble-rousing appealed. Not this sort of man, who calls Hitler by his first name.

"How will Hitler assuage Germany's grievance over the Treaty of Versailles?" Winston jumps right into the most alarming aspect of the strange leader.

"He has no intention of waging a war of

aggression, if that's what you are concerned about."

"I think that's what everyone worries about," Winston mutters.

"We did pass quite a lot of Brownshirts undertaking military maneuvers on our way back to Munich from the Blenheim fields. I thought that sort of thing wasn't permitted," I add, not mentioning the prohibition of the Treaty of Versailles by name. Salt in the wound and all that.

Putzi's smile never falters. *He must make an excellent press secretary,* I think as he says, "The Treaty of Versailles prohibits Germany from assembling an army of certain size, among other restrictions. It says nothing about political parties forming military groups for their own protection."

Ah, I think. *That's how Hitler is circumventing the law.* Winston glances at me with a half smile curving on his lips. I must have asked a particularly good question.

Leaning toward us with an eager expression, Putzi says, "Mr. and Mrs. Churchill, I think that if you met Herr Hitler, you'd be reassured."

"I'd welcome that opportunity." Winston makes no effort to hide his excitement over the proffered introduction.

Putzi leaps to his feet. "If you are serious,

I can bring Herr Hitler to meet you for coffee and dessert this evening."

Winston takes a big puff of his cigar and says, "I am deadly serious."

As Mr. Hanfstaengl hastens out of the hotel restaurant, the waiter returns to take our order. A nervous quiet settles over the six of us, until Lieutenant Colonel Pakenham-Walsh blurts out, "Well, that was an unexpected encounter."

"Was it?" Winston says. "I'm not so sure. It seems awfully coincidental that Mr. Hanfstaengl happened to know Randolph and happened to be here alone at the hotel bar when we sat down for drinks."

Randolph says, "Really, Papa. You do see conspiracy everywhere. He's just a chap I met on speaking tour —"

Winston interrupts him. "Why do you think he made an effort to meet you on tour in the first place? Why do you think he made an effort to be here today? Me, of course."

Randolph's face turns bright red in fury, and he stands up, sending his chair toppling to the floor with a clatter that startles nearby diners. "Not everything is about you," he yells, storming off into the hotel bar.

Winston puffs on his cigar, and the waiter arrives with our first course. Everyone grows silent in embarrassment at witnessing this very personal confrontation, and I do my best to make small talk about the next day's plans. We review our itinerary to tour the countryside around the Blenheim fields, and Pakenham-Walsh talks about the maps he's making for Winston's research. Sarah has not uttered a word, cowed by either the impending arrival of Hitler or the lurking menace of her brother's anger, or both. It's behavior I would have expected from the meeker Diana, not the more outspoken Sarah.

As the first course plates are cleared away, I excuse myself. I walk in the direction of the ladies' room but circle around a back hallway to the hotel bar, where I know Randolph is holed up. I want to make sure he doesn't overdo his drinking.

As I suspected, Randolph sits at a dark corner of the bar, downing a beer. He's on his third, by the looks of the empty glasses. "I don't think your father meant to insult you, Randolph," I say quietly.

"For once, I agree with you, Mama," he answers without looking at me. "I don't think it was his intention. But since he believes the entire world revolves around him, he can't help himself. You of all people should know that."

My body stiffens. "What do you mean by that?"

"Your whole existence focuses upon him and his requirements. He demands all of you, and there is no space left for your children to have needs."

I know this, of course; I've always known this. But it is one matter to understand a terrible truth deep within the darkness of yourself and quite another to have someone else say it aloud. Especially when the one speaking is your child, who pays the price of that terrible truth.

His words send me reeling, and I half stumble out of the bar. Leaning against the wall outside the restaurant, I take a deep breath and try to compose myself. I feel as though I've been slapped, and even as I wonder whether I'll recover, I know I must play my role. What else is left to me in any event? Randolph is right.

When I approach our table, I see that our main courses have been delivered and that Mr. Hanfstaengl has returned. But I see no sign of Hitler.

"Ah, Clemmie," Winston greets me. "It seems as though Hitler wasn't available after all."

"A pity," I say, although I'm relieved. After Randolph's statement, I'm not certain I could handle the stress of an encounter with the infamously intense Hitler.

"Yes," Mr. Hanfstaengl agrees. "I believe that, if you'd met Herr Hitler, you could have been put at your ease. Perhaps we can arrange a meeting for later in your trip?"

"Perhaps. In the meantime, there is a question you might like to put to him, which can be the basis of our discussion when we meet," Winston proposes.

"Of course," Mr. Hanfstaengl answers, ever agreeable.

"He's always railing about the Treaty of Versailles, a gripe I can understand and one that might be addressed at a future point. But he's also always ranting about the Jewish people. Please ask him from me: Why does he so dislike the Jewish people?"

I stare at my husband, resisting the urge to laugh at his challenge to the views of Hitler, the unsavory upstart who's desperate for power. This is the man I married, one willing to take risks and make the unusual statement — even if unorthodox or unpopular — if it serves the greater good.

CHAPTER TWENTY-FOUR

December 8, 1934
Westerham, England

"So you think India would be better ruled by some inexperienced native than by a seasoned British official? Just because he's an Indian?" Winston baits me. His tone is sharp, like the tip of the sword used by his infernal ancestor the First Duke of Marlborough about whom he continues to write that biography. I try not to wince at his words and instead glance out the window of the bridge room at Chartwell where Winston and I have retired to play an afternoon round of bezique.

How could the Liberal man I married utter such a sentiment? I wonder. *How could the man who challenged Hitler's anti-Semitic views hold such unpleasant opinions about the Indian people?* Each day, I endeavor to sidestep discussions about the political issues that divide us and that will cause another of Winston's eruptions. The list is long, and as Winston has become more entrenched in his Conservative views, it grows longer. From Irish rule to India's government to his obsession over German rearmament, our views do not align. Only one issue, the one dearest to me, has been settled and thus removed from conversation: the women's vote. It took two laws separated by a decade to deliver the vote women deserved; in 1918, an act passed allowing a limited category of women to vote, and finally, ten years later, all women in England had the same right to vote as men.

But I must be similarly cautious not to delve into conversation about the children. We diverge wildly over their treatment. While Diana and Sarah cause us mild dismay — the former already divorced after an unfortunate year-long marriage with a fellow who turned out to be a cad, and the latter intent on pursuing an unseemly acting career, focusing as it does on dancing in musicals rather than serious stage work — it is Randolph who truly divides us. Our impossibly self-important son, who now works as a journalist after his failure to get an Oxford degree because he left on that ill-advised speaking tour of America, appears regularly in the newspapers as a subject because of his drunken brawls and romantic dalliances. Even though his journalistic efforts have some merit, Randolph lords around town in a chauffeured automobile and does not earn enough to pay his bills, particularly because he is a regular gambler, which makes me nervous because of Bill and his insatiable habit. Just two weeks ago, even though Winston had promised to treat Randolph with a firmer hand, he covered Randolph's gambling debts of fifteen hundred pounds, a fortune we can ill afford. *But,* I often think, *how can I object when my neglect played a hand in creating the beast?* Only my twelve-year-old Mary seems fine, and I'm fairly certain that's because Moppet is parenting her.

Hoping for a peaceful afternoon, I return my gaze to our bezique game and decide to say nothing in response to his quip. I know he's trying to provoke me. He misses the posturing and grandstanding of Parliament, and while I am a poor substitute, he will utilize me when necessary. Given that his two favorite cronies — Brendan Bracken, an unmarried loner who's cast off his Irish family and is probably using Winston for some as-yet-unknown gain, and the Canadian newspaper magnate Lord Beaverbrook, whose reputation is as shady as his business

— have been unavailable to listen to his political tirades, I guess he deems me fair game for debate.

As I half listen to his diatribe on the question of Indian rule, I stare out the window at the Chartwell landscape from time to time, considering how I turn fifty this year and how my remaining days will most likely stretch before me in this precise manner, constantly walking the tightrope of Winston's needs while suffering through the maelstrom of his moods. How many times had I cried to Goonie after a family gathering? My only consolation is that he does not understand how his barbs wound me, because at day's end, I still love him and believe in him for the most part, and that makes me vulnerable to his onslaughts.

"Nothing to say to that, do you, Clemmie?" he pronounces, a triumphant note in his voice. "That silenced you on the topic, didn't it?"

His mouth opens again, wide enough for me to see the bits of scone on his tongue and in his teeth. Mercifully, a knock sounds on the bridge room door. Winston's valet enters bearing a silver tray heaped high with envelopes. All for Winston, no doubt. Even in political exile, his opinion is solicited. Although those very same supplicants wouldn't hesitate to walk by him on the street without a single word. I think about how, in the early years of our marriage, I wore our social snubbing as a badge of honor, an indicator we were pursuing righteous Liberal causes that ruffled the feathers of our entitled circle, but now, our marginalization, in large part, does not stem from the pursuit of such lofty goals.

With his butter knife, he begins slicing through the envelopes. I rise and excuse myself for a brief respite in my bedroom, but he barks, "Clemmie, there's a letter here from Moyne."

"Oh?" I answer offhandedly as I continue to walk across the room. I cannot see what this letter has to do with me. Walter Guinness, Lord Moyne had been financial secretary to the treasury when Winston was chancellor in the 1920s and remains his friend. He's not as odious as Beaverbrook and Bracken, but Moyne's public fondness for his mistress, Lady Vera Broughton, does not endear him to me. That said, Winston and I did spend a delightful few weeks cruise on his boat, the *Rosaura,* visiting Lebanon, Syria, and Palestine this past October.

"Yes. He's invited us to join him in a quest to capture a giant lizard known as the Komodo dragon. He wants the London Zoo to have a specimen."

"I see," I say, although I don't. Why someone with funds as vast as Lord Moyne would dedicate his time and attention to collecting a reptile, no matter how rare, is beyond me. It's not as if herpetology is his life's work. Weren't there more worthy causes or needier people upon whom he could lavish his money? I suppose a man like Moyne is in constant need of a new quest, and this Komodo dragon must fit the current bill.

"Odd pursuit that, but they're headed to the East Indies for four months."

I sit down at the table. "The East Indies, you say?"

"Sounds like a grand adventure."

"Are you thinking of going?" I ask cautiously, uncertain for what to hope. Four months of blissful quiet while Winston sails alone into the Indian Ocean? Or four months of sun, warm winds, and exploring exotic cultures with Winston at my side? Either way, I long for a change, away from the burden that is Chartwell and the needy, sometimes argumentative man that Winston becomes while there.

"How can I, Clemmie?" He lances me with another sharp tone. "My deadline looms. And I must keep my finger on the pulse of political developments." He deems it his public duty to watch over England, even though he has no power.

"Ah, yes," I say, hoping my voice does not betray the disappointment.

"I bet the Cat would love to sit in the sun and purr," he comments, and I wonder if he is taunting me. But when he continues, I hear tenderness in his voice. "The letter does invite you to come on your own if I'm occupied."

"It does?" I wish I could ask him to read the letter aloud, but I must tread carefully. If he senses a strong desire on my part to take this trip without him — no matter if it stems from nothing but a longing for warmth in this bitter December — he will be hurt. We are alike in our sensitivity.

"Surely you wouldn't think of taking such a long journey without me." His voice borders on petulant, and I understand at once that I'd sounded overeager.

"Of course not, Winston. The notion would never have occurred to me if you hadn't mentioned Moyne's offer just now. You heard surprise in my voice, nothing more."

Winston studies my face. "I know I'm hard work, Cat, and the next few months

265

will be all nose to the grindstone for me. Perhaps you should go. Perhaps a grand adventure is just the thing."

Funny how he slips between uncanny self-awareness and an inability to think of anyone but himself. While I appreciate it and, in truth, am surprised by his offer, I'm not certain he's in earnest.

I don't reply but instead run the toe of my shoe along the pattern on the blue carpet underfoot. I want to think over his overture, inauthentic though it may be, alone. We play an unusually quiet round of bezique, and I retire to my bedroom for my typical afternoon rest, although I feel anything but restful. The sky-blue dome of my bedroom provides a welcome refuge, and I lay down on my red silk moiré bedcover, hoping that if I close my eyes, my mind will stop whirring. As the experts on my "cures" taught me, I inhale a calming breath. Curious how Winston is always talking about his depression, but I'm actually the one with a nervous condition. One about which he has conveniently forgotten.

I open my eyes, and my gaze lands on the framed photograph of Marigold that I always keep on my bedroom desk. Even though I almost never mention her — so much so that, only two years ago, Mary asked about the identity of the little girl in the picture — she never really leaves my thoughts. Oftentimes, a powerful memory of her will suddenly wash over me. Images of Mary and Marigold populate my mind, along with the attendant self-criticism about my mothering. My heart begins to race, and anxiety and a familiar desire to flee take hold.

Do I dare go to the East Indies? I've taken holidays alone — usually "cures" for my nerves, at the doctor's insistence. Living with Winston means that I often need to live without him. But a four-month jaunt to the other side of the earth is quite a different matter, and we only just returned from a *Rosaura* cruise in October. I'd hate to appear self-indulgent. Another, better sort of mother might worry about the impact of a prolonged absence on her child, Mary in this case, but I am not that sort of mother. She has Moppet, who parents her far better than me. I worry more about the effect on Winston, how unraveled he can become without my structure and influence.

Rising from my bed, I wander into my bathroom and stare into my mirror. Why do people tell me that I am more attractive with age? When I examine my almost-fifty-year-old face, I see lines of worry, creases of fear, the sag of childbirth, and once chestnut hair tending toward silver. True, I've kept my figure, and I've learned how to dress for it, but I see a woman beset.

All at once, I make my decision. Slipping my shoes back on, I stride down the stairs into Winston's study, somehow both cozy and imposing with its high ceiling and exposed wooden beams, where tendrils of cigar smoke race out to greet me. He looks up from his desk, startled to see me at this hour of the day.

"I've made my decision," I announce with more confidence than I feel.

"About what?" His brow furrows in confusion. Can he really be perplexed? I realize then that he never really expected me to accept and so put the entire Komodo dragon adventure from his mind as soon as we started playing bezique.

His dismissal strengthens my resolve. "I am going to the East Indies."

CHAPTER TWENTY-FIVE

February 24, 1935
Bay of Islands, New Zealand
The wind whips my hair, and the relatively mild morning sun warms my cheeks, even through the shade of my wide-brimmed hat. I wonder what's happening at Chartwell and how they are faring since I've been gone these eight weeks. A mere week before Christmas, the entire family waved me off at Victoria station, and I hopped on the train to Messina where I joined Moyne's yacht, the *Rosaura*. Stepping on board the *Rosaura* initially reminded me of stepping on board Winston's beloved *Enchantress,* but there the comparisons stopped. A festive, devil-may-care mood imbued everyone and every occasion on board the *Rosaura* — not a whiff of political chatter to be found — and I surrendered to it. It is a lightheartedness I've never before experienced, certainly not in my own peripatetic, anxious youth.

Even the guilt of missing Christmas slips away.

I open my eyes, squinting into the delicious sunlight. The light blinds at first, and with the swaying of the boat as it courses through the Pacific Ocean, it takes a moment to orient myself. When I do, I see Terence, a wide grin spread across his handsome face.

"Why the smile?" I ask, grinning myself. I find it impossible to keep a straight face when Terence is beaming. His smiles are infectious.

"Can't I smile at a beautiful *brama?*" His bemused expression turns mischievous.

"Oh you!" I throw a towel at him for calling me the slang word for a pretty woman. It's an oblique reference to Brahma, the supreme god of Hindu mythology and, while geographically appropriate, has a hint of lasciviousness. Eight weeks ago, when I first boarded the *Rosaura,* I would have stormed off in a huff of righteousness when faced with such a comment. How my time on board this boat with Terence has changed me.

He suddenly strides over to the railing and peers into the distance. "Come here, Clementine. I think we are approaching the coast," he calls to me.

Pushing myself up from the deck chair, I quickly wrap my robe around my bathing costume and stand beside him. The air smells of sea and salt as well as something new and fragrant. Perhaps the magnolia-like flower I've seen growing along the New Zealand beaches?

Without thinking, I clutch his arm. "That's the island!"

He places his hand over mine. "It is indeed."

Our eyes meet, and I think about the moment I first met him. After changing in my stateroom after my arrival on board, I entered the dining room to join my host, Lord Moyne, and his mistress, Lady Vera Broughton, or so I thought. When I stepped into the room, it wasn't Moyne who welcomed me but Moyne's more agreeable cousin Lee Guinness and his wife, Posy. It seemed that Lord Moyne wouldn't be joining us for three weeks, not until we reached Singapore. I assumed that the Guinnesses and I would be a threesome for those weeks, and while three can be awkward, I consoled myself with the fact that it might give me the time alone I craved. Then a tall, attractive man strolled into the room. My old shyness overtook me, and when he was introduced as "Terence Philip, director of the

London branch of the New York art dealer Knoedler's," I could think of nothing to say. No longer.

"Should we ready ourselves?" I am eager to take the dinghy to the deserted island rumored to have pink sand beaches, created after decades of waves crushed the exquisite coral that rings the coast. The Bay of Islands in which we sail contains more than 140 islands, each alleged to be more beautiful than the next.

Terence reaches for the champagne bottle on the table between our deck chairs. "How about a drink first? We have plenty of time, and God knows, we won't need the same sober powers of concentration we would need if we hadn't so wisely abandoned the fishing."

The Clementine who mounted the *Rosaura* over eight weeks ago would have declined the champagne on the grounds that it was too early in the day and therefore unseemly. Or if I was at Chartwell, I would have eschewed the champagne because it was too costly and therefore a drain on my tight budget. But I am not that Clementine anymore. I reach for my crystal glass and hand it over to Terence to fill.

How have we become so comfortable with one another so quickly? I wonder. It usually takes me years to lower the barricade of my natural reserve, and even then, I've only allowed in a select few friends. Was it that both Guinnesses succumbed to seasickness as soon as we set off from Messina, throwing the two of us together alone for three weeks before we reached Singapore? Either way, by the time Lee and Posy Guinness disembarked in Singapore and we were joined by Lord Moyne and his mistress, Vera, Terence and I were already thick as thieves. We had spent countless hours alone swimming in the rigged-up pool on deck, dining in the salon, and talking as we watched the vast expanse of sea pass us by. When we were finally joined by our hosts — who generally spent the day in their own pursuits — we explored, on our own, Borneo, New Guinea, the uncharted Eilanden River, the eastern coast of Australia where all the geographical points were named after Captain Cook, and the geysers of Rotorua. Terence, Russian-born and English-raised, was a cultured sophisticate with a vast web of acquaintances and friends and no interest in politics. For the first time in decades, I listened to amusing tales about culture and society told by a lighthearted man, who inspired me to be the same.

After finishing our champagne and suiting

up for our decidedly nonfishing excursion, Terence and I meet at the *Rosaura*'s dinghy. Earlier, when we docked at a different point along the coast, the larger tender left to take the keen fishermen Moyne and Vera back to Deep Water Cove, a stretch of coast in the Bay of Islands known for its abundance of mako sharks, a prize catch for fishermen of our hosts' stature. After our experience with them yesterday — during which Terence and I not only failed to catch anything larger than a minnow but also suffered from paralytic seasickness in the pitching sea — we vowed to eschew fishing for the rest of the voyage.

We hop on board the dinghy, greeting the *Rosaura* cocaptain who's piloting us to the unnamed island. The little boat is jam-packed with baskets of food for our lunch, folding deck chairs, blankets, and two umbrellas, and Terence and I must squeeze tightly together on the bench to fit. The motor is too loud for us to talk, and I'm not certain I could speak anyway. In the close quarters of the dinghy, our thighs touch, and because the fabric of my dress is thin, I feel his skin against mine. I experience a wave of desire.

My body instinctively recoils at this swell of emotion and physicality. How can I simultaneously react so strongly to Terence and condemn those culpable of extramarital affairs? Perhaps I've been too harsh a judge of others' behavior. I feel confused and overwhelmed and guilty with the thoughts racing through my head, even though I haven't acted upon them. But I wonder, does one only cross the line to infidelity if one engages in their fantasies?

Unnerved, I move away from Terence, closer to the edge of the boat. I cling tightly to the side as we approach the island and peer at our destination, as if I'm seeking a better perspective. As the mere speck amid the vast azure bay materializes, the island delivers on its reputation. Pink beaches encircle a single mountain carpeted by green velvet, ringed by water so vibrantly blue, its color defies description.

The dinghy's motor stops, yet we are still a far distance from the beach. The cocaptain glances at us. "Sir, ma'am, this is as far as she'll go in this shallow water."

As our pilot loads up a portable float to bring our picnic and gear ashore, Terence rolls up his pant legs and hops out of the dinghy. He is knee-high in crystal clear seawater, and I can see the hair on his legs as plainly as if I held a magnifying glass. Stretching out his hand to me, he says, "Join me, Clementine. It's warmer than a bath!"

Peeling off my shoes and cramming them in my bag, I tie up my skirt and take his hand. Leaping into the turquoise water, its balminess prompts me to guffaw loudly. How is this temperature possible? It's as if Winston's valet had boiled the water and poured it into the Pacific himself.

We wade through the shallow water until we reach shore. By the time our feet touch the soft sand, the picnic has already been assembled on a blanket under an umbrella and the deck chairs arranged under the shade of the second umbrella.

Any residual tendrils of anxiety and worry that followed me here from London slip away. I inhale deeply, thinking how this ethereal sanctuary seems like reality, while Chartwell, Winston, the children, and politics feel like the dream. If only I could reside in this nether space forever.

I whisper, "It's what heaven must be like."

I must have spoken louder than I intended, because the cocaptain, sweaty from his efforts assembling our picnic, replies, "Aye, ma'am. That it is. I'll be back for you in three hours."

Three hours is not near enough time in this paradise. I drop my bag on the chair and sit before the food. Suddenly, I am voraciously hungry, and I begin to eat the sliced papaya. Terence plops down next to me and reaches for the tropical fruit. "It looks delicious."

"It is," I answer, juice dripping down the sides of my mouth. I don't bother to wipe it away. The seawater will take care of it soon enough.

Without waiting for Terence to finish, I slip off my dress, place it onto the chair alongside my bag, and wade back into the water in my swimsuit. Within minutes, he paddles beside me, and we engage in a merry game of diving for shells. The water is practically invisible up close, and we easily retrieve the plentiful cockles, snails, limpets, circular slipper shells, nerites, fan scallops, and blue mussels. Our hands grow full, and we decide to take a break and organize our treasures.

The blazing sun dries us in minutes as we build a large mound of shells to bring back on board with us. We stroll along the pastel sand, picking up delicate branches of white dried coral, while albatrosses fly overhead. "How do you think this island compares with others we've seen on our voyage?" Terence asks me.

"This is the most glorious by far." I pause for a moment, wondering whether I should say aloud the notion that's taken hold of me. "I never want to leave."

The ever-affable Terence laughs. "I think we'd run out of food without the *Rosaura* to send over provisions. And the *Rosaura* won't stay here forever."

For once, I don't laugh along with him. I know my wish is impossible, and yet I long to freeze this moment. To live within its exquisite parameters forever, with Terence by my side. He makes me feel loved and respected for myself — not for what I can do for him and not for who he wants me to be. It is a different sort of love and admiration than Winston has for me. And I feel a new person under his gaze.

I walk back toward the chairs, don my wide-brimmed hat, and lie back. How can I return to my prior existence after this bliss, unreal though it may be? But how could I ever leave Winston?

A few minutes later, Terence sits on the edge of my chair and stares at me. "If you were a sculpture, I could sell you for a fortune," he murmurs to me, sending a shiver down my spine.

A witty retort begins to form on my lips, but instead, I lean toward him. I have never, ever thought of another man in this way. Only Winston. Closing my eyes, I incline my face toward his for a kiss.

I receive the caress of his fingers on my cheeks rather than his lips on mine. My eyes fly open. Is he rejecting my overture? I'd believed the connection between us to be strong and mutual, but now I feel sick, and not only because he hasn't reciprocated. How could I have even thought of initiating something with Terence? I've become the people I've scorned.

"Oh, my dear Clementine." He holds my cheek tenderly, as if I was a child. "I'm not the marrying kind."

Not the marrying kind. What does he mean? I already know that he's a lifelong bachelor. All at once, I think I understand his euphemism. Could he mean that he prefers men to women as partners? He never felt for me what I felt for him. How could I have been so blind? I am a fool.

My face must betray my confusion and shock and mortification, because, with apology heavy in his tone, he says, "I thought you knew."

"I didn't." My cheeks burn as if I were standing directly in the Australian sun rather than under the shade of the umbrella. "I've grown to like you, Terence."

"And I've grown to like you." His smile is warm and open, as if nothing embarrassing had just passed between us. "Not that it's hard, Clementine. You are beautiful and wise and funny and brave. And I love you, in my way. If I were the marrying kind, you would be the woman I'd marry."

His words are small solace for his inability to fully reciprocate my feelings. And yet, as he beams at me, the warmth of his admiration spreads through me, and I realize that perhaps what I actually adore most about Terence is the courageous, exuberant woman I become in his company, not weighed down by others' cares and not rushing to judgment of others. And that is something I can bring home with me.

CHAPTER TWENTY-SIX

April 30, 1935
Westerham, England
Through the rain-smeared window of the car, I see the mechanical digger. What on earth is it doing here? Its incongruent presence among the familiar verdant landscape of Chartwell astonishes me until something niggles at my memory. Had Winston mentioned it in one of the "Chartwell Bulletins" he sent to me on my journey? I had studied the first bulletin with some interest, but by the time the second one arrived, I barely skimmed it. The combined magic of the *Rosaura* and Terence had already transported me to another realm by then, and I did not want the tethers of home to restrain me.

How unbelievable the voyage now seems against the drizzling backdrop of gray London, I think. Nearly as unreal as Chartwell had seemed while cruising through the Pacific and Indian Oceans. How will I navigate the return home while staying true to the person I've become?

The sound of tires on gravel increases as we near the front door of Chartwell. I'd prepared myself to feel the anxiety mount as I neared it, but I fought off the old demon with calming breaths and memories of blazing sunlight. By the time the driver opens my car door and Winston and a much-taller Mary rush out of Chartwell to greet me, my nerves and will are strong enough to survive the onslaught and all that might follow.

As my beautiful twelve-year-old daughter races toward me, I have a horrible flash of the moment I returned home from Egypt and Marigold didn't recognize me, and I feel sick. What have I done by leaving my sweet daughter for four months for purely selfish reasons? How will she feel about her often-absent mother? Will she even hug me?

"Mummy, Mummy, you came home!" Mary cries out, tears of relief in her eyes.

"Of course, my love! Of course I returned to you." Tears pour down my cheeks, and I am immensely grateful for her ongoing affection in the face of my desertion. I reassure my poor daughter that I'm home to stay, encircling her in my arms. I feel her body flinch within my foreign embrace, and sadness courses through me over her unfamiliarity with her mother's affection. At what price did I buy my peace of mind?

As I unwrap my arms from her narrow body, Mary returns to Moppet, with whom I exchange a thankful nod, although I can't deny a twinge of jealousy. Even though I made the decision to place Mary in Moppet's care, I can't help but feel a little covetous of their easy bond. Will I ever have that sort of connection with my children? Why couldn't I be the sort of mother who was content in her child-rearing? At what point will I rise up over my own unmothered childhood and give what I did not receive?

Winston rushes in, encompassing me in his embrace. "Oh, Cat, you cannot imagine how I've missed you. I worried that our domestic life might pale in comparison with your exotic travels, and, and —" He stammers out the final words. "I feared you might not come back."

"Oh, my poor Mr. Pug, I've longed to be folded in your arms." As I say this, I realize that it's true. This feeling is a relief. I wasn't sure it would come.

He releases a great sigh, saying, "I've been waiting for you to say that."

"How are Randolph and the girls?"

He points to a window on the second floor, where I see a lanky silhouette. "Randolph is still recovering from his tuberculosis. The cough lingers and his energy is low, but he'll be fine." His voice drops. "At least when he's ill, he's not creating mischief."

"Small mercies," I chuckle. "I'll stop up to see him in a moment. What of Sarah and Diana?" The girls are notable in their absence. Winston had written that Diana's divorce came through during my trip, and I know better than to think my presence would have helped her through the difficult time. Her passive personality has always been at odds with my own, and I am certain that Moppet, whose presence has always served as a comforting blanket for my children, provided better support for Diana in the courthouse and in the days that followed.

"Sarah should be back from dance class any minute. She wanted to skip it and wait for your return, but we didn't know exactly when you'd arrive, so I sent her off. Diana is in the city with a friend." Winston's volume drops when he mentions Diana's friend, but I ignore the matter for now. Is this friend a young man? Did I underestimate my daughter in the reason behind her divorce when I attributed it solely to her ex-husband's mercurial ways? There will be time enough for Winston and me to discuss this later.

Wide-eyed Mary watches us intently. Dropping Winston's hand, I stroll over to her side, unlacing her fingers from Moppet and relacing them with mine. I must reclaim her, for this moment at least. "I am so happy to be home with you. I cannot wait to hear all that you've been up to." Perhaps now is the time to begin forging a closer tie with my child. What am I waiting for?

As Winston leads us into the house, I think about the telegram I sent them during the *Rosaura*'s last stop, Bali. I didn't want to waste more than a minute of my remaining time writing a long letter, so I jotted a hasty telegram about being lost in the Pacific. How could I have been so flippant in my communication, so insensitive to the needs of these waiting souls, Mary and Winston? *And yet,* I think to myself as Winston tours me around the house and property to exhibit his projects, *it is Winston's incessant needs that drove me to take the journey.* I remind myself to tread cautiously as I reenter my old life.

The thought of Bali pulls me away from my surroundings. After the excitement of capturing five Komodo dragons — the ostensible reason for Moyne's trip — we made a final stop at the legendary East Indian island. Its terraced emerald interior was dotted with pagoda-like temples, or *pura,* and ringed by turquoise waters and golden sand; it lived up to its enchanted reputation. The only disappointment was that, although it was still relatively un-spoiled, tourists had recently "discovered" the island, and the English language could be heard in even the most remote villages.

On our final evening, Terence and I sat alongside Moyne and Vera, watching a traditional Balinese dance. Against the backdrop of chiseled, half-dressed men playing the Balinese gamelan, beautiful young native women engaged in intricate, traditional dances, their exotic movements at once lulling and jarring. But the ceremonial hut was far from the breezy shore, and the bodies and fire made the room stifling. Terence noticed me fanning myself and asked if I'd like to get some air.

We stepped out of the hut and followed the torches down a narrow cliff stairway to the beach. The breeze was refreshing, and I removed my hat, allowing the wind to tousle my hair and cool my brow. Huge ocean waves crashed on the beach, and a nearly full moon illuminated the scene. It was an unimaginably romantic setting for a walk with a man with whom romance wasn't possible. I almost laughed aloud at the incongruity but stopped myself. Terence and I had moved past our awkward moment to an even more authentic friendship, but I didn't know how he'd feel about such a frank reference to what I assumed to be his sexual preferences.

"Care to walk?" he asked.

"I'd love to." Actually, I longed to dive into the cooling Pacific waters, but stripping my dress off and swimming in my undergarments was hardly appropriate, even with Terence. Still, there was nothing wrong with strolling barefoot where ocean met sand, so I asked, "Should we walk along the water's edge?"

"You always make the perfect suggestion," he said as we removed our shoes.

We'd walked for a while in companionable silence when he said, "May I ask you something personal?"

I nearly guffawed at his question; we talked about nothing but personal topics. Over the past fifteen weeks, I'd shared stories from my youth as well as my concerns over my children, subjects I would normally only share with Goonie or Nellie. The only exception to our conversational range was Winston; I had never once mentioned my husband, except in passing, and Terence had never once asked.

I tamped my reaction down to a chortle and said, "I feel like there are very few lines of discussion we haven't tackled."

He smiled and said, "I'll take that as a yes, then. Why did you take this trip?"

"To capture Komodo dragons, of course." I delivered my answer with a straight face, but in seconds, we were both hysterically laughing at the memory of the long, grueling wait for a dragon to emerge from its cave toward the goat carcass in a trap as we lay in the tall, itchy grass in the hot sun. Afterward, we had confessed to one another that the infamous Komodo dragons had been the least of the lures of this trip, even before we learned how disgusting the process was.

"Really," he prompted me in as serious a tone as I've ever heard from him.

I wondered how to answer. I didn't mind discussing the topic of my marriage with Terence, but I wasn't sure I wanted to delve into the notion of Winston and his demands with only a few weeks left of freedom from them. "In my real life, the pressures sometimes mount uncontrollably."

"And who or what causes those pressures?"

"Oftentimes, I put those pressures on myself. I have unreachable standards, as I'm sure you've guessed by now."

"Standards that I admire," he answered, but he didn't waver from his line of questioning. "I think you know what I'm asking, Clementine."

"You are persistent, Terence." I sighed. "Here, with you, I've found the peace to hear my own voice. It isn't drowned out by the roaring demands of others." Once I opened the door to talking about Winston, I found that I couldn't close it. All my marital and parental struggles came pouring out.

When I was finished, Terence gently took me by the shoulders and said, "Clementine, you are a wise, beautiful woman with so much to offer the world. You can make your own path; you needn't stay on your current one. It isn't your punishment for your imagined sins of neglect. You can be happy."

As he wrapped his arms around me in a show of support, I whispered, "Oh, Terence, I don't think I'll have a happy ending unless I write the ending myself."

We climbed up the steep, torchlit staircase to the ceremonial hut. At the top, a tawny, wrinkled woman stood with a gray bird perched on her hand. Several other similar birds in wicker cages surrounded her feet. I supposed they were for sale and that this was her makeshift store.

Terence approached the bird, stroking it with a gentle finger. "Beautiful, isn't it?" he asked.

The creature wasn't as flashy as some of the tropical birds we'd encountered, and at first, I questioned why Terence seemed so drawn to it. But as I walked toward it, I noticed its bright coral feet, silvery gray feathers, its blush-colored belly, and the subtle patch of black-and-white-speckled feathers that encircled its throat like a necklace.

"Yes, it is," I answered. "What sort of bird is it?"

"A dove. Did you know that, in the Near East and Mediterranean, doves were used in artwork as symbols of various goddesses, like the Roman goddesses Venus and Fortuna? But in Christian artwork, the dove represents either the Holy Spirit or peace," he said, reminding me that Terence had a life outside this one and that, in it, he served as a trusted art adviser to the wealthy. I sometimes forgot about that life, just as sometimes I forgot about my own.

Before I could comment, he reached into

his pocket and pulled out some money for the woman. She tried to hand him one of the doves in a cage, but he shook his head and pointed to the bird on her hand. She hesitated for a moment until he offered her more coins, at which time she relented. As she reluctantly placed the dove inside an empty cage, I wondered if it was her personal pet.

"I hadn't pegged you for an animal lover, Terence," I said as we walked away from the woman.

"This isn't for me, Clementine, but for you."

"For me?"

"Yes. I want to send you home to London with a reminder of the peace you achieved on this journey. Of the person you truly are."

"Clemmie, did you hear what I said about the digger?" Winston asks.

We are standing before the digger, stuck in a great hole near the lake, and for a disorienting moment, I wonder how we got here. Then I realize that as we sauntered around Chartwell and the grounds, my mind was elsewhere, in my memory of Bali.

I am suddenly reminded of the Bali dove, to which I carefully tended in its wicker cage as we made the long voyage home. But the last time I recall seeing it was on the train. Or did I have it with me in the car from the station? *Oh no, where have I left it?*

Without a word to Winston, Mary, and Moppet, I dart across the grounds to the circular drive at the front of the house. To my immense relief, the car still stands in the drive, as the staff is still working to unpack my trunks. Pulling open the passenger door, I exhale when I see the Bali dove sitting in its cage on the back seat.

The thud of footsteps and the scrape of shoes on gravel follows me, and I turn to see Winston, Mary, and Moppet rushing down the drive. "Whatever is wrong, Clemmie?" Winston calls to me, panting.

I hold the wicker cage up high like a trophy. "I thought I'd lost him."

Mary sprints over to the bird, which I lower to her eye level. The dove sings out a *crou-crou,* and she giggles.

"He likes you," I tell her.

"He's delightful, Mummy," Mary says, and I watch Moppet's gaze turn wary. She has every right to be hesitant about my shows of affection toward Mary, and yet I can't help but resent it a little.

Winston sidles up to the cage and peers inside. To my astonishment, the dove bows to him.

"Now, there's an animal that knows how to pay its respects," he declares with a chuckle.

As Winston, Mary, and Moppet walk back into the house, I follow them, whispering to the dove between the thin bars of its wicker cage, "I think you will help me write my happier ending."

IV

CHAPTER TWENTY-SEVEN

September 1, 1939
London, England

I look down over the carved wooden railing to the proceedings a level below on the House of Commons floor. I sit at the very front of the Strangers' Gallery, intended for those watching the floor but who are neither members nor staff of the Parliament. I wonder about the peculiar name for this viewing place. How can I be a stranger to this proceeding when much of the four years since my time aboard the *Rosaura* has focused upon the momentous topics debated on the Commons floor beneath my feet?

Winston clears his throat and puffs on his cigar. Even though he has been out of power and without a political position for years — ostracized and lambasted for his views, in fact — he appears quite at ease as the House Members look at him and wait respectfully for him to speak. I am the one brimming with nervous energy as we wait for the events on the floor to unfold. The act that Winston has been predicting now for years has finally come to pass — Hitler has mustered the forces he's secretly assembled to conquer and lay waste to Poland. How different this reception is from the jeering and hissing he's received from Prime Minister Chamberlain and his cronies for the past two years and from Prime Minister Baldwin and his cohorts for the years before that. They were determined to appease Hitler at all costs, even when Germany breached the Treaty of Versailles and blatantly demonstrated its aggression in Austria and Czechoslovakia thereafter. They did not want to hear the truth Winston laid bare for them.

One would think I'd have grown used to the scoffing after so many years of my husband advocating unpopular positions — his immovable stance on keeping India under imperial rule as one example, and his support of King Edward VIII's right to remain on the throne even though he planned to marry twice-divorced Wallis Simpson as another. But it has never gotten easier to watch my husband derided, particularly since I am in complete agreement with Winston's views here today, about the evil of the Nazis and a call for rearmament. Ever since witnessing for myself the rise of Hitler's Brownshirts on the fields outside Munich, the British position of appeasement has been incomprehensible to me. I could not understand how, in Chamberlain's meeting with Hitler and Mussolini last September on the heels of the Anschluss, the prime minister could sacrifice western Czechoslovakia in exchange for promises by Hitler that he would make no further demands for territory — only to watch Hitler's troops invade the rest of Czechoslovakia six months later and Mussolini's armies take over Albania shortly thereafter. How had this not demonstrated to the English people the aggressiveness of Hitler's intentions? How much more proof did they need?

Considering the House of Commons floor now, it seems that they needed the tyrant to invade Poland — which Britain was honor-bound by treaty to defend — to finally see Winston's point. Even as recently as last week, when the German-Soviet Nonaggression Pact was announced and plans were made to evacuate children from London, the government was not prepared to take action. What have these supposed leaders been doing for the past several years while

Winston and I were gathering information about Hitler, besides turning a blind eye to Winston's relentless efforts to get them to see the truth? After Mussolini invaded Abyssinia in October 1935 and then Hitler defied the Treaty of Versailles in March 1936, Chartwell became a hub for those who shared our perspective. Winston recruited Professor Frederick Lindemann from Oxford University to provide necessary data for his speeches and articles, and Ralph Wigram, a lovely young man whose despondency over these terrible times led to his untimely death nearly two years ago, provided intelligence to us at great risk to himself and his position in the Foreign Office. I even recruited my own cousin, the journalist Shiela Grant Duff, to send us important information from her post in Prague. We also hosted like-minded military officers, civil servants, journalists, and businessmen, all of whom phoned, arrived, and met with us at all hours as part of our effort to prove the Nazis' plans to our reluctant countrymen. When the situation became too harried — or the stress of the children became too much or Winston's depression over world affairs and his own powerlessness overwhelmed my own anxieties — I excused myself for a holiday or a restorative trip to the mountains in Zürs, Austria, at least until the Anschluss happened. I would do whatever necessary to avoid slipping into the nervous exhaustion of my earlier years. Once again, there was too much at stake.

But no matter how often and how strongly Winston raised these threats in the House of Commons, England's leaders had refused to listen. In the face of mounting evidence about Hitler's intentions, they insisted on maintaining a steadfast "friendship" with the monstrous German. And this perspective was shared not only within the government but also among our so-called friends. Just this past January, while I was on a very different *Rosaura* voyage through the beautiful but impoverished West Indies, which incited my liberal sensitivities, Winston's opinions were vigorously attacked by Lady Vera Broughton as warmongering, and many of the other guests quite vocally agreed with her stance. I couldn't stand being on board with the myopic fools a moment longer, so after informing my host, Lord Moyne, I went ashore to Barbados and booked passage home on the SS *Cuba* the very next day.

Would all this awful appeasement finally

change now that Hitler thumbed his nose at England by blatantly invading Poland?

I turn my attention back to the chamber below. The murmurings grow louder, and the stares at Winston across the sea of green-cushioned chairs and benches grow more numerous. Still, as we had planned, he does not rise to speak. Winston will wait until Chamberlain gives his speech. The longer it takes and the more the restlessness grows, the clearer it will become that Chamberlain does not have what it takes to do the job. This is precisely our intention.

I wish I had Mary's hand to squeeze as I wait. Curious, how connected I feel to my youngest child despite the fact that Moppet has long served in my parental stead. Perhaps it's because of that. Could the concerted effort I make to have an annual skiing trip with her have contributed to this feeling? Despite the tense atmosphere around me in the House of Commons and tumult raging in my stomach, I smile to myself, thinking about the wide-grinned Mary and me skiing down the glistening Alpine slopes, five thousand feet above the clouds. Sometimes Jack and Goonie's only daughter, Clarissa, or Judy, my cousin Venetia's daughter, would join us — or even occasionally Diana and her husband, Duncan Sandys, or Sarah — but oftentimes it would be just the two of us, swooshing down the mountains or relaxing before the crackling fire in the cozy lodge.

Whatever the reason, I feel a tether to Mary that I have never felt to poor Diana, Sarah, or Randolph, who all continue in their troubled states: the domestically inclined Diana, the only one seemingly marginally content, in her second marriage but with a delicate nature that requires rather constant attention that Duncan's parliamentarian schedule does not allow; the aspiring actress Sarah, unhappily married to the Austrian-born actor Vic Oliver, with whom she'd eloped three years ago when Winston and I condemned a union with the peripatetic thespian eighteen years her senior; and the ever-troublesome Randolph, still a heavy drinker, whose entitled attitude has not been humbled by his three failed attempts at political office or his marginal, low-paid position as a journalist. I am reaping what I sowed.

Finally, the prime minister stands and says that, despite his many efforts at peace and resolution of Germany's actions, the German chancellor announced an imminent attack on Poland. He then informs us that ac-

303

tion is required in the circumstances, but doesn't call for war. As Chamberlain continues, I hear a rumbling, and it's growing louder. I recognize it from the many unpopular speeches Winston has given; it is the sound of discontent. They wonder, as do I, why Chamberlain isn't calling for war. Why we are hearing more explanations and excuses?

Chamberlain returns to his seat, and leaders of the two opposition parties, Labour and the Liberals, each give a speech in support of governmental action. Even after a special motion is put before the House of Commons to authorize five hundred million pounds to pay for war and the motion is voted for unanimously, war is still not declared by the prime minister. *What is Chamberlain waiting for?* I wonder.

The sidelong glances in Winston's direction mount. These garrulous politicians are used to my equally loquacious husband speaking his mind. They cannot believe he is still seated. But my husband stays quiet, puffing away on his cigar. This silence is calculated — and hard-won, knowing Winston — and meant to throw Chamberlain's weakness into bold relief.

We had decided that he should wait until the floor was very nearly closed for the night, no matter how late and no matter how hungry he might be, before leaving. But he should not linger until Chamberlain called an end to the session. He must walk just before the session ends — very slowly and very pointedly — to demonstrate the prime minister's failing. I watch as, for once, Winston follows his instructions to the letter.

"By God, has the man no courage?"

"After pandering to Hitler for so many years, he's finding it hard to change tacks."

"Even after the attack on Poland? How can he be so cowardly?"

I had been listening to this sort of talk for an hour. After the House of Commons session ended, members of Parliament Anthony Eden, Alfred Duff Cooper, Bob Boothby, Brendan Bracken, and Diana's husband, Duncan, had assembled at our flat in Morpeth Mansions, a redbrick, two-floor space within sight of Parliament. Although we sometimes struggle to maintain the apartment on Winston's income from his books and articles, Winston and I have continued to rent the three-bedroom London abode, complete with dining room, drawing room, kitchen, study, and secretary's room, since 1930, and it has become a gathering place for like-minded folks over the years.

The outrage of the men assembled today matches my own. Winston has been presenting evidence of Hitler's aggression for years, and it had been one thing for Chamberlain to ignore it then, but how could he not declare war now? I am tired of all this talk.

I rise from the table and glance out the window at the rain beating down on the spire of Westminster Cathedral. My anger simmers and then spills over. Turning toward the men, I say, "Chamberlain is a bloody fool, and he will take the coward's path until he's shamed into action. If we don't hold his feet to the fire, he will retreat into the safety of Downing Street until the Nazis march down the streets of London and plow over the fields of England." I give my husband an unwavering stare. "Winston, it is time for you to put pen to paper."

"Here, here," Duncan says, and the other men echo him.

Winston stands as well and walks to his small study. The men glance at each other, then get up and follow the trail of his cigar smoke. The clubby, wood-lined study overflows with the members of Parliament, and the smell of cigarettes, cigars, and sweat soon weighs thickly in the air.

I stand at the doorway to the study, listening to the men rally around Winston. They offer suggestions for phrasing, but I know Winston will choose the most precise and powerful words. It is one of his greatest strengths. Yet he is used to my input, and I hear hesitation in his tone. When I hear him speak eloquently of the injury done to the British people, I walk through the circle of men and say, "That's fitting, Winston."

As he finalizes the letter, the men vie for the honor of delivering it to Downing Street personally. Unable to settle on one of their number, they determine that they will *all* take the short journey from Morpeth Mansions to the prime minister's residence and office. All except Winston, who begs off, claiming that he wants them to share the recognition. But I know he's been simply too drained.

When the door closes, I take Winston by the hand and lead him over to the large window overlooking the street below. A web of black umbrellas covers the men as they stride toward Downing Street in the pelting rain. A clap of thunder does not send even a ripple of hesitation through the ranks; they proceed without a pause.

When I look into Winston's eyes, I see a familiar but long-unseen spark. *This is not*

CHAPTER TWENTY-EIGHT

September 3, 1939
London, England

We hover anxiously around the wireless. After receiving Winston's letter, Chamberlain issued an ultimatum to Germany, demanding that it cease its attack on Poland within two hours. We'd received word from a loyal source close to the prime minister that Hitler sent no such commitment, and as such, Chamberlain would be making a radio address. But after watching the clock tick for the past twenty minutes, we had still heard nothing from Downing Street.

"Clemmie." Winston interrupts my anxious reverie with a speech he's drafting in anticipation of Chamberlain's announcement. He feels certain that the prime minister will soon capitulate. We go back and forth on the appropriate phraseology, searching for the most powerful, until we settle on the right verbiage.

"Good, good. I'll make that change."

The black wireless crackles with life. We lean into it, as if we could hasten Chamberlain's words with our proximity. "Do you think he'll finally declare war?" I ask.

"After my letter, how could he not?" Winston says.

Chamberlain's clipped, aristocratic voice transmits clearly over the wireless. We hold our breaths until we hear the words for which we've been waiting: England is at war.

"Chamberlain finally did it," I say with an exhale of relief. I hadn't realized that I'd been holding my breath.

"Nearly too late. If he'd listened to me a year ago, it might not have come to this. Although it gives me no pleasure to be right in this particular instance." Winston hoists himself out of his chair. "Shall we watch London prepare herself for war, Clemmie? From the terrace?"

Stepping over puddles of rainwater, I follow him wordlessly up the stairs to the terrace on the roof above our fifth- and sixth-floor apartment, a space to which only we have access through a door close to the secretary's room. After the thunderous rain last evening, the day is fine and unexpectedly bright. I shade my eyes to gaze out over the London cityscape of Westminster and the Houses of Parliament, wondering what Winston expects to see up here. With the azure sky and the blinding sunlight making vivid the colors of the city, it seems an unlikely day for war. To my astonishment, I see three blimps float up and over the rooftops and church steeples of the city like low-hanging clouds.

"So soon?" I ask, my heart racing at this evidence of war.

"We are at war, Clemmie." He sounds surprised by my reaction. "And we are jumping in midstream. Its battles will often take place in the air. We must be prepared, and we must begin now." He says this matter-of-factly, but to me, the leap from declaration to action seems too short. I feel vulnerable and exposed and yet oddly thrilled. Once again, as we had in the Great War, Winston and I stand on the brink of history.

Suddenly, a deafening wail fills the air, and I automatically cover my ears with my hands. "What in the blazes is that?" I yell.

"I believe it's a first air-raid siren," he yells back.

He seems fixated on the skyline, so I tug on his arm. "It's blaring for a reason, Pug. Let's get a move on." He is immovable.

Threading my arm through his, I pull him toward the stairs. "You're not going to let your Cat stand in harm's way, are you?"

The reference to my well-being wakens Winston's sense of duty, and he begins moving downstairs. As we pass our apartment door, I nip in for a moment, bringing out a bottle of brandy and two glasses. "For medicinal comfort," I say, waving it toward him. I don't know how long we'll be forced to stay in the newly erected air-raid shelter on the street, and I know Winston will fare better with a brandy to pass the time. Should I change my clothes? I wonder if my pale-blue gabardine dress is suitable for a shelter. *Silly,* I think, *to be worrying about attire at a time like this.*

Near an underpass, a makeshift shelter has been constructed. As we approach the queue of neighborhood people waiting to enter, I hear a whisper pass through them: "The Churchills are here." I realize that from this moment forward, every decision we make and action we take will serve as an example for the people who only now acknowledge the truth of the warnings Winston has been issuing for years.

Ever impatient, Winston is tempted to rush to the front of the queue, as if early entrance means early exit. I place my hand upon his arm, holding him back. "Everyone is watching you. You must model the proper behavior for the people."

Chastened, he bides his time until we reach the entryway. Just as we are about to step into the arched space, a peculiar blend of indoor and outdoor, crowded with every manner of London folk — young mothers and children, shopkeepers, grocers, maids, barristers — the man who has been in front of us in the queue hesitates, then walks away. I call out to him as he wanders down a side street, "Sir, you must come inside where it's safe."

"I don't think the people will want me in there, ma'am." He has a heavy German accent, and I suddenly understand.

"Why? Because you're originally from Germany?"

"Yes." He will not meet my eye.

"But you aren't part of the German army, are you?"

He looks horrified. "No, ma'am. Of course not."

"And you are a naturalized citizen, are you not?"

"Of course."

"Then come along. All British citizens deserve protection from the threat of the Nazis."

■ ■ ■ ■

Hours later, the sun wanes, and the silver automobile idles on Downing Street as Winston meets with Chamberlain. My wristwatch, which I cannot help but constantly check, shows that half an hour has passed. Wrapping my tweed coat around me in the unexpectedly chilly autumn evening, I wish Winston had allowed me to spend these long minutes at Morpeth Mansions where I could distract myself with the stack of letters I must write, but he would have none of it. "This is our war, Clemmie, and this will be our position, one for which we've waited nearly a decade. You must be nearby when we are restored."

While I appreciate the sentiment — and I do believe my careful ministrations have allowed him to survive these long years with a modicum of success and self-respect — I don't think that whatever position he secures will be any less mine if I'm down the road instead of outside on the street. I wonder if he sees me as a kind of a talisman, bringing him luck for the meeting with Chamberlain, and yet, how could he? I haven't brought him good fortune these years away from the hub of power. In fact, there were several points when I contemplated leaving him alone in his unruly forest, as he is well aware.

Surely Chamberlain, Winston's nemesis and naysayer of his warnings, wouldn't have summoned him unless he wanted to restore him to power? Surely the prime minister understands that he must recognize the truth in Winston's long-held positions.

Another quarter hour ticks by and still no Winston. I'm tempted to instruct the driver to deliver me back home and then return for my husband when a thump pounds on the window from the cane Winston always carries, the legacy from my long-departed brother. *Poor Bill and Kitty,* I think. *How would they have fared in this war-trodden world?* I see Winston's half grin through the foggy glass.

He flings open the door before the driver can come around. It's been an age since I've seen him move so quickly. "What happened?" I ask.

He slides into the car as gracefully as a man of his formidable size can and says to the driver, "Please drive us to Admiralty House." His half grin becomes a full smile, and he turns to me. Regardless of the jowls, lines of worry, and receding hairline, I see the youthful Winston that I married in his jubilant smile.

"You are the first lord of the admiralty, *again*," I say with a mixture of astonishment and awe. I'd hoped and prayed that Chamberlain would give Winston a worthy position — it was a pragmatic, self-serving choice on the prime minister's part, after all — but I never believed that he'd be granted this lofty post for the second time in his life. Not that Winston didn't deserve it. He deserved it and more.

"Indeed, Clemmie." He beams at me, the smile of a man finally vindicated. "And we have work to do immediately. Naval yards to inspect, battleships to assess, an entire navy to review. All left to languish for far too long while Hitler has focused on nothing else but amassing his military might. We must shore up our country at sea."

"Yes, indeed." I smile back at him. How can I not? I have not seen my husband this vibrant for nearly a decade, and I am finally about to embark upon the work I've been preparing to do nearly my entire life.

"Are you up to the task, Cat?"

"I think you know I am, Pug."

"Thank God. You know I cannot do this alone."

We entwine our fingers. Whatever domestic issues have divided us, whatever familial disagreements have wedged between us, whatever toll the years of shoring up Winston's dream of Chartwell — his England in miniature — has taken from us, we are linked in this work for our country. Together, we will be serving in the Admiralty again, in another wartime nonetheless. How we have come full circle.

CHAPTER TWENTY-NINE

May 6 and 10, 1940
London and Hertfordshire, England

"Come, Clemmie. We've got a vessel to launch," Winston bellows.

I am finishing up my instructions to a secretary, so I hold up a finger. A collective gasp, quiet but still audible, emanates from the staff members scurrying around the room, carrying out Winston's orders. No one but me would dare shush the lord admiral.

Handing over the list of donors I'm targeting to raise money for minesweepers — civilian boats that have been commandeered and outfitted for military purposes — I look up at Winston. He waits for me near the door to the office outfitted with many desks now, though it had formerly been one vast office just for the lord admiral.

From the moment war was declared and Winston assumed the lord admiral role, the entire country moved forward alongside us with a sense of urgency and purpose. Within days of Winston's appointment, we'd moved into Admiralty House with Mary in tow and settled into a routine of working sixteen hours a day, seven days a week, surrounded by government staff used to only working for five to six hours a day under the lassitude of the Chamberlain administration. But how could they reasonably complain? Their new leader kept to this pace, as did I, and it seemed that the Germans would be moving at a rapid-fire clip as well. Since Winston took office, the Nazis bombarded British vessels, and we lost the aircraft carrier HMS *Courageous* in the North Sea, the ocean liner SS *Athenia,* and the HMS *Royal Oak* in the Orkney Islands, along with sixty thousand tons of British shipping loads. And we all understood that this was just the beginning, even when a lull set in after the initial wave of attacks.

Immediately upon moving from our apartment at Morpeth Mansions to Admiralty House, I knew we'd need a modern-day center of control with a suitable office for a hardworking first lord, not a bastion of old-world entertainment. We converted the expansive stateroom space and many living and entertaining rooms into a naval command center, moving our flat into the upper two floors of the building. What used to be our main apartment was cut into workrooms. Instead of the frivolous naval-themed and nautical-colored decoration with which the prior Lord Admiral Duff's wife had festooned Admiralty House, we simplified the fabrics and furniture into a somber style, more appropriate for laborious wartime. Chartwell had been boarded up, leaving only Orchard Cottage open for Moppet, Diana, and her two young children, Julian and Edwina, who'd been evacuated from London. Winston and I will be in London for the long haul, no matter how brutal this becomes, and we will have Mary at our side for now, attending school and working in a canteen and for the Red Cross.

The infectious sense of urgency permeating the nation even prompted Randolph to action, although not of the sort for which Winston and I had longed. After quitting his job to join Winston's old regiment, the Fourth Hussars, he focused his attention on securing a bride and an heir in the event he was killed in the war. He showered proposals all over London to any marginally appropriate girl he encountered — a rumored eight proposals to eight different women in the span of two weeks, much to our embarrassment — and received a resounding round of nos until he met Pamela Digby. The voluptuous auburn-haired eldest daughter of Lord and Lady Digby had grown up in the rather tedious world of the Dorset countryside, and while she professed to adore the equestrian life, I saw from our first encounter that she was thrilled to be at the epicenter of power. Even during the wedding we hastily arranged — along with so many other British families whose sons were about to deploy — at St. John's Church in Smith Square with a party in one of the Admiralty House staterooms afterward, in which the bride wore a dark-blue dress, beret, and matching dyed fur as there was no time for a gown, I saw that it was becoming a Churchill that intrigued her, not necessarily becoming Mrs. Randolph Churchill. Still, I found the girl endearing, and I resolved to support this new member of the family, which I knew she'd need in a marriage to Randolph. And I had trouble enough with Randolph as it was to not befriend his bride.

"Clemmie, the frigate will not wait," Winston chides, although softly. I am accompanying him to launch a new airship carrier, which he still insists on calling by the archaic term of frigate.

"Are you all set then?" I ask the secretary.

"Yes, ma'am. I'll reach out to these pro-spective donors today," she answers with a nod, and I hope I'm leaving this important project in capable hands.

When Winston received his appointment, I'd decided that I would no longer wait for him to include me in his work but that I would seek out critical projects of my own. For every battleship I inspect at his side and boat I launch alongside my husband, I undertake projects for which Winston does not have time but that I think merit atten-tion, the running of Fulmer Chase Mater-nity Hospital for soldiers' wives, for exam-ple. I forge ahead on meritorious tasks, unwilling to be solely ceremonial, joining Winston on those difficult meetings with relatives who'd lost their sons and arranging a special enclosure for bereaved families on the Horse Guards Parade, for example. The long-lasting legacy of the *Rosaura* means that I will wait for no one to invite me into history.

This may well be our last chance to serve close to the inner machinations of Britain's power, I realize, and I do not want to lose this opportunity. As I assume this mantle — again becoming the lord admiral's wife after almost thirty years — I experience an almost embarrassing sense of exhilaration and calm. Strange how I thrive under the stress of crisis and falter under the weight of normal existence.

"Clemmie," Winston says again, his voice more impatient.

"Coming," I call back and stride toward my waiting husband.

I dab away Nellie's tears with my damp white handkerchief. *How well my poor sister is bearing up under the burden of her dual loss,* I think. Her long-suffering husband Bertram, who had been enduring the pain of his injuries from the Great War for decades, died only four days ago from cancer, and then, a mere two days later, she received word that her son Giles was captured in Norway by the Nazis. Although Winston hadn't wanted me to leave his side, my sister deserves my consolation and assistance, so I went to her home in Hertfordshire as soon as possible after Giles's capture.

"Has Winston found out more about Giles's situation?" Nellie asks, her heavy, inky eyebrows casting a shadow under her eyes, making the dark circles there even darker. As soon as I reached Hertfordshire, she'd begged me to have Winston do some digging into Giles's whereabouts, and the housemaid had just delivered a letter from the morning mail.

"The note I received this morning contained no new information." I do not tell Nellie that the missive didn't even mention Giles, only a series of tasks for me to handle and a query about how best to manage the challenge by Conservative Leo Avery to Chamberlain's fitness to serve. Should he join in the chorus of members of Parliament calling for Chamberlain to step down, he wondered, or stay uncharacteristically silent. These are the matters most pressing in Winston's mind; sadly, not Giles.

It is only a matter of time before Chamberlain is forced out, I'd cautioned a very impatient Winston before I left. The rumblings about the prime minister had turned into a roar, and Winston needed to allow that roar to grow even louder on its own, without his prompting. But forbearance has never been Winston's strong suit.

"Giles wasn't even a soldier. He was just a reporter for the *Daily Express,* for God's sake," Nellie says. I'd heard this lament many times over the past two days.

"I know, Nellie." I take her into my arms. "Sadly, I think it was enough for the Nazis that Giles was British. All we know is that Giles is classified as *Prominente* because of his relationship to Winston. That should get him better treatment and some protection, at the very least."

The phone rings, and we jump. "It could be someone about Giles," Nellie says.

Nellie's young housemaid, a pretty girl with bouncy chestnut hair who reminds me a bit of my new daughter-in-law, Pamela, enters the parlor. "Mrs. Churchill, the call is for you. It is the lord admiral."

My sister gives me a hopeful glance as I scuttle out of the room, into the hallway where the phone is located. I place the receiver to my ear. "Pug, is that you?"

"Cat." Winston is breathing heavily. Why is he so winded? "Thank God, I've got you."

"Of course. Is everything all right?"

"The Nazis have initiated an offensive through Holland, Belgium, and France — with the goal of invading the channel. It is only a matter of days or weeks before the Germans could be beating down our door."

"Oh God." I feel sick. From all the secret military information to which I was privy, I knew, of course, that this was possible. But I never fathomed that it could come this soon. "What is to be done?"

"I've just come from Downing Street.

Chamberlain summoned me and Halifax."

My heart begins to beat quickly, and I find I cannot speak. Winston and Halifax are the two natural contenders for Chamberlain's position, so I can guess about the reason for the summoning. Is this the moment to which we have been building our whole lives? Has Winston been called to save his country, as he predicted decades ago on our engagement day?

"Clemmie, are you there?"

I force myself to speak. "I am, Winston. I'm here."

"Chamberlain advised us that he has decided to stand down as prime minister, albeit reluctantly. He asked Halifax and me who we thought should be his rightful successor. My natural instinct was to throw my hat in the ring — point out my longstanding arguments about the Nazi threat and the dangers of appeasement — but I thought of you. All your warnings about letting the rumble turn into a roar and all that. So I stayed quiet."

"And what happened?"

"Halifax acknowledged that the war leader needed to be a member of the Commons, which effectively put him out of the running. Chamberlain's eyes turned on me. The duty to save the country, it seems, has fallen

326

to me." His labored breathing is audible. "I feel as if all that I've imagined for so long ago is finally coming to fruition."

"Oh, Winston, I knew it would. You are the only one who can do the job."

"How Mother would have loved to see me assume this role, although I wish it had not come at this cost," he says with a sigh. "But I can only do it if you're by my side. The summons to attend the king at the palace — and transfer power — will come soon."

"I will get on the next train to London. I should be there by late afternoon."

"Hurry, Cat. I'll want you with me at the palace. Your Pug needs you. And so does your country."

CHAPTER THIRTY

June 17–18, 1940
London, England

How does one support one's husband when he stands as the guardian to one's country's freedom? From the moment King George VI invested Winston with the titles of prime minister and minister of defense, I consider this question, one that I first contemplated decades ago when Winston began his climb during the Great War. While I know the guiding hand I provide in his speech-making along with the help preparing him to present those speeches will be more critical now than ever, I understand now — as I did during Winston's earlier days in power — that my husband's brilliant ability to see the larger picture and to design both political and military strategy often blinds him to the powerful needs of the individuals serving him as well as the needs of those he serves. I decide that, in order for him to vanquish the Nazis, I must serve as the lens through which he views and treats human-kind, almost as his social barometer and conscience. Without the consideration of all these souls, we will not prevail. He cannot, indeed does not, fight alone.

"The prime minister asks that you review his speech within the hour, ma'am." One of Winston's typists, a Miss Hall, hands me the papers at my desk in the White Drawing Room at Downing Street. As we had during our brief stay at Admiralty House, we've converted the prime minister's residence and workplace into a hub for the war effort. Despite its modest exterior, Number 10 is a very large building. I've maintained the ground floor's dining room, the Cabinet Room, and the prime minister's office, as they are absolutely necessary, but the first floor's drawing room is now overrun with makeshift work spaces for the many staff members, military men, telephone opera-tors, and dispatch riders, among others. I've limited the family space to the passage room, where Winston and I dine alone or with Mary, who still mostly resides with us, as well as our children and their families from time to time, and to the bedrooms, with their eggshell-blue walls, bright-red carpets, and sash windows with views of the gardens. The White Drawing Room, which was used as a private reception room for guests, is now an office for my own endeavors, those critical tasks that Winston has not the time to tend. But I've decided my first and foremost priority is awakening him to his people.

The mousy-haired Miss Hall appears nervous and browbeaten, undoubtedly from the yelling and berating Winston unleashes on all his staff members. The more pressure he's under, the more he rebukes them. And we have had nothing but pressure in the month he's been in office, beginning with the German offensive in western Europe and continuing with the success of the Germans in the Netherlands, Belgium, and now France. As prime minister and minister of defense, Winston holds the future of Britain in his hands, and he is not handling it with grace. Not that he has ever handled anything with grace exactly.

The girl clearly needs to settle her nerves before she returns to my husband or risk a total dressing-down. Winston loathes reticence and nervousness, even if he is its cause. "Miss Hall, why don't you join me for a cup of tea? It will calm you." I simultaneously gesture to the chair opposite me and smooth the skirt of my charcoal-gray dress. Since Winston assumed office and our days became unimaginably hectic and unpredictable, I decided upon a uniform for my days — a well-cut dress in a serious, but not funereal, shade with my double strand of pearls — but I settled upon a splashier coat to top it off when we go out to give the people a lift and a smile when we are among them. A leopard-skin coat has become a particular favorite.

"Oh, no, I couldn't, ma'am. The prime minister might need me. He wants to finish his review of the day's confidential documents before making any final changes to the speech." Her hands are visibly shaking at the thought of disappointing Winston. But I know that Winston and I will go around and around with the speech before we conclude, so there is time. He will not be delivering it until tomorrow after all, and not until we are both satisfied with it. I edit and review all Winston's speeches and rehearse them with him; they must unify and inspire the British people, especially now that we stand alone. It is a role I've undertaken many times, but never has it been more crucial.

"Isn't Miss Watson there?" Winston keeps a stable of typists on constant rotation. He has announced that no orders emanating from Downing Street are to be followed unless typewritten and signed by him personally. This step, necessary to maintain the sort of absolute control he believes necessary in wartime, has increased the typists' work multifold.

"Yes, ma'am," she answers warily.

"The state of your nerves is critical to us, Miss Hall. We are all doing the crucial work of protecting our country. You are ensuring that the prime minister's important speeches are ready for their delivery."

She gives me a cautious smile and perches on the chair opposite me. "Yes, ma'am."

"You mustn't let the prime minister rattle you." In a ritual that I've repeated with several other staff members exhibiting stress over Winston's treatment, I pour her tea. These key individuals deserve appreciation for their efforts and a listening ear, rather than the screaming mouth they usually encounter. I know what my husband demands of these staff members, but I also know how critical they are to Winston's success and, consequently, to the success of our country's war efforts. I make a mental note to speak with Winston about his treatment of staff, particularly since Jock Colville, Winston's private secretary, recently told me that Winston was in danger of losing the best results from those with whom he works because of his behavior. My husband, so perceptive when it comes to the broader swath of political developments, has long had a blind spot for those in close proximity and his impact on them. I must reassure them they are supported.

Not that I begrudge the staff, but my task would be easier if they had the thick skin of Grace Hamblin, who I have invited to join us from Chartwell to serve as my secretary. When Grace first arrived, the more experienced, urbane Downing Street staff underestimated the modest, unassuming woman from the countryside, and I occasionally heard sniggers about her. After only a brief stint in which they'd observed her efficiency and doggedness, she'd earned their respect, and they now came to her for advice. I'd delighted in watching this pale country rose bloom in the murky London air, much to everyone's astonishment — except me.

"Sometimes, ma'am" — Miss Hall's voice is quivering — "it isn't what he says but where he says it from."

She doesn't need to elucidate. I know that sometimes he dictates letters to his typists from behind the closed door of his long afternoon bath, a ritual he has not altered since he returned from the wilderness of Chartwell to the center of power.

"I will speak with him about that. But please remember this. No matter what he says in the heat of the moment, he appreciates you. As do I," I continue, realizing that I must have one-on-one conversations like this with each member of his staff if we are to avoid a mutiny.

Her blue eyes glisten. I watch as she squares her shoulders and stiffens her resolve, ready to face whatever dressing-down Winston might give her. In her now stalwart expression, I see the eyes of all Britons, who are in need of inspiration for the battles ahead but who will rise when they are called.

"Winston, you must use simpler words." I hand him back the papers when he arrives in the White Drawing Room two hours later instead of the threatened one hour. Although he holds everyone else to a high standard of absolute punctuality, he has never been on time himself. The difference now is that he is literally shouldering the fate of our nation, so how can I complain? How can any of us?

When he took office, we discussed the power of his speeches, one of the few ways he could reach and empower every Briton. But Winston often becomes enamored of his own oratorial skills and "forgets" our conversation.

"What's wrong with my words?" His voice is rising, and I remind myself to stand firm. He becomes wedded to his own language and must be shaken from his attachment to it.

I stand up to face him. "You must keep in mind your audience."

"Whatever do you mean?" His tone becomes quizzical, an affectation of course.

"Your job is to deliver the truth, even when the news is dire, while inspiring *all* the people of Britain, not just the ones who benefited from a public school education like your usual parliamentarian audience. If you use complicated language instead of plainer words, you will alienate the regular people who don't use that sort of parlance." I pause to be sure he's still listening. "Do you remember how the people responded to your first two speeches? The stirring speech you gave in May, three days after you took office, just after the start of the German offensive —"

He interrupts. "Yes, I recall that speech."

"What sort of reaction did you get from the people?"

"Rousing," he answers, his eyes shining. He'd reveled in those moments.

"And what about the speech on June 4? When you had to rally the people at the same time you had to deliver the news that the Germans had overtaken the Netherlands, Belgium, and France north of the Somme? When you urged them to stay strong and patient while we evacuated thousands of men from Dunkirk?"

I had spent nearly a day listening to versions of the June 4 speech and vetting the language with Winston. I'd believed then, and believe now, that the simple recitation of all the places the British forces would continue to fight created a powerful image in the minds of the people, strengthened their resolve to go forward.

"The people seemed emboldened."

"Exactly. And what was the common denominator of all those speeches?"

"The simple, inspirational quality of the language. I see your point, Clemmie. No need to hammer it home." Papers in hand, he wanders around the room, taking a distracted puff on his cigar. He returns to the speech at hand, suggesting one word in place of a few.

Hadn't I just suggested that change? No matter. I recite the sentence with the new phrase. "That is powerful, Winston. That is precisely the sort of rhetoric that will rally the people to your cause."

"The people will be despondent at the news that France has fallen to the Nazis, but this must inspire them to not surrender their will." Winston and I had been devastated at the fall of France, and not just because Britain was left to fight the Nazis alone. We did not want the British people's dejection over France's fall to impact their will to prevail.

Winston reaches for a pen from his jacket pocket. His papers are already covered with changes in blue pen, but now he inks the alterations in red, a signal that we are nearing closure.

He squares his shoulders, an indicator that he's about to recite the speech from the beginning. This has become our ritual before every public speech and every radio broadcast. I prepare to listen. Again and again.

When Winston stands up in the House of Commons to give this speech the next day, I stare down at him from the Strangers' Gallery as I have many times before. I fix my gaze not on Winston but on the ranks of members of Parliament surrounding him, perched on the edges of their green benches. My task is to watch his listeners intently to assess whether we've hit our mark, to operate as a weather vane of sorts. As the cadence of his speech rises and falls dramatically, I note that he's swapped out certain words but that the speech is otherwise delivered as practiced.

He reaches the climax, his volume surging and his words ringing out over the House of Commons. Even though I've heard these sentences countless times over the past few days, I feel uplifted as Winston utters them so powerfully in this setting. I see from the faces of the men around him that they are galvanized as well. I pray that the citizens of our country feel the same.

CHAPTER THIRTY-ONE

July 2–6, 1940
London, England

She isn't very tractable, is she?"

I hear the low voice of one man talking as I walk down the overly warm corridor of Downing Street's first floor. I am looking for Grace, but I stop and strain to hear the reply from behind the nearly closed door of an antechamber that branches off the hallway. Who on earth is speaking, and, I wonder, who are they discussing? I pity the poor girl being gossiped about so unpleasantly; I can only imagine the sort of tractability about which they speak. I hope no one ever talks about my daughters in such a revolting manner.

"No, she's not at all like Chamberlain's wife," a second man replies in a low voice.

"That was a PM's wife as she should be — rarely seen and even more rarely heard," the first man comments.

The unseen men chuckle, and the first man continues, "We've got an entirely different sort of breed now."

These men are speaking about *me*. I know that the public-school men who populate Downing Street and serve as my husband's staff and advisers don't care for me, but I never fathomed that they'd be so audacious in their criticism. They don't have to like me, but they should respect my role and the virtue of my goals for the British people. How dare they be so petty at such a time. How dare they speak of women like this, any woman, at any time.

The men's voices drop to an undetectable level, and I am tempted to barge into that anteroom and give them a good dressing-down, then turn them over to Winston, who'd likely dismiss them. Nowhere does Winston's rage flame more wildly than in the matter of my treatment, unless it is at his hand, of course. I reach for the door handle, and as I'm about to push the door open, one of the men laughs loudly. In that moment, I realize that I recognize the voice of the second speaker. It is Jock Colville, Winston's trusted private secretary. Despite his youthful age of twenty-five, the ambitious, sharp-dressed man — the younger son of a younger son — sets the tone for the rest of the staff. If Winston learned of Colville's comments — even though not as negative as the other speaker — it would crush him, and given the precarious state of the war, neither I nor the country can take the risk.

But another idea takes shape in my mind. Perhaps I can use this overheard conversation and Jock as leverage in my plan to involve women in the war in a meaningful way.

Wearing an uncharacteristically somber dark-blue coat, I keep a steady clip as I stride toward the makeshift stage that the navy hastily constructed at the harbor for this occasion. As Winston cannot attend the christening of this vessel, he'd asked that I serve in his stead. Instead of checking my schedule to see if I had availability, I seized the opportunity when he mentioned it and then suggested to Winston over a private dinner that Jock might be the perfect person to serve as my escort for public appearances when he was otherwise engaged. Winston agreed.

Jock, nattily dressed as always in a charcoal-gray pin-striped suit, scrambles to match my pace, as I'd hoped. I am aware this makes him appear strained in his ability to move at my speed, and I enjoy listening to his labored breath. As I mount the stairs to the stage, the naval officers and their men cheer, cries that grow almost deafening as I break the champagne bottle on the ship's prow. I glance back to make sure Jock is listening to the crowds.

In the ride back to Downing Street, Jock seethes at the task he's been asked to do today. His expression alone tells me what I suspected — that he believes chaperoning the prime minister's wife is beneath a senior aide such as himself. I orchestrated his attendance not to punish him for his words about me, although I was sorely tempted, but to extract valuable support, which I will need in the days to come.

"Winston and I have decided that you will accompany me to these sorts of events when he is unavailable," I say, although it is not precisely true. And then I patiently wait for the reaction I know will come.

The young man almost snorts in derision and then, after a pause, announces, "I believe that it is a job more suited to your own secretary, ma'am, as she may be able to provide you with the sort of conversations you might like, focused upon more appropriate topics, like the arts." He squares his shoulders and says, as if my gender has caused me to forget, "I am, in fact, the prime minister's private secretary, and my focus is war. I don't have the time to keep abreast of the cultural events about which you might be more familiar."

This is the reaction I expected. In fact, it is the precise reaction upon which I'd depended. "You give yourself airs if you object to assisting the prime minister's wife, Jock. We are all doing the important work of our country," I say calmly and then add, "And, in case you haven't noticed, I prefer to discuss politics and the intricacies of our wartime challenges above all else."

"You are an unusual woman in that regard. I suppose, ma'am, that is because your husband is the prime minister," he concedes dismissively.

The serene facade I'd been carefully maintaining begins to shatter, and my voice rises as if rebelling against my will. I must keep it under control if I am to be successful. "You would be mistaken if you believe that the only reason I am well versed in politics and military developments is because of my husband's position. Every single citizen of this country — women included — has necessarily become immersed in this war. And winning this war will require every single citizen of this country, women included."

"Excuse me for questioning you, ma'am, but won't it be our soldiers who win this war for us, along with the leaders, like your husband, who direct those soldiers in battle?"

"Oh really, Jock? Who will do all the necessary work of war while all the men are fighting as soldiers?" I am so furious that I could slap this arrogant, cocksure young man, but that simply wouldn't do for the prime minister's wife, even though it is fully justified. And it would undermine my plan. "Who will manufacture the weaponry that these soldiers will need for the battles? Who will plow the fields to make the food that the soldiers will need to sustain them? Who will build the ships, the tanks, and the airplanes while the men are fighting? Who will care for the wounded so that they might return to the war?"

He grows quiet, and his arrogant expression fades. As his gaze moves from my face to the floor of the automobile, he looks unbearably young. And he does not speak.

"You don't have any answer to my questions, Jock? How unlike you not to be ready with a quip. I'll help you with the answer. It is, of course, the women." I inhale deeply to maintain my composure. "But I guess I shouldn't be surprised by your perspective, Jock. After all, I heard your opinion of me and your views on women generally when I overheard your conversation three days ago."

I hear a sharp intake of breath as he realizes what I know. "Ma'am, it wasn't me that made those remarks."

I refuse to look at him as I reply. "No, but I didn't hear you defend me either."

Peering out the window, I'm surprised to see that we have already arrived at Downing Street. The driver races to open my door, and without a glance back at Jock, I step out of the car. I don't need to see his face to envision his expression, undoubtedly a blend of shock and fear. A wide smile spreads across my face as I step into Number 10; I have laid the foundation of my plan.

Later that afternoon, I wait for Winston and Jock to arrive. Our meeting was set for two o'clock, and in anticipation and perhaps as a lure, I have asked our cook to prepare a sumptuous afternoon tea. Because I understand well the importance of food to Winston's well-being, I'd lured the indomitable Mrs. Landemare to Downing Street and its Annexe; she had been trained by her

345

husband, the former French chef at the Ritz, and her cooking for us at house parties at Chartwell had been exquisite. Grace sits alongside me, and as we check the clock, we review the documents we've prepared. In order for this endeavor to be successful, it is imperative that I paint a clear and compelling picture of my vision for Winston, complete with supporting documentation. From our early years in which suffragette issues divided us, I know I may face resistance, so I must present him with a thoroughly supported position that he has no choice but to accept.

After a buss on the cheek, Winston settles into the chair across from me, and Grace and Jock take the remaining seats. Jock holds his pen and paper, ready to take notes as usual, but he looks visibly uncomfortable, and I wonder if he's expecting me to reveal the overheard conversation. I do nothing to assuage his unfounded fears.

The maid pours tea and offers the cakes Mrs. Landemare manages to make with rationed wartime ingredients supplemented by our farm at Chartwell. We spend a few quiet moments enjoying these indulgences until Winston interjects, "So what's this all about, Clemmie?"

"I am delighted you asked, Winston." I

nod to Grace, who distributes the plans we've drafted.

Before I speak, I take a page from Winston's own book on delivering speeches by pausing dramatically. Only then do I begin. "Winston, if we are to win this fight against the abominable Nazis, we will have to enlist all of Britain's citizens. I am not suggesting that women stand alongside men in the trenches or fly beside them in the air. But we need vast numbers to serve in supportive, administrative, and manufacturing capacities, and there are not enough men to fill the thousands and thousands of roles that will be necessary. But we can meet these numbers if we use women. They can serve in administrative capacities in fighting units, staff armament factories, help build equipment, run farms, and, in limited capacities, could fill military roles such as the operation of antiaircraft batteries."

I race on to my next point before Winston can mount any objections. "I know that various parts of the government have begun to fill certain roles with women, as they did in the Great War." I nod to the papers laid before him by Grace. "In those pages, I have laid out the vast gap in the necessary numbers, a gap that will grow wider and wider as this war progresses and we send more and more men into the breach. We can fill that gap if we appeal to women. They are every bit as worried about the war as men, and they have every bit as much to lose. Winston, the wolves are at the door, and the women must help defend us. I want you not only to help plant the seed with the governmental powers that be and approve supplications made to you in this regard, but also to begin the process of inviting the women to join in this war."

Winston is silent. I know this means that he is either moved by my presentation or about to explode. I take a slow sip of my tea and wait. If he does not detonate in the next minute, then I've won the point. He lifts up the papers and skims them as I watch the clock.

The minute passes, and still, he doesn't speak. He merely studies the pages. "Clemmie, how can you be certain that the women of Britain would react favorably to my invitation?"

"Winston, if you make this call to action, the women will answer. You have promised the people victory, and victory will depend on the involvement and strength of women." I shoot Jock a pointed glance. "Don't you agree, Jock?"

This is the decisive moment. Will Jock

support me? He knows I have information about him that could damage his relationship with Winston irreparably. And perhaps — a big perhaps — I've managed to bring him around to my point of view.

Jock meets my gaze. "Absolutely, Mrs. Churchill."

CHAPTER THIRTY-TWO

October 25 to November 1940
London, England

Dusk settles over the autumn London sky in a bold pink display, and a sense of satisfaction courses through me as I examine the papers spread across my desk. My plans are proceeding apace. As soon as I received Winston's imprimatur, I began rolling out my assessment of the different departments and then the recruitment and placement of women in these key roles, which had previously been done by men, thus freeing up British men for frontline combat. My plan, executed not directly but through conversations with Winston or well-placed letters, meetings, and lunches with key governmental officials, involves women and girls serving in more traditional capacities such as secretarial, code, clerk, accountant, shorthand-typist, telephone operator, signaling work, and agricultural work, but also in many nontraditional positions such as decryption, radio and air mechanics, maintenance, torpedo and boat crews, radar detection finders, cinema operators, gunnery dome operators, submarine attack teacher operators, meteorologists, bomb range markers, vision testers, and antiaircraft target operators. Even the Special Operations Executive, established in July to engage in the more unorthodox tactics of espionage, has leeway to use women in its corps. Some of the organizations had already conceived of the notion to include women and only needed assistance getting their ideas before the right people, and others had utilized women in the Great War and needed only a gentle prod to begin using women again. I will push them apace to create our very own female home front. I am not alone in this desire, but I am well placed to effectuate the plan.

As I labor to secure these places for women, I realize that the arc of my life mirrors that of many women. With both feet, we leap into life with our spouses, ready to offer whatever skills we have to the marriage and engage with the world, only to face marginalization at some point along the way. In my case, the door to the world of purpose reopened when Winston's years exiled from power ended, and I believe there is no reason why that door cannot be reopened for *all* women. It had been flung wide for them during the Great War, and why shouldn't it be for this war? Once open, I see no reason why it must ever be shut again.

I'm looking for the sheaf of papers describing women in the Special Operations Executive when I hear a loud explosion. I drop the papers and race to Winston's office. *Please,* I pray, *please let Winston be safe.* If he has been injured, not only do I lose my husband, but the people lose their leader. But when I push open his door, his room is empty, as are the halls. I run to the parlor next, where I know he'd been planning to have a drink and a private discussion with Sir Archibald Sinclair, Oliver Lyttelton, and John Moore-Brabazon before we dined with them, but it is barren as well. Where is the bustle that normally infiltrates every corner of Downing Street?

The nighttime bombing raids on London and the British countryside began in earnest last month after the Nazis failed to defeat us in the Battle of Britain. Winston tells me that the goal of this Blitz, as people are starting to call it, is to disrupt military production and terrorize our citizens, and after a few weeks of the relentless noise and destruction, I see that the Germans might achieve their goal if we do not maintain the people's spirits. We are aware, of course, that Number 10 is a target of these raids and have taken the necessary precautions of steel shutters, strengthening beams, and an air-raid shelter on the garden level, but neither Winston nor myself thought it would benefit the country's morale to abandon Downing Street. Not yet anyway.

"Winston!" I cry out, but no one answers. Does the silence mean that no one is left to respond? Terror takes hold, and for a moment, I am utterly unable to move. I will myself to scream my husband's name again, and the spell of immobility breaks.

I run from room to room, searching for someone, anyone, to tell me what has happened. Time moves strangely, as if both painfully slow and incomprehensibly fast. I pass by typically chockablock workrooms now completely bare, with papers scattered about as if dropped in a hurry, and as I race past more formal spaces and the family's quarters, I see no one. All the offices and hallways and anterooms are empty. Not even the heavily pregnant Pamela is visible, and she's usually omnipresent since she began living with us once Randolph's military duties — of a low-risk sort, as per Winston's insistence — required him to be in and out of London. Aloud, I thank God that Mary is safe in the countryside visiting family and friends.

Then suddenly, I hear the sound of shattered glass. Running toward the noise, I descend to the kitchen level where the sound grows cacophonous and the crowd grows large. Threading through the serving staff and governmental personnel standing at the periphery of the kitchen, I see Winston staring around the room. All around him are heaping piles of splintered glass that used to be the twenty-five-foot-high plate-glass kitchen window, great white mounds of fallen plaster, doors torn from their hinges, and shards of broken wood from smashed furniture.

"Winston, are you all right?" I scan the staff lining the hallway to the kitchen. "Is anyone hurt?"

"No, no, Clemmie, not to worry." He puffs heavily on his cigar, which I know sometimes serves to mask his nerves. "I was having a few drinks in the parlor with our guests when a bomb fell quite close, out on Horse Guards Parade, and a compulsion overtook me to check the kitchen and have the staff evacuate. I'd just ushered them out when another bomb fell even closer, causing the impact and damage you see here." He gestured to the debris. "But no one was hurt. At least not here."

I hug him and whisper, "Thank God for your foresight."

The call was too close, killing three civil servants who were on Horse Guard duty, and we decamp to the Central War Rooms, a secure underground complex for the chiefs of staff of the army, navy, and air force and their deputies as well as the war cabinet that had been prepared in 1938 in anticipation of the aerial bombardment we are just now experiencing. This extensive warren of hallways and tiny offices and slightly larger conference rooms — underneath the strong, modern concrete New Public Offices and close to Downing Street and Parliament — had, until quite recently, been the building's basement, overrun with rats, dust, and forgotten government files. The War Rooms are accessible only from within the building; after entering through the building's main door, one climbs a few more steps to a guarded, internal door opening to "Staircase 15," wide, spiral stairs that lead to the basement and, from there, the War Rooms. The space works well for war cabinet and planning committee meetings, and for a time, we continue to entertain and conduct work in the fortified Garden Rooms in Number 10 Downing Street by day and, by night, sleep in the basic bedrooms in the War Rooms.

But as the months progress and assassination reports pour in, this situation proves untenable. Among other problems, sleeping in my appointed subterranean concrete bedroom — thoughtfully decorated with a flowered bedspread and upholstered chair — is an impossibility with the din of round-the-clock meetings, alarms, and the echoing clap of footsteps, as well as the fug of cigarette smoke, and Winston refuses outright to retire to his assigned bed during the air raids, preferring to watch the bombing from the rooftops. We identify a set of offices in the New Public Offices building directly above the War Rooms — and linked to them with an internal staircase — that we transform into living and working apartments with further structural support and steel shutters over the windows and leave Number 10 behind, for now. This Number 10 Annexe, as it is known, becomes our office and home for as long as necessary, and I do my utmost to make the space a welcoming refuge, painting it cheerful colors and arranging for the delivery of our own furniture, carpets, and paintings for the space.

But I worry that the British citizens will not be able to bear up under the strain of nightly bombings. I insist that we stay in the public eye so that the citizens can see us. In between meetings, we constantly travel around the country, visiting ammunition factories, shipyards, and the troops and, increasingly, those affected by the Blitz. The people need to know that we are among them.

But this proximity to the suffering people is not enough for Winston. As soon as the bombing ceases on any given night, he begins to roam through the destruction, regardless of the fact that the bombs may still be coming. Over the years, I'd grown accustomed to Winston's disregard for his own safety; after all, I'd literally saved his life before when he was oblivious to the danger around him, certainly once in Bristol and possibly two other times, in Belfast and Cairo. But this new behavior — sneaking out after a raid with a torch to inspect the damage personally — is too much. His private secretaries, ministers, and military officials share my alarm, but he will listen to no one, not even me, in this regard. When I object, he points to the people's immediate needs, to which I respond with the people's long-term need for him.

I cultivate a few of my own spies, who share these nightly excursions with me. My duty, first and foremost as I see it, is to keep my husband alive. After a failed scheme to have Winston's valet hide his boots to stop him from venturing out after a raid, I develop another plan.

Despite the sounds of far-off explosions, my sleep is unusually deep, so the hand on my shoulder becomes intertwined with my dream at first. As the hand begins to more vigorously shake me, I awaken with a start. Sitting upright and more than a little disoriented, I stare at the interloper, only to realize that it's Grace.

"I have been informed that the prime minister is getting ready to inspect the raid damage," Grace whispers.

I know this means that, as usual, Winston has waited out the raid upstairs in the Annexe — he refuses to sleep in the protective bedrooms in the War Rooms, preferring to sleep in the flat when the bombing stops — and the poor valet has been enlisted to dress him for his nightly excursion.

I rub my eyes and answer, "Thank you, Grace."

She hands me the coat, headscarf, and

boots that I've set out precisely for this occasion. I slip them on over my pale-blue nightgown and rub some red lipstick over my lips. When I walk toward Staircase 15, I bump into Winston as he's exiting from the internal staircase into the Annexe flat. I greet him with a hearty, "I'm all set, Pug."

He whips around to face me. His eyes are wide with shock. "What on earth are you doing here, Clemmie? Post-raid London at night is no place for you."

I arch an eyebrow and pull myself up to my full height. "If it's a place for you, then it's a place for me." I link my arm with his and say, "Let's go."

He hesitates, and I sense that he's torn between the compulsion to investigate the bombing and my safety. I've counted upon this conflict. Finally, he follows.

We step out onto the night street, and an armored car awaits us. "What's this?" he asks his bodyguard, Lieutenant Commander Tommy Thompson, with whom I'd planned this in advance. "I won't ride in this metal box. I'll ride in your police car."

"I apologize, sir, but there are no other cars available," Thompson answers, and I suppress a smile. I'd ensured that no other automobiles would be in the vicinity at this time.

Winston's mouth opens, and I surmise that he's about to order poor Thompson to find another car for him. I intervene and say, "Winston, you wouldn't want *me* to drive about the city in an *un*armored vehicle, would you? After all, we don't know when the bombs will stop coming down, and there could be firing and shrapnel. I could be struck by metal flying about in the air."

Without waiting for him to answer, I step into the car and climb under one of the plaid rugs I've arranged to be in the back seat. I sit alone for a moment, then call out to him, "Aren't you coming?"

Grumbling, he settles into the back seat beside me. When I tuck a striped rug around him, he shoves it aside, but I place it back on his lap. "The country will not thrive if you're unable to work because you've gotten ill. The night is cold. You must take precautions."

"The soldiers don't have the luxury of precautions, Clemmie. Why should I?"

I ignore his comment, as any protest on my part will only make him dig in his heels. Instead, I ask, "I understand the bombs landed near Richmond Park. Shall I instruct the driver or will you?"

He looks at me in astonishment that I

mean to carry this out. But what he doesn't understand is that I mean to accompany him every night going forward. Because I know he will not expose himself to unnecessary danger if I'm with him, I intend to use his concern for my safety as a means of constraining his dangerous activity and keeping him secure. We can appear among the people and buoy their spirits without stepping directly into the path of bombs, I tell him.

As the car proceeds and, as I'd predicted, shrapnel rains down on the roof, I restrain myself from commenting on the good fortune of traveling in an armored car. In fact, we do not speak until we reach Richmond Park, and I step out of the car ahead of him. My mouth drops open when I observe that the entire side of a smoking building bordering the park has been sheared off; I can no longer suppress myself. "Oh, Winston, our poor people."

He reaches for my hand. "That's why I come out here, Clemmie. To help the people and show them they're not alone."

Holding hands, we follow Thompson as he weaves through heaps of bricks, ragged strips of wood, and irregular gray stone blocks the size of horses. We grip our torches in our free hands, and the beam cast

361

from mine lands upon a small stuffed tan teddy bear, smeared with dirt. Releasing Winston's hand, I reach down for the toy, wondering about the child who dropped it.

"Winston, I'd like to see a bomb shelter. Is there one nearby?" I know that he often speaks with and helps Londoners who've just lost their homes or people stranded in the rubble, but I don't recall any conversations about the visits to the ever-multiplying brick, concrete, and metal shelters used in addition to tube stations. The little boy or girl who'd lost this bear would likely be ensconced within one.

"Yes, but I don't know why you'd want to do that."

I hold up the teddy bear and say, "I want to see how the people are riding out these storms."

After talking with one of the soldiers accompanying us, Thompson locates the closest shelter. He directs us to an arched brick structure, not larger than a bus, and after opening the rough wooden door, gestures for us to enter. The pungent smell of sweat, urine, and excrement overwhelms us before we even step inside.

As the light from our torches illuminates the tiny space, a sea of exhausted faces, mostly women and children, stare up from the dirt floor and grimy corners. *How are the people withstanding these horrific conditions?* I think but do not say. Instead, as they recognize Winston and excitedly stand up and gather around us, I reach out to shake their hands, whispering to myself, "Pray God we don't let the people down."

CHAPTER THIRTY-THREE

November to December 1940
London, England

What began as a mission to protect my husband becomes a passion project. After witnessing the squalid conditions in which the British people are being forced to spend ten to fourteen hours every night, I make it my goal to transform the shelters. I begin with the people's own requests. I will not let our citizens go without a voice, just as I will not let this war proceed without giving women a part. I wonder if this is part of my own destiny, a concept Winston discusses often, to expand the understanding of women's capabilities in this war and beyond. In a way, it is an expansion of my suffragette beliefs.

"Here are today's letters, ma'am," the young blond boy, likely too young for military service, says in a heavy accent as he places a bag nearly half his size on the chair adjacent to my desk.

"Thank you," I answer and gesture to Grace to help me begin sorting, a daily chore. We have developed a system to categorize every missive sent to me. I am determined that every message — whether complimentary, sensible, abusive, or futile — will receive a response from me directly in another effort to let our citizens know that their concerns are being heard. With Winston too engrossed in the military parts of the war to handle the domestic issues, this has become my job among many tasks that directly affect the welfare of our people.

As Grace and I form piles of letters according to the concerns raised within their pages, I note how tall the shelter pile has grown. It seems that each day brings more and more complaints about the state of the air-raid shelters. Just last evening, I completed a monthlong tour of a cross section of shelters, accompanied by Mrs. May Tennant of the Red Cross and occasionally Jock Colville, who, of his own accord, has shown interest in this project. Sadly, I've learned that the litany of issues raised by these letters does not begin to encompass the list of problems I've identified on my own.

The image of an older woman from one of the shelters last night inhabits my mind.

Her face covered with grime and without any possessions save the flimsy green coat she wore and her purse, she'd been crying into her handkerchief when I spotted her. Her cheeks were striped where tears had wiped clean the black soil, and a young man sat by her side, clutching on her free hand. Glancing up at the sight of our torches, she rose when she saw me and waved her blackened handkerchief. "Mrs. Churchill, what an honor," she called out, forgetting her own worries for a moment.

As she reached out to shake my hand, one of my security detail intercepted her, not wanting to allow the poor, filthy woman to touch me. Brushing aside the guard's arm, I took her damp hands in my own and said, "The honor is all mine, ma'am. I am here to help. Will you please tell me what happened to you and your family?"

Her house, a small, two-room stone concern where she lived with the mentally disabled son who stood at her side, had just been bombed out, and she'd lost absolutely everything. "This will have to be our home for now," she answered when I asked where she'd be staying, gesturing around the godforsaken hovel.

I shudder as I think about the freezing-cold shelter with frozen beads of water on the walls and two overflowing buckets serving as latrines, where the poor woman and her son will live until more permanent housing can be found, a project I undertook as soon as I returned home. Incredibly, her shelter is by no means worse than many of the air-raid shelters around London I'd visited in the weeks prior; in fact, it is representative of them. I am determined that the British people will receive better.

"Grace," I say, "I think I need to add a few more items to my memorandum to Winston."

"Of course, ma'am," she replies, rising to fetch her paper and pen.

When she settles back next to me, I enumerate four more categories for the memorandum, which already details my primary concerns about the outbreak of disease and illness in the crowded, often unsanitary conditions. I insist on waterproofing shelters, stopping the spread of disease through clean bedding, and providing sleeping conditions conducive to families. When I move on to the topic of latrines, I notice Grace's note-taking slows down.

When I stop speaking, I notice that Grace has paused altogether. Her thoughtful face, glasses perched on her long nose, seems frozen. "Did I speak too quickly, Grace? I'm sure you've noticed that this has me quite upset, so I might be rattling on too rapidly."

"No, ma'am. It's just that" — she hesitates — "that I wonder if these topics are seemly for the prime minister's wife."

Grace's reaction surprises me. She is quite the stoic, and I cannot imagine what she finds objectionable, particularly at this critical juncture in the war. When the Nazis are bombing people nightly in the streets and in their homes. When we might lose hundreds of innocent civilians to typhoid if the shelters aren't sanitary. "If these conditions are seemly enough for the British people to endure, they are seemly enough for me to discuss with the prime minister."

Grace's words ring in my head five hours later when I push open the door to Winston's office, and I'm faced with my husband and three of his ministers, the minister of health, the minister of home security, and the minister of supply. Typically, when I meet with Winston to discuss an issue or project I've undertaken, Jock Colville might be present, or one other pertinent official, but rarely anyone else. Today, he has assembled all the key players in the matter of the shelters. I appreciate his trust, but he might have warned me.

"Clemmie." Winston reaches out a hand for me to join him in the open chair to his right. "I was just describing your Red Cross tour of shelters to these gentlemen. It's been quite the endeavor, taking you nearly a month."

"Mrs. Churchill, you have gone above and beyond the call of duty, trudging out to these dangerous locations in the dead of night. It really wasn't necessary." The minister of health, Malcolm MacDonald, says with a chortle as I sit down. "They are temporary shelters after all. Just to keep the people safe during the hopefully short duration of the Blitz."

I am tired of the arrogance of the senior members of government, so often raised in luxury with all the advantages of their class and education. While I was born to an aristocratic family, I know the striving of working people as well as the disdain they face. Whatever good these men do in their current roles, this issue cannot be ignored.

"Sadly, Mr. MacDonald, my tour was absolutely necessary. I wish it wasn't. If we are concerned about the health of our citizenry, we must do something about the abominable state of our air-raid shelters. They may have been rudimentary and improvisational at the outset, but now that we are into the third month of the Blitz and the winter season is upon us, we cannot allow the situation to continue." I had not intended to begin my conversation with an unyielding tone, but that is what they shall receive. "Have you ever been in an air-raid shelter?" I ask, knowing full well that the answer will be no.

He shakes his head, but before he can make another remark, I say to all the ministers, "There seems to be a general uncertainty as to the policy regarding the creation and maintenance of air-raid shelters, perhaps, in part, because their administration involves so many ministers and it is an issue involving local governments as well. The reason — or excuse — offered for doing nothing is that, as Mr. MacDonald has just said, the shelters are temporary and it is not worthwhile to spend money on them, particularly given the costs of war. However, the people you represent are living in those same shelters for upward of fourteen hours a day in terrible conditions of cold, wet, dirt, darkness, stench, and, I fear, disease. We must meet certain standards of hygiene and comfort."

Winston chuckles softly under his breath, although when I turn to him, he tries to hide it with a puff of his cigar. I know he's not laughing at me, but he is thoroughly enjoying the treatment these ministers are receiving at my hand.

I glance back at Minister MacDonald, whose face is nearly apoplectic with anger and astonishment. His expression telegraphs his thoughts: How dare I, a woman with no appointed or elected position, take such a firm stance against governmental leaders? *Indeed,* I think. How dare *we* fail so miserably in his duty to the British people?

But I do not speak my thoughts aloud. Gesturing to the copies of my memorandum I have placed upon the table, I say, "I invite each of you to read and study my report. You will see, in the cross section of shelters we toured and examined, that this is a systemic, widespread problem. And it must be rectified."

The shrill cry of an infant resonates throughout the room. The ministers look around, as if the source of the jarring, unexpected sound might be found in here. It seems that our grandchild, Pamela and Randolph's newborn son, has done me an unplanned favor.

"Ah, that will be young Winston, our newest grandchild. Imagine if you will, gentlemen, allowing your own young grandchildren or perhaps your own offspring to

371

pass ten or twelve hours of a cold winter's night in pitch darkness on a dirt floor with the smell of an overflowing bucket latrine filling the air. Night after night after night."

"No?" I ask rhetorically to the ministers, whose faces have clouded over with shame. As if on cue, young Winston cries even louder. "It seems our grandson can't envision it either."

CHAPTER THIRTY-FOUR

December 2, 1940
London, England

I stand as close to the edge of the rooftop as the soldiers will allow. I'd wanted to serve my shift as fire watcher without the meddling presence of Winston's personal guards, but he would not hear of it. In fact, we'd had quite a row over me serving as fire watcher at all.

I'd argued with Winston. "If you hadn't wanted your citizens to serve in this so-called dangerous role, then why did you push for the Fire Watchers Order?" This law, introduced in September, required business owners to ensure that someone was on-site to scan for fires at all times — both at the building and beyond — so as to prevent further fire damage, particularly from the ubiquitous incendiary bombs that were raining down on London nightly.

"By citizens, I did not mean to include

373

the prime minister's wife. You do quite enough for your country, and the prime minister needs you by his side. It's not the place for you," he barked at me as if I were one of his many underlings.

His behavior only reinforced my commitment to the role, so I stood up and announced, "Winston, I have only informed you about my shift as a courtesy to your schedule. As you know, I publicly responded to Home Secretary Morrison's complaints that the fire-watching service was understaffed by urging him to request that all middle-aged women of independent means assume shifts as fire watchers. Now that I've called on women to serve as fire watchers, how can I urge them to clamber onto rooftops in the dead of night if I won't do it myself?" I pause and use one of his own arguments against him. "Just like you do when you venture out onto the city streets during the nighttime bombings."

Sighing heavily, Winston puffed on his cigar for a long moment. His silence told me that I'd won this point but that he would exact some sort of concession from me. "You will take some of my guards with you."

I wanted to protest, but I knew he'd be worried the entirety of my shift unless his men accompanied me. So I acquiesced, but in this respect only.

My arrival on the rooftop flusters the older, white-haired gentleman from whom I'm taking over, a Mr. Peacock. Despite the fact that he appears to be over a decade older than myself, he's remarkably spry, which he demonstrates by jumping at the sight of me. "Mrs. Ch–Churchill? What on earth are you doing here?"

"I'm here to take the shift after yours as fire watcher," I answer calmly with a smile, trying to imply that my appearance on this rooftop is no more unusual than his own.

"Fire watcher?" he blurts out, then his hand flies to his mouth. "My apologies, ma'am. I'm just so surprised to see the prime minister's wife up here on the roof."

I fear the poor man may never recover. In the hopes of smoothing his nerves, I ask, "Can you show me the ropes? This is my first time after all."

After a moment's hesitation, he undertakes the instructor role so naturally that I guess he must have been a teacher at one time. Slipping on this seemingly familiar hat, he calms and explains the tasks I'll be performing for the next eight hours. As he hands me a pair of greasy binoculars, he says, "The most critical part of the job is scanning the horizon for incoming bombs as well as smoke and fire." He walks me around the perimeter of the rooftop, pointing out the various buildings in the skyline, although, of course, I recognize St. Paul's myself.

He leads me to a telephone that appears as though it's been hastily installed on the rooftop wall. "The moment you spot anythin' like that, you're to give a warning to the staff in the offices below. The proper number is posted here. That way, they can protect themselves and the building and get the word out to those in the other targeted buildings by sounding an alarm for the staff to get to the basement shelter and with other telephone calls."

Pointing to the piles of sandbags and buckets of water and sand scattered about, I ask, "What are those for?"

"For shelter if the Germans fire on you directly," he answers quietly, as if he's hesitant to share the reality of this post with me. As if I was unaware — until this very moment — of the risks. "And water and sand in case their fire and bombs start a fire up here."

Ah, I think. *They serve the same purpose as they do in the War Rooms, which are lit-*

tered with buckets of water and sand.

I nod briskly and say, "Well, sir, thanks to your excellent instruction, I feel ready to assume my post."

"Are you certain, ma'am?"

"Quite. We all need to do our duty." I see that my words do not mollify him. Gesturing to the soldiers lining the rooftop wall, I say, "Not to worry. Those fellows won't let a thing happen to me."

"Wouldn't let the prime minister down, ma'am. He does so much for us."

I clasp his gloved hand with my own. "I'll be sure to share your sentiments with him. But now, I must begin." I sling the binoculars around my neck, place the required helmet on my head, and begin to patrol the perimeter. I'm thankful that I broke protocol and wore pants.

I try to ignore the guards as I undertake my rounds, but their constant surveillance of me and the rooftop itself makes it challenging. I nearly trip over one silvery-blond young soldier as I round the corner to check the north side of the building. After a few hours of this rather monotonous work, the soldiers begin to relax their vigilance, and I am able to linger at each vantage point and study the cityscape below me.

Even though it is dusk, I can make out

the outlines of our citizens scurrying about their evening tasks. Men in topcoats and trilbies returning home from the office, although perhaps to empty houses and apartments as their loved ones have been evacuated. The occasional woman strides down the street, purposefully carrying parcels. The only evidence of the war that I see from my vantage point is the shelters, dotted across the cityscape.

I am lost in thought, admiring the resiliency of the British people, when I hear a clatter of gunfire and the roar of plane engines. Instinctively, duty calls, and I lift the binoculars to my eyes. Biplanes streak through the sky, and huge fiery incendiaries rain down over buildings, streets, and parks. The smoke billows from the ground toward the dusky sky, and the smell of sulfur fills the air.

Immediately, I race for the telephone to alert the workers in the building below, but I am intercepted by the guards. They form a circle around me to ensure my protection. I know they are simply following instructions, but I am determined to do my job.

"Gentlemen, I have a call to make."

The blond soldier says, "Ma'am, we're under orders to protect you. We cannot take the risk that a stray bullet or bomb will harm you."

"You may follow me to that telephone, but I will make that call."

The soldiers in tow, I race to the phone and inform the building staff about the bombs in close proximity so they can run to the basement shelter, even though this particular building hasn't been hit. Returning to the perimeter of the roof, I scan the horizon again with my binoculars. I see nothing except the gleaming dome of St. Paul's Cathedral rising above the billowing smoke and scattered fires. *I have seen the devastation firsthand on the ground, but how different it looks from the air,* I think.

The sound of gunfire grows faint, and then the scream of dropping bombs ceases altogether as the action moves into the distance. The soldiers refuse to leave my side, even when the night grows completely quiet. As the smoke clears, through the binoculars in the dim moonlight, I see the detritus left behind on sidewalks as people ran to safety. The outlines of a wrapped parcel of food here, an umbrella there, even a woman's shoe. I am relieved that I do not spot any human casualties. How terrible is this war.

One of the soldiers clears his throat behind me and then says, "Ma'am, since there is a lull in the action, this might be a good time to return to the Annexe."

I turn toward him and respond in an unwavering voice, "I have every intention of staying for the entirety of my shift. I must fulfill my duty."

CHAPTER THIRTY-FIVE

December 12–13, 1940
London, England

Winston raises his glass of Pol Roger, a scarcity in wartime and hoarded specifically for special occasions, in toast. "To France." He clinks glasses with General Charles de Gaulle who, the day after Premier Reynaud's resignation in June, had flown to England in a British plane. With the collapse of France and the subsequent establishment of the pro-Nazi Vichy government, this man, the only member of the French government publicly willing to continue the fight against the Nazis, is the representative of Free France. Even with his limited power, we need him; we are otherwise alone in this conflict.

The general touches his glass to Winston's. The chime of crystal rings out over the Downing Street white dining room, and for a moment, with the golden champagne sparkling in the candlelight and crispy Cornish hens on the white bone china, it almost feels like peacetime.

"To *Free* France," the general, nostrils flaring, corrects Winston, who nods in apology and gulps the champagne down greedily. He's missed his favorite indulgence.

"Madame, I could not forget to toast you," de Gaulle says and touches his glass to mine.

While the Free French will continue to work with us against the Nazis, unfortunately, those French soldiers and sailors who did not defect must be treated as enemies, as they are aiding in the Nazi cause. As a result, shortly after France fell, Winston had to order the Royal Navy to destroy the French fleet anchored at Oran in North Africa so it would not fall into the Nazis' hands. It was a decision that troubled Winston terribly, particularly when he received reports that thirteen hundred men had died. But he couldn't allow such a powerful weapon to be wielded by the Nazis; Britain might never have recovered.

"Here's to the Free French fleet's support of the British." I raise my glass in my own toast.

Instead of clinking his glass with ours, the mustachioed de Gaulle places his crystal champagne flute down on the table. In a tone that quickly transforms from hospitable to hostile, he says, "Madame, it may be that many French would prefer to fight the British — with whom they've often been rivals — than the Germans." His narrow face pinches tighter together as he glares at Winston, adding, "Particularly after North Africa."

I am aghast. While I understand his dismay at the deaths in Oran, his comment is utterly unacceptable; he understands better than almost anyone how necessary — and hard — the decision was for Winston. We have harbored him in our country, facing the heightened wrath of the Nazis for our sins, and given him support for whatever endeavor he wants to pursue against our common enemy. How dare he lash out at us instead of his true adversary, the Nazis!

I glance over at Winston, who sits silently, nursing his Pol Roger. I am shocked at his quiet, but as I study Winston and wonder about his muted reaction, I'm reminded of a recent disagreement in which he'd exhibited similar behavior. We had learned that his brother Jack's son was planning on sending his own daughter off to Canada, despite the fact that we'd asked our immediate and extended family to stay in the country unless their war work took them outside it. We had explained that it was critical for the country's morale to see that the prime minister's family had every confidence that we would ultimately be victorious. But when we discovered his nephew's plan, who himself was stationed in Dunkirk as a corps camouflage officer, Winston hadn't wanted to intervene or utter a remonstrance — not unlike now when faced with de Gaulle's incendiary proclamation. Even after all these years, I sometimes find Winston's actions perplexing and frustrating.

"How can we ask the people of Britain to bear up and fight but allow our own family members to escape?" I asked Winston then in a voice that sounded surprisingly calm to my ears. It belied the rage I felt mounting within me. How could Winston be so harsh and demanding with his staff but so yielding with his own family?

"Clemmie, the girl is five years old. Don't you think your position is a bit on the harsh side?" Winston said.

I almost laughed at the irony of my husband — notorious for his own harsh outbursts — suggesting that I was being unyielding, particularly when he has publicly demanded that the British citizens never surrender. Only this was no laughing matter.

"Harsh? You didn't think it was harsh when we insisted that Diana keep her children in England, and her youngest is not quite two years old. How can it be harsh to stop your brother's son Johnny from shipping his five-year-old daughter off to Canada?"

"But you have surreptitiously intervened and had the girl's passport held at the point of embarkation," he exclaimed.

I stood up to stare him down. "Only after we specifically requested that your nephew keep Sally in the country — and he defied your request by making arrangements to the contrary. He could have sent her out of London and into the countryside and *not* defied your order."

Winston glanced down at the ground, unwilling to meet my gaze. "It wasn't an order, Clemmie. He is a private citizen with all the attendant rights. And those rights do not prevent him from evacuating his daughter. Not yet anyway."

"You are the prime minister, and we are at war. A request is tantamount to an order, particularly since his father is living with us at Downing Street and he's your nephew to boot." I knew I had to stand firm. Winston had always been soft in the matter of his brother's family. "Not to mention you've disapproved of the government's proposal for a plan to evacuate women and children from the country quite vociferously."

He barked, "Because it would be a bloody stampede." Then realizing he'd conceded the point, he grew quiet.

I continued. "You would be a hypocrite to condone his action. It would be as if we'd enlisted the whole of the country to help in the war effort but allowed our own family members to sit it out, instead of insisting that they participate in the war just like every other citizen." Winston and I have ensured that our children had been put to work: Diana as an officer in the Women's Royal Naval Service; her husband, Duncan, as a territorial officer with the Anti-Aircraft Regiment; Randolph as an officer in Winston's old regiment, the Fourth Hussars; and Mary, who still lived at home, as a canteen and Red Cross volunteer. The only exception was Sarah, who continued to act, although she'd promised me that she'll join the Women's Auxiliary Air Force, and Randolph's new wife, Pamela, who was pregnant with their first child at the time of our conversation and understandably sitting out war work. My own sister, Nellie, had complied with this request as well — taking refuge in the English countryside near Chartwell — even though her sons could not, through no fault of their own. Her elder son, Giles, was still being held captive by the Nazis, albeit in relative comfort in Colditz Castle in Germany, and her younger son, Esmond, who had long rebelled against all aspects of English society and, with his distant cousin Jessica Mitford in tow as his wife, decamped to Spain to fight in their civil war before moving to America, had joined the Royal Canadian Air Force when war broke out.

Anger passed across Winston's face like a storm cloud and then disappeared. He sighed, saying, "You're right, Clemmie. We can't have a Churchill child show a lack of confidence in Britain. What would the rest of little Sally's countrymen think?"

"Precisely," I said, thanking God Winston had come around.

But now, with de Gaulle, I see no hint that Winston will come around. In fact, he sits rather placidly, puffing away on his blasted cigar. How can he stay silent in the face of de Gaulle's insults? This man has overstepped our hospitality, and I will not ignore his disparagements.

In French — so that de Gaulle will not misunderstand me — I say, "General de Gaulle, your words are inappropriate from anyone, let alone someone who purports to be our partner."

De Gaulle simply stares at me, and I meet his gaze head on. Winston may not have understood my French exactly, but he certainly comprehends this tension. In an abject tone, he interjects an apology on my behalf.

I cannot believe that Winston is apologizing for me. I will not be cowed by my husband or anyone, not even the leader of the Free French, whose alliance with England is important but fragile. If I do not adhere to what is right and just, what are we fighting for? For the first time in a long time, I realize that I must adhere to my own beliefs rather than ignore them to advance Winston and his positions.

Without shifting my gaze from de Gaulle, I disagree with Winston, again in French. "Winston, do not apologize for me. I am not sorry for my statement. General de Gaulle needs to hear those words."

Both men are rendered speechless. I sip at my champagne and wait for someone to speak.

"You are absolutely correct, Madame

Churchill," De Gaulle finally offers. "Please accept my apologies." When he rises from his seat to kiss my hand, I nod in his direction and allow it.

The next morning, I hear a loud rap at my office door. It sounds like Winston's distinctive knock, but it cannot be. The hour is not yet eight, and my husband does not typically rise until nine at the earliest, even in wartime. The door swings open with a thud, and to my surprise, it is indeed Winston, beaming in his striped pajamas and robe.

"You must come and see this, Clemmie," he says, striding out of the room with an unusual energy for so early an hour.

"Whatever is it, Winston?" I call back at him. Glancing over at Grace, who has been helping me with correspondence since seven o'clock — it seems the more I respond to the people personally, the more letters they send. Grace, usually placid in demeanor, appears as perplexed as I feel.

"It simply must be seen to be believed," he yells back, waking whatever members of the house haven't already risen.

As we near the foyer, my skirt swishing in the quiet of the still Annexe, a fragrant smell overtakes me, and I almost swoon with delight. It has been months since I've inhaled the heady scent of flowers. We step into the foyer, which blooms with overflowing vases of fuchsia, yellow, and cornflower blue like a spring meadow.

Winston hands me a card, which, I see, he has already opened. "Dear Mrs. Churchill. Please accept my most abject apology for my misbehavior last evening. I have only the greatest respect for you and your husband. Sincerely yours, General Charles de Gaulle."

He squeezes my free hand and says, "As I first said many years ago, you are indeed my secret weapon."

CHAPTER THIRTY-SIX

December 24, 1940
Buckinghamshire, England

What is it about a crisis that draws us closer to our loved ones? Why do the differences between us — minuscule and vast — seem to disappear against the backdrop of mounting catastrophe? It seems that a world war is necessary to erase the divide between Winston and me and our children and to remind us of the familial threads knitting us together.

As I gaze around the Christmas Eve dinner table, I am incredulous and grateful that every one of our children and their spouses — however tenuous their marriages — have been able to join us at Chequers, the designated country retreat for the prime minister. I smile at the unusually content Diana and her husband, Duncan; their sweet young children, Edwina and Julian, have retired to bed upstairs under their nanny's care. The

391

less contented Sarah sits adjacent to her husband, Vic; he has been the recipient of several withering glances from his wife because Vic, born in Austria but now an American citizen, wants to relocate to the United States, despite Sarah's obvious loyalty to Britain and despite Winston's orders that no member of the Churchill family should flee England. The birth of now-three-month-old little Winston has reunited Randolph and Pamela for the holidays, but I fear for the longevity of this reconciliation. Randolph has had some success as of late — he won a seat in Parliament in the fall, albeit an unopposed Preston seat, and his military work has been moderately successful, despite the dislike his men have for him — but his achievements have not slowed his gambling or philandering. It is only Pamela's bond with Winston and me that incentivized her to join him here. Mary alone, who spent the summer safely in Norfolk with the family of my cousin Venetia and her daughter and the fall here at Chequers working for the Women's Voluntary Service, remains unchanged by the war, and her even-tempered kindliness is a great solace to me and Winston. Of all our children, only poor little Marigold is not with us tonight, and quite against my wishes, I feel the melancholy pang of her absence after all these years. I brush away the unwelcome tear welling up in my eye with a quick motion of my finger and engage in the animated conversation among my children and their cousins about the "genie's cupboard" where I used to store all their Christmas presents.

Our extended family has managed to join us as well, including Moppet, who sits happily by Mary's side. Nellie seems surprisingly merry, despite the situations of both Giles and Esmond. Even though Goonie has been ill, Winston's brother, Jack; Goonie; their children Johnny, Peregrine, and Clarissa; and their spouses and grandchildren rally for the holiday and gather around our table, and I overhear Winston say to his brother, "How I wish Mother were still alive to enjoy Chequers with us. She would have adored spending Christmas at the prime minister's estate." Strangely, his remark makes me long for my own mother, even though our always challenging relationship had grown more strained in the months before she died in Dieppe, drunk and broke from gambling, nearly fifteen years ago.

Even though we are not spending Christmas at the family home in Chartwell, I had wanted to make Chequers glow with my usual Chartwellian Christmas spirit. Although Chartwell is boarded up for the duration of the war, several weeks ago, I invaded its storage to bring the familiar holiday decorations to Chequers. During my brief jaunt to Chartwell to organize the precise boxes to bring to Chequers, I passed by the kitchen garden. The sharp peak of the sundial peered over the hedge, and I stepped onto the garden path and walked toward the chest-high structure, which also served as a memorial to the dove Terence Philip had purchased for me in Bali years ago. I ran my fingers along the inscription at the sundial's base, from a poem by W. P. Ker about not straying from one's home and lingering on islands too long. I'd had the inscription made during a wistful stage.

How long ago those days on the Rosaura *seem,* I thought to myself. In each life, it seemed that there was one dispositive choice, the choice that narrowed and excluded some possibilities but expanded and enlarged many others. Even though there'd been a time when I believed I should circle back and change my definitive choice and select another path for my life — the time period around the *Rosaura* — I now know that I'd been terribly mistaken. My dispositive decision was and had always been Winston, and the expansive, unorthodox life I've shared with him was the exact one I was meant to experience.

I glance around the room, pleased with the usual ornaments decorating the Christmas tree, and hope the children take notice. I want to remind them of the singular occasion of the year in which I commit myself entirely to bringing our family unity and joy. I do this in the hopes they will experience the same feelings, even in these tumultuous times.

But I have held back a little in honor of wartime, particularly in my selection of food and decor. I cannot invest fully in a lavish meal when I know many are eating cheap mutton for their Christmas dinner rather than the traditional goose and turkey and will be serving the conventional pudding with carrots instead of the unattainable fruit called for by the recipes. And how can I decorate every corner of Chequers when I know many will not even be able to celebrate in their homes? For many British citizens, Christmas, which has come to be known as Blitzmas, because the Nazis show no sign of ceasing their nightly bombing for the holiday season, will be spent in an air-raid shelter. Even though I know the British people, resilient beyond imagination, will endeavor to imbue the holiday with the Christmas spirit, I try to soften this terrible blow. I orchestrate underground canteens — I've heard that shelter Christmas parties will be organized around them with singing, skits, and dancing — arrange for the larger shelters to have Christmas trees, and plan for a costumed Father Christmas to visit many shelters as well. I can do nothing about the cancellation of street-side caroling, deemed unsafe with the bombings and blackouts, or the requirement that factory employees must work on Boxing Day instead of enjoying the holiday.

Winston knows all these details, of course, but his mind soars high over the battlefields and oceans. It does not often land in the streets with the ordinary folks as does mine. So guilt doesn't factor into his mind when he sips his Pol Roger and raises his full champagne flute now. "To my family. This has been a year brimming with hardship and toil, and yet here we sit, most of us, safe and in the warmth of one another's company. May we all reunite here — or at Chartwell — next Christmas, unharmed and a long step closer to victory."

Every family member stands, careful to clink his or her flute with everyone else's. When my glass touches Nellie's, I see that her eyes, direct and frank as always, bear a sadness and worry too profound for tears, despite the merry smile painted upon her lips. *What an unfathomable weight she carries,* I think, *with one son in a Nazi stronghold and another in Canada preparing for the war's most dangerous role, that of pilot.* And yet, here she stands, toasting to a happier new year. How resilient she is, and how forgetful are we of her plight.

We must honor Nellie's nobility and sacrifice. I raise my glass again. "Here's to Giles's speedy return home from Germany. And here's to our fighting boys, especially Esmond, who is not with us tonight. May they have victorious missions and safe delivery home."

"Hear, hear." The words echo throughout the cavernous Chequers dining room, followed by the melodious chime of crystal.

My sister nods to me in thanks and reaches across the table to clink my glass in a private toast. "To our other loved ones who are gone and missed — Bill and Kitty. And Mother as well." The unbidden tears that I'd managed to hold back earlier now return, and for a brief, wondrous moment,

Chapter Thirty-Seven

January 9 to February 10, 1941
London, England

We must enlist the Americans in this war. We are alone in this fight, and I wonder how long we can last. The *Luftwaffe* is flattening the country, and the Nazi U-boats are destroying our ships with critical supplies. *How will we make it through the winter without some kind of commitment from the Americans?* This is what I'm thinking as I discuss a luncheon menu with Mrs. Landemare.

Winston and I are hosting a luncheon for Harry Hopkins tomorrow. This emissary of President Roosevelt, a member of his inner circle, landed in England yesterday evening and would arrive at Downing Street late tomorrow morning. We understand that Roosevelt's right-hand man — decidedly anti-British — has been sent in a fact-finding mission to assess whether America should strongly aid us or should even consider entering the war. Until now, America has been noncommittal at best about sending troops and equipment into the fray, and yet, we desperately need them.

Jock pokes his head into my office. "Winston is wondering if you have a minute?"

My husband knows better these days than to summon me for unimportant queries, so he must have something critical to review. Turning to Mrs. Landemare, I ask, "Any more questions about the luncheon?"

"No, ma'am," the ever-pleasant, full-faced cook answers.

"I know you will work your magic with whatever we manage to forage for you." Somehow, Mrs. Landemare manages to whip up the tastiest confections from the most basic of ingredients, making her an indispensable weapon in the rationing of wartime.

Striding past a queue of staffers waiting to procure a moment of the prime minister's time, I open the door to Winston's office. "You sent for me, Winston?"

"How are the plans for Hopkins coming, Clemmie?"

Has he really called me down to his office to discuss a menu? I'm irritated, so I fiddle with my double strand of pearls as I answer. "As we discussed. A luxurious meal in the basement dining room at Downing Street, which I'm having elegantly decorated —"

Winston interjects, "Insofar as a reinforced subterranean space with steel shutters and metal pit props in the ceiling can be 'elegantly decorated' —"

I interject right back, "Precisely, meaning that I've had the space painted a soft coral color and arranged to have silk curtains and paintings by French masters Ingres and David hung. It looks surprisingly lovely."

He barks, "But is it lovely *enough?* You know we've been told that while this Hopkins professes to be anti-British, he's susceptible to the finer things, to the aristocratic life. We must bring him around to the British cause." He huffs and takes a deep draw on his cigar. "Don't make me regret calling you my secret weapon."

How dare he brandish his compliment around like a carrot and stick? I raise my voice to match his volume. "So you are placing the success of wooing the Americans into the war on my shoulders? If that is the price of your compliments, please don't bestow any others upon me."

I march out of the room, letting the door slam behind me. Looking straight ahead, I ignore the queue of staring faces and return to my own office. Fury builds within me, threatening to spill out between my carefully stitched seams. I pace around the confined space, seething at the pressure Winston has put upon me. After everything I undertake on his behalf, after all the projects I assume myself, how dare he. I have served as a sort of prime minister's wife like no other before me, and Winston demonstrates his gratitude by burdening me with a Sisyphean goal? One he's been unable to achieve himself?

I take a deep breath in and remind myself about my recent epiphany about the reasons behind my labors — the greater good of the British people. By the time I hear Winston's knock on the door, I have composed myself. I've also conceived of an approach to Winston and Mr. Hopkins.

I allow him to grovel and apologize, as I knew he would, and then I take command of the conversation. "Winston, let's not focus on what divides us but what unites us. Right now, we are unified in our desire to bring the Americans into this war, to give Britain a fighting chance. This visit by Mr. Hopkins is a unique opportunity to make that happen, but we can only do so if we work as a team. Together, if we follow the plan I've devised, I know we can entertain, persuade, and charm Mr. Hopkins into becoming *our* emissary." I pause and ask softly, "Can we do that, Pug?"

He almost purrs, "Of course we can, Cat."

"Good," I answer briskly. "Then by the time he leaves, we shall be one step closer to having an ally in this bloody war."

"Come, Mr. Hopkins, let me show you." I gesture toward the gaunt gentleman, who, I must remind myself, is the second most powerful person in America. With his sunken cheeks and hollow eyes, he appears so sickly, his influence is difficult to fathom. From the moment he stepped into our makeshift dining room, I understood that Mr. Hopkins has survived thus far on sheer will alone. His body — ravaged by stomach cancer that left him permanently malnourished — had long ago abandoned him. I resolved in that moment to deliver him a constant stream of Mrs. Landemare's delicacies, no matter the cost, such that his memory of the time spent with us would be cast with the glow of health and goodwill. Savory soups, tender beef, fresh green salads, fine cheeses, sponges, rich coffee, and rare wines from Winston's own stores made regular appearances at lunch and dinner until the American glowed with health, an impossibility in the White House, I'd heard, with its notoriously poor cuisine, and I vowed that this would be his fare the entirety of his six-week visit. I employed a parallel tactic in the matter of his accommodations — which always had roaring fires and hot water bottles tucked in between his bedsheets — and our weekend abode, ensuring we stayed in the finest English country house manor at Ditchley Park, Ronald Tree's estate in Oxfordshire. How could he think anything but favorable thoughts toward us when he was so well fed and comfortably cared for?

The weekend at Ditchley proceeded even better than we'd hoped. The quintessential country house experience I arranged for Mr. Hopkins — no mean feat in wartime — entranced him and softened his harder edges. The man who'd been described as irreverent, even contentious, proved a delight, and we spent two pleasant evenings gathered around the great hearth at Ditchley. Yet this cosseting was hardly the most critical aspect of our plan. In London, we would unfurl the key components of our project to woo the Americans.

Silence reigns behind me, where there should be the sound of footsteps crunching through debris. I see the backs of Winston and two military escorts ahead of me, but where the devil is Mr. Hopkins? I turn around to discover that he stands stock-still in a rubble pile where the church entrance had once been, staring at the ripped-out walls of the destroyed church. His face appears incredulous at the very notion of entering this burned-out hull of a place of worship. This is his first time accompanying us on one of our regular Blitz tours, and he appears every bit as shell-shocked as the buildings we have passed.

I retrace my steps through the piles of stones and rocks to where Mr. Hopkins is frozen in place. Linking my arm through his, I say, "Would you lend me your arm? These ruins can make for unsteady walking." Chivalry can make for strong motivation, as I've learned from Winston.

"How often do you undertake these Blitz tours, Mrs. Churchill?" he asks in his flat American drawl when he recovers himself.

"Winston and I take them whenever his schedule allows. But I take them alone — with guards or Red Cross representatives, of course — every night I'm in London."

He looks aghast. "You trudge through this dangerous debris every night?"

I stop walking and stare directly into his eyes. "Mr. Hopkins, the British people do far worse than trudge through this debris every night. They live and die through it. The Blitz destroys their homes, their schools, their churches" — I gesture around — "their families. The least I can do is bear witness to the devastation. That and create safe air-raid shelters for them, of course."

"Air-raid shelters?" he asks.

Does he really not know about the shelters? Where does he think the people ride out the nightly bombings? Of course, to the Americans, the actual threat seems unimaginably far away, but for us, havoc arrives every evening like Swiss clockwork.

As I explain the shelter system to Hopkins, we approach Winston. Whispering in his ear about the detour I'd like to take, he assigns one of the men to escort us. As we walk to a shelter that I hope will leave a lasting impression upon Hopkins, I describe the Anderson shelters, the most common type, made of curved steel sheets, partly sunken in the ground, freely distributed by the government, and installed in the private gardens of a million homes. I explain that because the Anderson shelters often become insufferably cold and damp, many citizens prefer the sturdier, communal shelters such as the surface shelters, long brick-and-concrete structures built on sidewalks or beside buildings, or the sunken shelters, often heavily reinforced basements or trenches.

"And of course, many people choose to use the Underground as shelter, even though we don't specifically sanction it. Each type, of course, has its benefits and drawbacks," I finish.

His mouth, already off-kilter with a slightly mangled jaw, gapes. "How on earth do you know so much about the range of shelters?"

I glance at him and answer matter-of-factly, "Mr. Hopkins, the adequacy, cleanliness, and sanitary conditions of these shelters is my special project. Winston and many of the governmental leaders are overwhelmingly busy with the military aspect of the war, as you might imagine. The Nazis are literally in the air above us and in the sea on our shores. So when I identify a domestic problem, I take it on — with the assistance of the requisite governmental agency, of course — to free others to focus on the war itself."

"That is admirable, Mrs. Churchill. You go above and beyond what duty demands."

"No, Mr. Hopkins. It's our people that go above and beyond. They stare down the barrel of the Nazi artillery every night and summon the courage to face that barrel again the very next day, oftentimes losing everything and everyone they have in the process. I have simply become the prime minister's wife that these brave citizens deserve. Or at least I strive to be."

As I say these words, I wonder at their truth. Indeed, I try to serve our deserving people and ensure they aren't forgotten. But do I undertake this work for their sake alone or for my own sense of self-worth as well? Or a combination of both?

Although his face has grown pensive, Mr. Hopkins doesn't respond to my statement, and I suspect that my message will be emblazoned upon his consciousness once he sees the people in the shelter for himself. We approach a squat concrete structure on a wide sidewalk. I have inspected this particular shelter before. It accommodates up to fifty people, a surprise given its small footprint.

I nod to our military escort, who opens the door for us. As we step inside, I tell Mr. Hopkins about the alterations we made to this particular shelter to make it more habitable. "After all, they regularly spend ten to fourteen hours here."

"Fourteen hours?" Mr. Hopkins sounds astonished. I'd been whispering, but he makes no effort to keep his volume low.

His voice and the light from the torches rouses some of the women and children. As they slide out of the triple-stacked bunks, I hear them whisper, "Mrs. Churchill."

A young woman whose hair appears inky black in the low shelter light, with two young girls clinging to her legs, approaches me with a tentative step. To assuage her trepidation, I reach out and clasp her free hand with both of mine. "Thank you for your bravery and patience," I say.

"Ma'am, Mrs. Churchill, I mean, some other mums and I were chattin' over there" — she points back toward the bunks — "and we're ever so thankful for the work you did to fix up these shelters. They were downright horrible before."

I answer her in a practiced phrase about what an honor and privilege it is to serve the English people, one I've uttered hundreds, if not thousands, of times before. Yet when I look into this lovely creature's eyes — the shelter is dark, and I can't discern their precise color — I mean it, and I know with certainty that I serve the people, in large measure, out of my sense of duty toward them.

I chat with the young mothers for a few minutes, marveling at their tenacity in these circumstances. With their husbands off fighting the war — one husband was at sea, two others on land in France — they are not fraught with nerves and fear, as I would have been. They are not sick with worry over the children they've sent off to the safety of strangers' homes in the countryside or the toddlers and infants who still cling to them. They are better wives, mothers, and human beings than I've ever been.

Mr. Hopkins is still quiet as we stroll back toward Winston and the bombed-out church. "I suppose you wish to know what I am going to say to President Roosevelt on my return," he finally says.

I stop and turn to him. My heart beats wildly, and I feel my stomach churn. The fate of thousands depends on his decision. "Most desperately, Mr. Hopkins."

"Please call me Harry."

"I most desperately wish to know what you're going to say to President Roosevelt, Harry."

"Where you go, I'll follow." Then he adds softly, "Even to the end."

CHAPTER THIRTY-EIGHT

March 10 to April 15, 1941
London and Buckinghamshire, England

Even Harry's recommendation does not sway President Roosevelt to enter the war. I establish a regular correspondence with him, and reports filter back to us at Downing Street that he told Roosevelt that America must do all it can to help Britain with munitions, equipment, even ships and planes. Roosevelt was apparently incredulous that the once anti-British Hopkins had been moved by the courage and resolve of Britain and her leaders. America has decided to provide us with armaments and the necessary financial aid — even to sing Winston's praises — but still will not abandon its isolationist stance to join us in the fight.

More persuasion is necessary, Winston and I decide. Once the proappeasement American ambassador Joseph Kennedy Sr.

is replaced by Gil Winant, a former Republican governor who, I'm told, shares some of my more liberal social views, we focus our efforts upon him. We arrange for Mr. Winant's train to be met by King George VI in a rare breach of royal protocol and for an invitation to stay at Windsor Castle to be extended by His Majesty.

I scramble to arrange a welcome dinner once I learn, to my delight, that Mr. Winant has declined the king's invitation in order to hasten to London and start working. Feeling even more optimistic about this American and his willingness to help when I hear that he's chosen not to live in the official ambassador's residence but in a modest flat, I arrange a relatively sumptuous dinner but hold back on the more luxurious details. I don't want to overwhelm, or alienate, the reportedly humble Mr. Winant.

Over our initial dinner and the many meals that follow, I find Mr. Winant to be warm and, more importantly, principled. While he and Winston connect on the broader wartime strategy about which my husband is brilliant, he and I share kindred political views on the duty to serve the less fortunate. He joins me on some of my Blitz tours in London and throughout the countryside, quietly telling me that the American people are with us.

I arrange for Mr. Winant, Gil as he's asked me to call him, to join us for a weekend at Chequers, even though Winston's security advisers now find it inadequate from a safety perspective as they've heard that the Nazis have the estate on their maps. In particular, we want to connect him with another American guest arriving at Chequers this weekend in the context of our company.

Chequers consists of a large Tudor country house nestled in a sheltered hollow and fifteen hundred acres of parklands, working farms, and Chiltern beechwoods. While Winston prefers Chartwell, the magnificent house at Chequers, with its great hall, impressive art collection of Constables, Turners, Rubens, and van Dycks, historical relics, and deep fireplaces, is better suited for a prime minister, particularly one who travels with an entourage of cars ferrying secretaries, telephone operators, and security detail and hosts an ever-evolving array of military officials and dignitaries.

Gil arrives at Chequers after traversing the forty-mile distance from London by automobile, and once he has settled in, I invite him to join me for a walk. As we traipse through the maze on Chequers

413

grounds and out onto the Buckinghamshire countryside surrounding the estate, always with a military escort in tow, of course, Gil asks, "Where does the estate get its unusual name?"

"History is more Winston's subject than mine, but it is my understanding that the name might derive from an early owner whose coat of arms contained a checker-board — also known as chequer, in the French — or, more simply, it might stem from the chequer trees that grow here on the grounds." I point to a few of these trees in the distance, near the foot of the Chiltern Hills.

"Speaking of the French, please tell your husband how much I enjoyed his recent speech. It was quite brilliant. I particularly enjoyed the references to de Gaulle and the Free French. Would I be correct in guessing that you had a hand in that speech?"

I glance over at him, amazed at his insight. How had he known? Very few people other than family and staff comprehend the synergistic relationship that Winston and I enjoy regarding his speeches. Gil's eyes, hooded by thick, bushy eyebrows, reveal nothing about the origin of this observation, and consequently, I merely smile at the compliment.

"Tonight, we will be four for dinner. Our daughter Sarah will be visiting," I offer by way of a subject change, but lest he think we have dragged him out of London for a family weekend, I add, "A parade of other guests will begin arriving tomorrow morning, commencing with a dinner for twelve, and they will include some individuals helpful in your projects." I do not mention that, among those other guests, will be more family, our daughter Mary and Pamela, Randolph's estranged wife. Given that Winston and I work every day, if we want to see our children at all, they must join us in our more official duties and meals.

We finish our tromp through the grounds and enter through the estate's back entrance, nearly colliding with Sarah, who arrived for the weekend. After kissing one another on the cheek, I introduce her to Gil. The usually reserved American seems animated in Sarah's presence, and I try to see Sarah as Gil must see her. Her lovely, fair English skin with a rosy tint from the brisk air is complemented by her reddish hair that falls in waves around her face, and the khaki of her uniform enhances her coloring. She has recently entered the Women's Auxiliary Air Force as an interpreter of aerial photographs — one of the more critical roles that women occupy — and she looks especially becoming in her uniform. What Gil cannot know about my Sarah is her inner conflict — constantly vacillating between indulging in her aristocratic status and pursuing the independent life of an actress — and the tentative state of her ill-advised marriage to fellow actor Vic, who'd decamped to the United States against the will of our entire family and from whom she's secretly separated. Not that Gil would judge Sarah for her marital state; I'd heard that Gil was all but divorced from his own American wife as well, who allegedly prefers socializing to social reform.

Over dinner that evening, Gil listens politely to Winston's military updates. He commiserates on America's reluctance to enter the war, but it is Sarah who captures his attention. What a twenty-seven-year-old veritable girl and a fifty-two-year-old seasoned politician find in common baffles me, but commonalities they do indeed find. Although, I suppose an older man is a comfortable fit for Sarah, as Vic was nearly eighteen years older than my daughter.

"Are we witnessing the birth of something inappropriate?" I ask Winston after Gil and Sarah retire to separate wings for the evening.

416

"Whatever do you mean?" he asks distract-edly, glancing up from a pile of papers on his desk. It will be hours until he makes his way to his bedroom, and his military offi-cers will soon arrive in the study to review developments and plans.

"Did you not sense a frisson between Gil and Sarah?"

"No, but even if some flirtation transpired, surely there's no harm in it? She's a good girl." He seems unperturbed, but then his mind has zeroed in on military matters. Not to mention his reaction is undoubtedly clouded by what he considers to be my exaggeration in matters concerning our children, although it is usually Randolph about whom he accuses me of overreaction.

"Anyway, Clemmie," he says, softening, "Winant seems like a fine man. She could do far worse. In fact" — he chuckles to himself — "she has done far worse with that damn Austrian actor husband of hers."

I allow the concern to drop. Who knows? Perhaps Winston is right. And perhaps I am exaggerating the interaction between Gil and Sarah. Anyway, in the scheme of the war, what danger can there be in a bit of flirtation?

The next morning requires a flurry of

417

preparation, and I'm forced to leave Gil in the care of a distracted Winston and an attentive Sarah while I work with the staff on the final details of the welcoming dinner for our new guest, Averell Harriman. Roosevelt has sent the wealthy businessman to London for the specific purpose of setting up his new lend-lease military aid program, in which the United States would "rent" key armaments to us in return for assets rather than cash, a boon to our cash-strapped economy. Roosevelt's adoption of this program was the direct result of Harry's time with us. When he returned, he persuaded Roosevelt to proceed with the program, and Harry now serves as its administrator, overseeing many billions of dollars. Harry is the one who sent Mr. Harriman here and tasked him with delivering the planes, ships, weapons, and equipment we need to fight Hitler.

Winston and I arranged for a naval aide to pick Mr. Harriman up when he landed in Bristol and usher him onto a waiting biplane to bring him directly to Chequers for the weekend. This morning, we received word that he was en route and would be arriving at the estate in advance of dinner. Now we just needed to woo this Mr. Harriman.

By the time the tall, tanned Mr. Harriman strides into the grand dining room at Chequers, I've arranged for every surface and nook in the vast space to gleam, despite my reduced staff. From the burnished woodwork on the walls to the sparkling faceted crystal on the chandeliers and goblets to the crisply ironed ancient Belgian linens on the table — but never ostentatious, never opulent, simply a polishing of historical furnishings — the room appears every bit the quintessential country estate. My reconnaissance on Mr. Harriman, by all accounts a suave, wealthy businessman who appreciates all the trappings of luxury, suggests that inviting him to step into our world might be a first step toward bringing him around to embracing our cause and supporting it wholeheartedly with American armaments.

He marches toward me with a bag of tangerines in the crook of his arm. "It is a great pleasure to meet you, Mrs. Churchill. Your hospitality is legendary on the other side of the pond, but I must say, to be kidnapped on my arrival and swept away to this grand manor house, well, you have outdone yourself. I am embarrassed to admit that all I have in the way of a hostess gift is this paltry sack of tangerines that I picked up in Lisbon." He hands me the bag.

My mouth actually waters at the sight of the vivid orange fruit. I cannot recall how long it's been since I had a tangerine, or any tropical fruit, for that matter. "It is our pleasure to host you, Mr. Harriman. But don't you dare call this gorgeous array of fruit paltry — it's been eons since we've had anything so decadent as tangerines," I exclaim.

"Hear, hear," Winston chimes in, never one to be left out of a conversation, especially about food.

Winston and Mr. Harriman stroll off, launching directly into a discussion about munitions. I glance toward Gil, thinking that perhaps we could continue one of our conversations about American social reforms, but I see that he and Sarah are deeply engrossed in conversation. Pamela, who stays with us on Chequers weekends despite the fact that she and Randolph are estranged, no surprise given his string of affairs and gambling debts, which he's inexplicably demanded that she pay, mercifully chats with two of Winston's military officers with whom I'd rather not engage. Sweet Mary proudly wears her Auxiliary Territorial Service uniform, and I approach my youngest, threading my arm through hers and offering congratulations on her decision to join the unit, where she'll be working at antiaircraft batteries. It is one of the military posts in which I'd hoped women might find a place, and I am beyond thrilled that my daughter is serving in one of these roles.

As we sit down to another miraculous meal by Mrs. Landemare and toast to our shared venture, I gaze around the room. Through our joint efforts, Winston and I have fueled the British fight against the Nazis in ways unimaginable only months ago. Soon, we may have equipment, munitions, ships, and planes to make success possible, if only we can keep the British spirits high. For so long, the focus has been solely on survival.

A welling forth of laughter, like a spring bursting from the frozen earth, breaks into my reverie. Scanning the table, I realize that Pamela is laughing at something Mr. Harriman said. When had I last really studied her? The youthful, eager expression she used to wear like a playful puppy has disappeared, as has the fullness of her face and the soft, voluptuous plumpness of her figure. She is almost chiseled yet still curvaceous, and she has caught Mr. Harriman's eye. She seems to be relishing his attention, even returning it. It feels inappropriate, yet how can I begrudge her a flirtation after the reprehensible misbehavior of our errant son?

A rogue notion creeps into my consciousness — how the flirtations of Sarah and Pamela with Gil and Averell might help our cause — before I banish it. Good heavens, how can I even think about utilizing Pamela's and Sarah's innocent coquetries, even if it is for the greater good? At what cost am I willing to win this war?

CHAPTER THIRTY-NINE

August 4 and 9, 1941
London and Buckinghamshire, England

The hands of the grandfather clock in my study refuse to move. The time on my wristwatch clings to its position. I will the hours and minutes to pass more quickly, but the day stubbornly adheres to its normal routine. Will it ever reach noon? I yearn for the release it will bring.

Why am I surprised at the unhurried passage of time today? After all, I feel as though I've been treading in increasingly viscous, torpid waters for the past few months, desperately waiting for some form of relief to emerge from the depths. I'd sensed that the seams of my composed exterior were coming unstitched during our campaign to woo the Americans into the war. The strain of forging and maintaining those ties — compounded with the pain of watching my husband chase after the recalcitrant Presi-

423

dent Roosevelt — was tremendous. But I felt I could bear up with my duties and maintain my steadfast facade until the reports poured in enumerating the loss of life, and I could see no way through to the end of this conflict except through more bloodshed. All the brisk sense of purpose that had arrived with Winston's return to power started to disappear, only to be replaced with anxiety.

How to return to my state of calm determination? This was the question that plagued me in the middle of the night, when I couldn't sleep and my long list of worries worked its tentacles into me. I longed for the sort of respite I'd taken in the past, one of my rest cures, not a *Rosaura*-esque excursion, but I could never leave Winston. He relied upon me completely for support and advice, and our routines and rituals were a solace to him. I would not, indeed could not, permit myself the luxury of a break, especially when our country's women were truly suffering, like my poor sister Nellie, who was constantly awaiting word of her sons' fates. Not when young men were dying and my husband was in charge of their destiny.

But then, in July, Harry Hopkins sent word to Winston that Roosevelt was anxious for a meeting. Finally, the news for which we'd been waiting. He and I rejoiced at this missive, seeing it as one step closer to having America as an ally in this war.

The weeks that followed were a flurry of planning, a great feat of scheduling interconnected land, sea, and air travel under the cloak of secrecy. No one person, aside from Winston, me, and a few key advisers, knew his complete itinerary, as Hitler would like nothing more than to bomb Winston in the air or sea as he made the crossing to America and claim victory.

I promised myself that if I could just make it through one more week, then one more day, then one more hour before Winston left for America, I could take the respite I need before I splinter. Casting around for a secure, private establishment for a focused rest cure, I read about Dr. Stanley Lief and his unique work at Champneys, a health retreat in Buckinghamshire. Dr. Lief holds some unorthodox but compelling views about the negative impact that stress and nervousness have on one's health. Thinking back over the course of my life — the times when my nerves overwhelmed and the consequent maladies, both physical and emotional — this made perfect sense to me, even though most other doctors I'd consulted held no such view. I booked a week-long stay for the time when Winston was away and stuck to my plans even when Winston dubbed it a madhouse.

The door shudders with a knock. Has the hour come? Glancing over at the grandfather clock, I see that it is eleven thirty on the nose, earlier than the designated hour. Is Winston eager to leave? "Come in," I say.

Jock peeks his head in the door. "The prime minister is ready for you, ma'am."

How my relationship with Winston's private secretary has change since our early days, I think. In the past, he'd have bristled at the lowly task of notifying the prime minister's wife.

"Thank you, Jock. Where is he?"

"In the entryway of the Annexe, ma'am. Ready to push out."

Nodding, I push myself up from my chair, straightening my dove-gray, serge wool dress, and follow Jock down the hallway. When I round the bend into the foyer, I see Winston from the back, a great hulking presence of a man, intimidatingly fierce to so many but my needy, sensitive Pug underneath. He turns toward me, his eyes soft, and my heart tugs unexpectedly. Why am I suddenly feeling so sentimental about Winston's departure for this trip when we've been separated so many times before? Is it the risk associated with the travel? Or my guilt over wishing away the time before he leaves?

"I'll miss you, Cat," Winston whispers into my ear. He seems unusually sentimental as well, perhaps for much the same reasons.

"And I you, Mr. Pug," I whisper back, and even though I need this span of time alone to reassemble myself, I mean it.

A sliver of morning sun streams through a small gap in the two billowing seafoam-green silk curtains that cover the French doors leading to my private patio. The shift in my bedroom's brightness awakens me, and I stretch like a cat awakening from a nap, thinking that I could sleep forever. *How relaxed and at ease I feel at Champneys,* I think.

I experience a curious sense of lightness here. It did not settle upon me when I stepped into the attractive facility five days ago but in stages. The first bit occurred when I surrendered my wardrobe of wool dresses and suits for the Champneys' loose-fitting, soft cotton dresses; I felt as liberated as I did when fashion no longer dictated corsets. The next layer happened when I was encouraged by the staff to sleep as

427

much as my body permitted; I slipped into the cool, pressed cotton bedsheets and slept away the fatigue that had plagued me since the war began. The final stage transpired during my sessions with Dr. Lief. In them, we built up to confessional discussions about the restlessness I experience around motherhood and the anxiety I feel when tending to Winston. When the doctor validated my emotions and explained their interrelationship with my physical health — something no other medical professional had ever done — I felt an almost tangible lifting sensation from my shoulders and back and a new openness across my chest.

Since then, I stopped questioning why I must leave my family and responsibilities to arrive at myself. I halted my self-criticism about my inability to bring a sense of wholeness and peace to my everyday life. And I no longer felt angry at Winston for indulging his depression but being unable to understand — or empathize with — my own struggle with nerves. After all, it took this particular doctor and establishment for me to comprehend it myself and give myself permission to heal.

I understand what I must do to maintain this sense of self-tranquility and fortitude of purpose. I will do what's necessary so I can meet Winston at King's Cross Station when he returns from his meeting with Roosevelt, restored and ready for whatever Hitler inflicts next.

CHAPTER FORTY

December 7, 1941
London and Buckinghamshire, England

Come, Clemmie," Winston urges as the train pulls into the remains of a station. We have four stops today, the areas most heavily bombarded by our enemies, and to make each one and interact meaningfully with the people, we must proceed apace.

But I cannot disembark without my headscarf, not in this chill. I adopted the bandana style of headscarves as soon as I saw that the female factory workers throughout the country tied up their hair in this style for safety and to keep out dirt and dust. I wear it in solidarity with the women supporting our country's war effort, and I've been told my wardrobe of scarves has become my trademark, aligning me with the British women and showing my support of them.

"One moment only, Winston," I call back and select a simple cotton scarf, in a navy that matches my dress. I tie it around my hair and anchor it with my earrings.

Winston is waiting for me at the door of the special train he had outfitted explicitly for the purpose of traveling to these scarred and devastated sites. I take his arm, and we step out onto a ruined street. Crowds have already gathered around the train, and we move through the cheering people, shaking hands and making inquiries. We visit families — usually only mothers and children, as fathers are away at war — who emerge from the shambles of their homes to greet us. Winston and I are often left crying at the bravery and tenacity of our citizens after these visits, in the privacy of our train car.

As always, the visit culminates with a speech, each a slight variant on another. Today, he finishes with a rousing call to action, in which he praises the British people for their tenacity and urges them to remain strong.

Now, more than ever, Winston serves as an emblem of hope and courage, imparting to the people the strength to endure the unendurable for another day.

As I stare out at the crowds desperate for a lifeline that will buoy them, I wish that Winston's speeches had the capacity to help my poor Nellie. Only a week ago, her son

431

Esmond was out on a bombing raid over Germany with his Royal Canadian Air Force squadron when he was shot down over the North Sea. Winston and I delivered the news in person to Nellie, and I don't think I will ever recover from watching my sister crumple like a tissue when learning that her son, whose unorthodox political views, not to mention his elopement, had given her much cause for concern during his life, had died. As I clutched my sister, sobbing alongside her, I glanced up at Winston, who looked as helpless as I felt. Remembering that powerless moment, a rage rises within me, along with a hardening of resolve. All the control and calm I'd mustered this summer during my rest cure vanished. Because I know that while these visits to bomb sites act as a tourniquet for the injuries to people's spirits, we must find a way to stop the bloodshed at the source.

Sitting before the roaring fire at Chequers feels wrong after witnessing the devastation through which the people are suffering. How can we be enjoying a glass of port after dinner when the citizens are living in rubble, thankful for the shelters to offer protection not only from the air raids but the elements as well? Winston seems comfortable enough, and in some ways, I envy his ability to compartmentalize the devastation we've just observed.

Surrounded by Gil, Averell, as we now call Mr. Harriman, his grown daughter Kathleen, Winston's chief military assistant General Pug Ismay, Winston's private secretary John Martin, Commander Thompson, and Pamela, Winston and our guests are lamenting the state of the war. Through my peripheral vision, I study Pamela and Averell, who sit near one another but do not touch. My suspicion about the attraction between them has recently been confirmed by Winston via his crony Lord Beaverbrook. The spark I saw at the Chequers dinner in April apparently ignited in the spring when Pamela paid Averell a visit in his Dorchester Hotel suite. Beaverbrook was among the first to discover the affair, and once he explained to Pamela how beneficial the relationship could be to Britain, she began passing along information about the Americans' decision to enter the war. And vice versa. Pamela began doing what she could to influence Averell's decisions about armaments and America's participation. Who would have believed that the solicitous and coquettish but otherwise innocent young woman who joined our family only two years ago could become the epicenter of such intrigue? Who would believe that I, who'd once been routinely called a prude and a prig, would tolerate such behavior? Is it another legacy of my time on the *Rosaura?* Or borne from the necessities of wartime?

Another woman might have been enraged if she discovered her daughter-in-law was cuckolding her son, but I am no longer that woman. Randolph has treated poor Pamela terribly, with no remorse whatsoever, and I cannot begrudge her this affair, which, by all accounts, she initiated. I do occasionally berate myself for assessing the benefits Britain might reap from the relationship — what sort of a mother am I, after all — but I now realize the lengths to which average citizens will go in the national interest. Is it acceptable to change — or even lose — one's moral compass in the miasma of wartime?

"I wish your Roosevelt would bloody well make up his mind," Winston says to Gil and Averell with a slam of his fist on a side table, interrupting my musings about Pamela. His scotch splashes out of his glass at this outburst, and I signal to the staff for a cloth.

Despite the fact that we now technically have an ally — after the Germans attacked

Russia in June, Winston aligned with Russia despite his aversion to Communism — we are essentially still alone in our fight. Even though the Russians watched while Britain suffered at Hitler's hands pursuant to the pact of nonaggression toward Germany that Russia signed in 1939, the now-beleaguered Russia has no compunction demanding troops and assistance from Britain while offering no military help. The reports from the front remain disheartening, despite the military aid that America has offered, and Winston is simmering. Consequently, everyone is on edge, bringing the mood in the room low. *How many people rely on Winston as an external source of courage and inspiration?* I think. And yet, of all his many complaints, that is never one.

I glance at the circle of people commiserating around the fire. I know I've been instrumental in knitting together this cadre of British and Americans — bringing the Americans as close to involvement in the war as they'll come — but I wonder if my influence here has reached its natural end. I wonder, in fact, whether the American supplies and assistance, which I worked hard to help secure, will even impact the outcome of the war. It simply may not be enough without the Americans actually fighting.

But what more can I do? I feel helpless, as helpless as I'd felt while consoling my grieving sister. Surely there must be some project I can undertake, some task I can conquer. I must take action instead of submitting to this despair, and a restlessness takes hold of me. I take deep breaths as I'd been taught at Champneys, and I remind myself that there is only so much I can control. But those measures do not alleviate the mounting anxiety. Pushing myself up from the high-backed brocade chair, I stroll around the room as if I'm taking inventory, and while I've been known to undertake such a task, it is odd timing. But I simply cannot sit idly by for one more minute.

"Clemmie?" Winston asks when he finally notices I'm not sitting in my chair alongside everyone else.

"Over here, dear," I call back, knowing he doesn't really want anything in particular. He just needs to know where I am at all times. I try not to let his needs add to my own sense of disquiet.

What course should I take? I ask myself as I pace around the room. Since February, I've served as president of the Young Women's Christian Association's wartime appeal, raising thousands of pounds for hotels, clubs, and canteens for female war workers and the increasing ranks of service-women, a task I've relished. *Should I work on my BBC script for my YWCA appeal?* I wonder.

Perhaps I should turn my attention to my work as the chairman of the Red Cross Aid to Russia Fund. I'd conceived of the idea of a Red Cross fund specifically dedicated to sending medical supplies to Russia when I received a petition from the wives and mothers of servicemen requesting a second front to help relieve the pressure on Russia. I knew that a second front wasn't possible yet, but I felt compelled to show the petition to Winston. When he confirmed my suspicions — offhandedly mentioning that the only support we could offer for months if not years was supplies — a seed was planted. In order to demonstrate the desire of our country to help the Russians, even though we are cash-strapped ourselves, I headed up the fund and spearheaded the effort. I am nearing my goal of a million pounds, with the hopes we'll soon send over emergency operating outfits, surgical needles, medicines, and cotton wool to help the wounded soldiers and the civilian population in a good faith show of support, even though we can't yet send troops.

Although I've happily shouldered both

these jobs in addition to serving in my regular nighttime shifts as a fire watcher, none have lessened my responsibilities to Winston or my other family members, who have suffered their own losses this year. Diana's husband was injured in a car accident this spring, necessitating a departure from the military, and Sarah and Vic officially parted ways, though I suspect that Gil has filled that gap. I had to insert myself into an ill-fated, war-hastened engagement that Mary entered, and we all grieved for the loss of Goonie from cancer, my longtime friend and one of my few confidantes. I often find myself thinking that I must discuss a particular issue or story with Goonie, only to remember that she's gone. But I cannot allow myself to give way to sadness or grief, as I know the actions I take can assist the thousands in distress.

Stop, Clemmie, I tell myself. This is the sort of circular thinking that nearly caused me to crack. *Restorative sleep and personal space are what I need, what Dr. Lief would prescribe,* I think.

I excuse myself for the night and retire to my bedroom. Perhaps in the morning, the path will be clearer and so will I. Just as I drift off to sleep, I hear pounding on my door. Groggy with sleep, I smell Winston's cigar before I feel his hand on my shoulder. Suddenly awake, I sit bolt upright.

"What's happened?" I ask, instantly thinking of the children and then our beloved Britain. "Have we lost the war?"

Winston sinks beside me on the bed. "Something wondrous and terrible, Cat."

"Stop speaking in riddles. Say it plainly."

"Gil and I have just gotten off the phone with Roosevelt. We are no longer alone in this war."

"You finally convinced Roosevelt?" I exclaim.

"I wish I could ascribe it to my power of oratory, Cat, but it took the Japanese to bring the Americans into the same boat as us."

He is too excited for clear conversation, so I admonish him again. "Speak plainly, Pug."

"The Japanese have attacked Pearl Harbor, the American naval base in Hawaii. America is going to declare war."

CHAPTER FORTY-ONE

October to November 1942
London and Buckinghamshire, England

I rise from my deep curtsy to King George VI and Queen Elizabeth and lock eyes with Mrs. Roosevelt. Photographs do not do her justice. In the monochromatic black, gray, and white of the newspaper pictures, she appears dowdy with her unkempt hair, unflattering dresses, and prominent over-bite. But her piercing blue eyes, intelligent and discerning, draw me in, making one forget about all her other features, even the sack-like remade gown she wears.

Before I make her formal acquaintance, I must make my way through the throngs of other guests. We exchange pleasant small talk, but I never let Mrs. Roosevelt out of my line of sight.

Finally, the protocol permits Mrs. Roosevelt and me a brief conversation. "I have been looking forward to making your acquaintance, Mrs. Roosevelt, ever since you and your husband hosted Winston at the White House last Christmas. I will be forever in your debt." I mean, of course, that we are *all* in America's debt for finally entering the war and fighting these past ten months — far more than hosting Winston for Christmas — but I suppose she understands my sentiments.

Last December, after America made its declaration of war, Winston traversed the Atlantic through a frightful series of gales and ensconced himself at the White House through the December holidays into January. I've heard from the staff who traveled with my husband that the tension over Winston's drinking habits and unusual schedule of sleeping and working was palpable and tried the patience of the Roosevelts, Eleanor in particular, who was a teetotaler after suffering through her own family members' alcoholism. Harry wrote me that Winston had done his valiant best to be good-natured, but in a White House with unpleasant food and a hostess who did not deem it her duty to pamper her husband, let alone her guests, I could only imagine how he must have acted. Still, Winston came away from the overlong visit with a strengthened relationship with Roosevelt, which was indeed the purpose of the encounter.

Winston had known that a strong connection would facilitate the critical next steps for a total and unconditional surrender by the Nazis. Both men agreed that a massive invasion of mainland Europe was necessary to accomplish this goal, and in this first meeting, they'd begun to hash out a multi-stage plan. But internal and external pressures about the details of that plan would necessitate further meetings, Winston had reported on his return, and the many conferences that have followed have been the focal point of Winston's energies and time. Yet the war has not stopped while the leaders map out strategy at these conferences. At first, the new Allies dealt with the surging Japanese military and the fall of Tobruk in North Africa with the surrender of thirty thousand British troops, but they finally celebrated the success of regaining ground against the Nazis, including the momentous Egyptian victory of securing the Suez Canal, as I celebrated my own success of maintaining my health throughout this tumult by adhering to my Champneys' teachings.

"I feel the same, Mrs. Churchill. Your husband certainly sang your praises during his time with us, and the opportunity for us to get to know each other better is an opportunity to unite our countries further as allies." She speaks with warmth, although I imagine that she did not come away from Winston's visit feeling particularly warm toward him.

"Indeed, Mrs. Roosevelt. Beautifully said."

We are swept up again in the tide of mindless court chatter. When the current recedes and she and I have another moment alone, I say, "I am delighted that I will be serving as your tour guide while you are in London. Also, I'm happy to have the chance to repay your kindness to Winston by hosting you at Chequers over the weekend."

"Oh, Mrs. Churchill, that's very kind of you, but I don't think I need a tour of the London sites. Since he cannot make the trip, I am here to serve as my husband's eyes and ears and assess wartime England." I'm assuming she alludes to her husband's infirmity, if nearly full paralysis can be described as an infirmity. But it is well understood that his condition is not to be labeled out loud.

"How perfect. Because that is precisely the sort of tour I have planned."

After her three-day stay at Buckingham Palace with the king and queen, I sweep Mrs. Roosevelt up in a flurry of visits over the following days. I want her to witness the endeavors of our women, so we stop at branches of women's military services, talking to girls staffing antiaircraft gun crews. We meet with female pilots shuttling planes between RAF stations as part of the air transport auxiliary services. We tour munitions factories where women keep working despite the sound of sirens. But, of course, she must also see the indomitable British spirit, so I arrange a visit to the bomb-torn East End. There, after Mrs. Roosevelt is received by cheers, we talk with an older couple who elect to stay in the remains of their house by day and sleep in a shelter by night rather than evacuate to the country-side: "This is home, and we won't let the Krauts take it from us," they insist.

She is boundless in her energy, defeating even me in her indefatigability. The final afternoon of our week of visits, with days beginning at eight o'clock in the morning and ending at midnight, we planned on traveling to three locales in rapid succession: first, a nursery for evacuated or wounded children, then two locations of the Women's Voluntary Service, which moved into neighborhoods that had just been bombed and assisted with everything from food to laundry. After a day of Eleanor's long strides and fast pace, I find myself breathless by the time we reach the second Women's Voluntary Service location, a clothing distribution center to be exact, not a state in which anyone else has ever left me. Watching Eleanor take two steps at a time up to the second floor of the building, I realize that I simply cannot proceed one step farther, and I sit down upon a staircase. Noticing that I am not at her side, Eleanor slows and glances down the marble stairs at me.

"Oh, Clementine," she exclaims, pronouncing my name with an American inflection, "shall I join you for a moment?"

As she descends a few steps to my level, I laugh and say, "Please don't slow your pace on my account. Eleanor, you might be the first person to have ever winded me."

She guffaws, almost as loudly as I do myself, and I join her. "You aren't the first person to say that."

"I'm usually leaving everyone in *my* wake." Smoothing my moss-green skirt out to cover my legs, I look up at her. "Please go ahead. I only need a moment, and then I'll join you."

"If you're sure?" she asks, but before I can really answer, she is already up the stairs again.

I find Eleanor, as she insists I call her, fascinating, with her easy, familiar manner and her ability to put people at ease, whether they are factory workers, air-raid victims, American soldiers, reporters, or aristocrats. Man or woman, royal or regular, she has the unique ability to move calmly and purposefully through the world, pursuing her own egalitarian agenda. *Was she always this way, I wonder, or like me, is it a skill she's had to learn?* From the reception she receives and the dignified manner in which she carries herself, I see that she is a public figure in her own right, no mere backdrop for her husband.

As we travel to Chequers for her first weekend in Britain, Eleanor shares her astonishment at the resilience of our people in the face of the constant assault and the vast array of roles undertaken by women. I am flattered, and I tell her so. "Those are the first two projects I undertook when the war began: providing safe shelters to ride out the nightly Nazi storm and ensuring that women serve in meaningful capacities. Of course, by now, I have a long, long list of other projects I oversee as well, typically those of domestic importance that Winston hasn't the time to tend, given the overarching international emergencies. Not to mention serving as Winston's confidante and partner, although I'm certain you understand what that is like." I arch my brow in a knowing expression; I don't need to tell Eleanor Roosevelt all the work involved for the wife of one of the most important men in the world.

Her brow furrows in confusion. "I must say, I'm surprised, Clementine."

"Whatever about, Eleanor?" Did I say something unusual? Surely this woman, sometimes referred to as "Madame President" by the White House staff because of her far-ranging influence, would find nothing shocking about my desire to place women in key jobs in wartime. Other women, yes, but Eleanor, no. Nor can I imagine anything else I said that could have startled her.

"In his visit to Washington last Christmas, your husband told us with great pride that you did not engage in any public activities or services of any sort. In fact, he praised you for your inclination to stay at home and tend to him." She says this slowly and tenderly, as if she intuitively understands Winston's statement might pain me, now that she knows me and comprehends the falsity in my husband's remark. But she is not one for dishonesty.

447

I am speechless. To have Winston diminish me and my contributions, to make the whole of my life so small, is more injury than I can bear. I have not minded serving in the backdrop of public life — I know my worth and actively dislike the spotlight — but to have my contributions publicly discounted and privately dismissed is another matter. How could Winston have brushed all my work aside as if it was meaningless? As if all I did all day was cater to his needs? I begin to process his statement — why he might have said it and how it makes me feel — when Eleanor clears her throat, interrupting the silence that has overtaken the automobile.

She says, "I'm sorry, Clementine. I know better than almost anyone else how hard it is to be married to the leader of one's country upon whom the additional enormous burden of saving the free world now rests. I understand how much they need from us, at least at certain times, and yet how we're sometimes shut out or relegated to the back seat, to use an American phrase. In the early years of our marriage — when Franklin was just starting out his political career and our marriage was admittedly quite different —"

She pauses, and I see that she is weighing

whether she should elaborate, whether she can confide in me what everyone already knows — that her husband keeps a veritable harem of adoring women at his beck and call and that his marriage is primarily a political alliance.

She decides against the intimate disclosure and continues more generally. "We shared political views, particularly on the domestic front, and I felt very much in partnership with him in our work. But as he became president and his power has expanded onto the international stage, my place has diminished. Once his focus changed from welfare to weapons, I decided I would operate independently of him."

Her path sounds so like my own. Without even consciously planning it, I add, "Shoring up the breech in the areas they've forgotten, as it were."

She meets my gaze. "Exactly, Clementine. We have our own sacred role, don't we? Separate from theirs."

Is my role truly separate from Winston's? While I certainly undertake my own projects, I'd always thought of the work as intertwined. Regardless, I feel compelled to disabuse Eleanor of the notion Winston planted. I enumerate my various and sundry ventures, including the daily role I play with

Winston himself. Her eyes brighten at the description of my air-raid shelter work and my advocacy for women, but that light extinguishes when I detail my full immersion in Winston's war work. Suddenly, I regret my words, for I see precisely how much she misses being part of the inner sanctum of power.

Desperate to change the tenor of our conversation, I ask about her children. She describes her five children, focusing most on her eldest, Anna, perhaps because she'd recently moved into the White House to serve as de facto hostess whenever Eleanor is busy with her own causes. But she is unusually hesitant in her speech, and she quickly turns the question back onto me. I realize that I'll have to report on the status of my own children, including Randolph, who is furious with me and Winston for permitting — if not exactly condoning — Pamela's affair with Averell. Even though he himself has had several mistresses, he felt entitled to indulge in a fit of righteous anger against us, and he stormed off in the spring to take a military position in Cairo, where he was injured returning from a long-term raid on Benghazi and returned back to England as an invalid. I'd known that my chickens would eventually come home to roost, but I hadn't thought it would happen quite so soon.

Quite uncharacteristically for me, I begin with my private truth. "It can be difficult to serve as both a wife to a husband such as Winston and also as a mother to the children of that marriage."

How could I have said aloud the words that I can barely acknowledge in the privacy of my own thoughts? That I only discussed openly with Dr. Lief while in treatment at Champneys? And to Eleanor Roosevelt, of all people? What on earth did I do?

Eleanor stares at me in astonishment, and my hand instinctively raises to my mouth, as if I could cram the words back inside. But from the gleam in her eye, I realize that she is not appalled but relieved. "I thought I was the only one. It is a gift to know I'm not alone."

"Why on earth would you tell Eleanor that I did nothing but tend to the home and hearth?" I had waited six long hours, through an interminable formal dinner at Chequers, to get Winston alone and say this.

He chuckles, "She said that, did she?"

How dare he laugh! "So you admit that you described me that way."

"Ah, that was back last Christmas when

451

Roosevelt and I were just getting to know one another. You know how bossy and free-thinking Eleanor can be, unconcerned with how she appears in dress or speech and the impact it has on her husband, not to mention her willingness to spout off her own opinions in utter disregard for Roosevelt's beliefs. Well, I didn't want to give her any ideas about similarities between you two."

"Do you think so little of me?"

"Now, Cat." He softens his tone, misguidedly believing that it will soften me.

"Don't Cat me." I am as furious as I've ever been. I'm tempted to pick up the little figurine on the side table and hurl it at him — I've thrown things in the past — but nothing at Chequers really belongs to us. It is on loan to us while Winston is prime minister. So I refrain from indulging in my impulse.

His voice assumes a groveling tone. "You know I rely on you for absolutely everything. You know I couldn't do this job without you at my side. But I can't have her thinking that, can I?"

Another terrible question rises up within me, and although I believe that I already know his response, I must ask it. I must hear him speak the answer aloud.

"Who do you think I am?"

He appears perplexed by my question. "Why, you're my wife, of course." Then, as if he is a student trying to please a particularly mercurial headmaster, he adds, "You are the prime minister's wife, in fact."

If he had slapped me, I could not have been more wounded. He only thinks about my identity and my worth in terms of the possessive, in terms of what I mean and what I do *for him.* I realize for the first time how dependent I've been on Winston for his admiration and how reliant I am for his permission to assume my own power, even if it is power derived from his own. No longer.

Winston is oblivious to the transformation taking place within me. He continues in this same vein, "And anyway, Eleanor serves perfectly detestable food, probably some sort of long-term punishment for Roosevelt's affair with that Lucy Mercer, which admittedly is detestable itself. But to instruct their cook to serve me creamy soup when my loathing of it is famous, well, Clemmie, you would never make such an error. You keep actual files on our guests' food preferences, by God. Your hospitality is legendary."

Unbeknownst to Winston — contrary to his intention, in fact — his words only confirm my discontent and my determination to change. Without speaking, I leave the room. So engrossed is Winston in his own verbiage that he does not even notice my departure. His voice continues to drone on in conversation with me even as I walk away and down the hall.

Ten days later, after Eleanor and I undertake an extensive tour of the English countryside bomb sites, I arrange a farewell dinner for her at Downing Street. Winston's guest list consists primarily of men — Brendan Bracken, now the minister of information; Field Marshal Sir Alan Brooke, chief of the Imperial General Staff; and Henry Morgenthau Jr., secretary of the U.S. Treasury — but I add a few women whose work deserves merit and further discussion with Eleanor, namely Lady Denman, head of the Women's Land Army, and Lady Limerick of the British Red Cross. The dinner conversation is lively, but as the discussion settles on the concept of peace, all the politeness and restraint Winston has exercised in his dealings with Eleanor reach their limit.

With a puff of his cigar, Winston pronounces, "The best way of achieving peace, a durable peace that is, is an agreement between England and the United States to prevent international war by combining our forces." He glances at Eleanor to gauge her reaction, which, knowing her social views, I can already predict will be negative. Why is he stirring up discord?

"The only way to achieve and maintain peace is to improve the living conditions of the people in all countries," she replies, meeting Winston's stare.

Neither will back down; I see that clearly. The rest of our dinner guests are visibly uncomfortable, quaffing drinks, squirming in their seats, and staring off into odd corners of the room. Why doesn't Winston understand that a complete accord with the United States — as represented by Eleanor right here and now — is necessary for peace today and that stirring up animosity with her will not bring us any closer to that desirable goal?

Mercifully, the staff enters with coffee and desserts, and I use this as an opportunity to end the standoff. "I think the time has come for us to leave you." I rise, and the women follow in the tradition of the men and women separating after dinner, an antiquated ritual with which I feel somewhat uncomfortable in Eleanor's presence.

We retire to the salon, where we feast on Battenberg cake and small talk. When a silence settles among the women, Eleanor rises and takes her leave.

I walk her to the front door, where her car awaits. "Let me get Winston for you. He will want to say his farewells," I offer.

"Let him enjoy his after-dinner talk with the gentlemen. I would like a moment alone with you, in any event."

"It would be my pleasure." *What would Eleanor like to speak with me about privately? I wonder.*

"I cannot thank you enough for all the time you've dedicated to showing me wartime Britain. Experiencing the courage of the British people firsthand has left an indelible impression upon me. The city of Canterbury, in particular."

My eyes well up with tears, thinking about our visit to Canterbury, where we were greeted by crowds of women and children, only to learn that they were bombed the next day and that many of the people who cheered for us had likely died. "It was my honor."

She reaches for my hand and gives it a reassuring squeeze. "I also want you to know how grateful I am for the insightful look you've given me into the British women and their war work. I plan on adopting some of your programs in America."

"It was my pleasure, Eleanor. We women are worth more than anyone knows."

"I wholeheartedly agree. In fact, it is about women's worth I'd like to speak. In the days to come, the alliance between our two countries will become ever more critical."

"Indeed." Eleanor is stating the obvious, and I wonder where she is leading.

"And I don't need to tell you that, with diplomacy being such a personal undertaking, the relationship between our husbands will be a key aspect in the success of that diplomacy."

I begin to understand her endgame, but I will not rush her. I will wait until she asks. "Of course."

"You and I are uniquely situated to play a role in that alliance, and I know what strides you've made in uniting our countries in your relationships with Misters Hopkins, Winant, and Harriman. So please forgive me if I'm being presumptuous, but I like to think we might be able to call upon one another when that alliance seems" — she fumbles for the correct word, a rarity for the typically articulate Eleanor — "less than peaceful."

"You can count upon me, Eleanor. I think you know by now that you are not alone."

CHAPTER FORTY-TWO

August 1943
Quebec, Canada, and Washington, DC

I take a seat by Winston's side at the conference table. Several of the men do not bother to mask their irritation at having me in attendance. I can nearly hear them think aloud, *Why in the devil did that blasted Churchill bring along his wife? As if we don't have enough impediments to peace.* Certainly none of the other world leaders brought their spouses, but then, I am accustomed to being the only woman at important political meetings and occasions. In the ten months since Eleanor's visit to England, I've sought out those situations more and more, in part because of her words and her husband's actions.

Since my time with Eleanor, shifts have abounded in the world and in my life. Many have been public and dearly welcomed. Although the war marches forward on all fronts, the newspaper headlines contain victories among the more troubling reports: while Russia begins to retake its lands, for example, the Germans are driven from North Africa, and the Allies invade Italy, but the Americans struggle against the Japanese in the Pacific. Some successes have been privately enjoyed, such as evenings playing bezique with my husband and attending the occasional play due to the slight relief the military successes bring. Other shifts have been less welcome, such as the toll on Winston's health from family tension over Pamela and Randolph's separation and from the travel required by far-flung conferences, arranged to bring world leaders in the same room to solve the jigsaw puzzle of the new military landscape.

Yet for me, the most potent shift has been quietly building within. My hypervigilance has become fine-tuned on the heels of my transformative conversation with Eleanor, and while I continue my work with the YWCA, the Russia fund, and British women, I seek out more opportunities to become involved in the war's bigger picture, beyond the usual vetting I do with Winston. I seek those areas where he's shown himself to be historically blind, even when my involvement requires me to challenge my-self.

By midsummer, from discussions with Winston, I sensed a certain coolness from Roosevelt, paired with a heightened admiration of the American president from my husband. I hinted at this, but my husband clung to his faith in the singular association between our English-speaking countries and to his confidence that Roosevelt shares this vision. When we learned that Roosevelt requested a secret meeting with the Russian leader Joseph Stalin that specifically excludes Winston, even my husband, who favors the American president beyond realistic measure, began to recognize that Roosevelt's convivial surface might not be without latent complexities. On the heels of this discovery, I suggested that I attend the upcoming conference in Quebec with him, and while I did not explain that I could help monitor the personal dynamics between Winston and Roosevelt, the rapidity with which he accepted my proposal told me that he understood on some level.

"Brilliant. I shall have the chance to cement my relationship with Eleanor," I offered as an explanation instead of the truth, although I was indeed looking forward to seeing Eleanor again. I was concerned about the dynamics of the highly secret military Quebec Conference, which was code-named Quadrant, and not only because of Roosevelt's recent outreach to Stalin. The chief participants in the conference were supposed to be Winston, Roosevelt, and the host, the Liberal prime minister of Canada, W. L. Mackenzie King, but when Winston suggested that King participate in all the meetings, Roosevelt strangely vetoed the idea, forcing King into a ceremonial role. Why would Roosevelt not want King present, an excellent man I'd come to know personally?

"Yes, yes," Winston concurred without a hint of his usual grumbling. "You'll be a boon to Anglo-American relationships."

Smiling at his compliment, I dared to go one step further. "What would you think if I brought Mary? She could even serve in an official capacity as your aide-de-camp."

He clapped his hands in delight at the thought of our favorite child — in the privacy of our chambers, we cannot deny to each other that she shares a special place in our hearts — joining us on this excursion. Mary and I have enjoyed many evenings alone together during her military leave, and I often stare in wonder at the steady, moral, and kind young woman she's become. *What did I ever do as a mother to deserve a child as marvelous as Mary?* I think. Every time the question enters my mind, the answer appears also: I turned over her parenting to the steady, moral, and kind Moppet, who remains a fixture in all our lives. Regularly, I thank God for Moppet and for Mary and ask forgiveness for the raggedy, inconsistent parenting I bestowed upon my other children, including poor little Marigold.

"I'll cable Roosevelt that you and Mary will be joining us in Quebec," Winston said.

I reached even further. I wanted to meet this president in person and assess the situation for myself. "Maybe he will even invite us to the White House afterward?"

"Ah, that would be grand, wouldn't it? Another chance to woo Roosevelt back into the golden vision of our alliance. Just think of the success you had with Harry, Gil, and Averell. I sometimes think that lend-lease — which set the stage for our current partnership, of course — was your doing."

After an arduous journey on the *Queen Mary* that left me anxious and physically drained, we finally reached Quebec. When the conference commenced, Eleanor was not present, as I'd hoped. I learned that once Roosevelt received our cable that Mary and I would come to Quebec, he sent Eleanor to visit U.S. troops in the Pacific. I guessed that he did so to ensure that there was no possibility she'd attend the conference. Rather than being delighted that Mary and I would be in attendance, as he'd suggested to Winston, it seems that he was ill-pleased and wanted to ensure that Eleanor would not follow suit.

I finally met the famous Roosevelt at the dinner before the first day of meetings. Mary was seated to Roosevelt's left, and I was assigned the chair to the president's right. He was already seated when we entered the room, but even immobile, even physically compromised, he exudes self-confidence and power. Beneath his glasses and the veneer of age, I could see the shadow of his younger, handsome self. *This is a man well accustomed to his way,* I thought. I would certainly recognize the quality, having lived with it for over thirty years.

He immediately engaged me in conversation about our voyage and the city of Quebec. His social skills were highly polished, but his manner contained a false, overconfident note, and he discussed nothing of substance. He's clearly used to creating an instant intimacy with others, because within the hour, without even asking for permission, he referred to me as "Clemmie," a nickname I reserve for family and close friends. Against my nature, I did not object, but this overfamiliarity makes me wary. I know my job is to charm Roosevelt, but I bristle against his presumptuousness. And while I admire his track record of social justice and reform, I perceive a certain vanity and speciousness in him that I do not like.

Why do I feel this negativity? I wonder. *The Americans have been our saviors in the war, and we remain dependent on them for food and military aid through the lend-lease plan.* Is it born from a sense of protectiveness for Winston, who blindly idolizes the man? I fight against my impression of Roosevelt because I know forging a tie with him and Eleanor is partly why I'm here.

Throughout the conference, I appear at some of the meetings and debrief with Winston afterward if my attendance is inappropriate. The meetings focus on Operation Overlord, the planned mass invasion of France that has been on the horizon for some time, and the resolution to concentrate more forces on the removal of Italy from the Axis by unconditional surrender, although other topics are considered, such as the coordination of efforts to develop an atomic bomb. From what Winston tells me, my impression of Roosevelt is confirmed. I think Roosevelt intends to assume the full mantle of control in this war and marginalize us. Perhaps this is what I'd sensed in Roosevelt from our first encounter, but when I suggest this to Winston, he dismisses it outright.

Given what I suspect about Roosevelt, how can I connect with him? If I confess this to anyone, they'd laugh at the ridiculousness of being chary of the charming Roosevelt and not the sometimes selfish or unruly Winston. Yet with Winston, one always knows precisely where one stands — even if one doesn't care for his self-indulgent behavior or his principles. With Roosevelt, the ground upon which one stands feels unsteady due to his inconstancy. In the days that follow in Quebec, I cannot summon up the necessary falsity to engage with him, and I fail to match the success I had with the other key Americans, Harry, Gil, and Averell.

After a restful stop in the Laurentian Mountains to help Winston with his lingering cold and fatigue, we stay at the White House as guests of Roosevelt and Eleanor, a place as lacking in charm and tolerable cuisine as had been rumored. While I delight in reuniting with Eleanor, I find it even more difficult to connect with the president in her presence. I think it's the coldness in his dealings with her. I also find her much more reserved in his presence than when it was just we two, and I wonder if I'm the same with Winston. I decide that even if I cannot call upon her in the ways that we'd discussed, I may be able to take a page from Eleanor's own book in order to fulfill my purpose here.

"Mummy, you're going to be perfect," Mary exclaims as I pace back and forth across the bedroom with my black silk dress swishing around my legs, practicing my speech. While I've given plenty of speeches in the past, this is my first press conference, and much depends upon it. *I am placing much on it,* I correct myself. *No one else is.* But that has always been my way.

"Thank you, darling," I say with a squeeze of her dear hand. "I think I'm ready."

"I'm certain you are," she says with an assured grin. We collect our purses and hats, and together, we descend the stairs to the waiting car.

When we reach the foyer, Mary asks,

"Shouldn't I get Papa?"

I squeeze her hand a little bit tighter. "No, darling, let him tend to his work." I don't think I could withstand the anxiety of this event with Winston watching my every move and analyzing my every word, much as I've been doing to him for the past thirty-five years.

My stomach lurches as we step out of the car to the facility where throngs of reporters await me. I climb the steps to the platform, with my sweaty hands clutching my prepared speech. After introductions are made, I launch into my speech, delivering it passably well due to my zealous preparation. But the pressure mounts when the time arrives for questions, when I know I must put aside all remnants of my natural reserve to achieve the goal for which I crossed the Atlantic. The goal I could not reach directly with Roosevelt in Quebec or Washington.

Squaring my shoulders, I remind myself of the friendly, direct manner Eleanor used with reporters, and I channel it. I charm them, joke with them, spar with them, all while highlighting serious issues. When several of the reporters break into a verse from "Oh My Darling, Clementine," an old American ballad with lyrics that lament a missing Clementine, I even joke back that, despite their serenading, unlike the song, I am not missing, but I am very much here to stay. I refrain from mentioning that the English pronunciation of my name — it rhymes with *Josephine* — varies from the American and thus doesn't even work with the song, because it would dampen the mood.

Funneling every ounce of charisma I have into the moments on the platform, I manage to accomplish with those anonymous reporters what I could not with Roosevelt, what Eleanor has managed to achieve despite the way her husband has marginalized her in the war. I bypass the president altogether and directly woo the reporters into embracing our country, and through them, woo the American people.

CHAPTER FORTY-THREE

December 16, 1943, to January 14, 1944
London, England; Carthage and Tunis,
  Tunisia; and Marrakech, Morocco

By the time I receive the envelope holding the cable, I have already sensed the message that lies within. Winston has been suffering from bouts of illness — including pneumonia — from the stress and the travel of his international conferences for nearly a year. The letters, calls, and cables about Winston's declining health have been arriving at the Number 10 Annexe almost from the moment he left for his most recent meeting with Roosevelt on November 11. In one of my recent cables from "Colonel Warden to Mrs. Warden," our current code names, Winston admitted to his belief that he *might* be suffering from the beginnings of pneumonia again, and Sarah, who is traveling with Winston as his aide-de-camp, wrote me about one startling evening in which, as he fell into a fevered sleep, he told Sarah not to worry if he dies, because he'd mapped out the winning strategy for the war. But nothing I say will make him return home until he feels ready.

Winston has been acting like a jilted, desperate suitor since we left Quebec and Washington in October. When we first returned home to London and reestablished ourselves at the Number 10 Annexe, he'd been delighted with the newspaper reports about me and my "witty, daring, and direct manner." But then he spent six sick, unhappy weeks at the Soviet legation in Tehran where he watched Roosevelt pursue Stalin as his primary cohort among the Allies, while he himself was ignored and even taunted by the other two leaders. My success with the American people — through my press conferences and tours — had done nothing to improve his relationship with Roosevelt, it seemed. Winston sat by as they overruled his doubts about a cross-Channel attack on France in spring 1944 as part of Operation Overlord.

I received these desultory reports while I remained in London, putting out fires among upset cabinet members, reviewing reports on Parliamentary debates and giving advice, and dealing with constituency matters. Despite my pleas that he was too ill to continue, he'd insisted on flying from Tehran to Cairo to pursue Roosevelt, and after that, despite his worsening condition, he'd refused to abandon a subsequent flight to Tunis to meet with General Eisenhower. All because he didn't want to appear weak to the American president.

But when I slice open the envelope with my silver letter opener, I see that the cable comes not from Winston's doctor, Lord Moran, as I'd guessed, but the cabinet. It contains a secret request that I fly out to Tunis, because Winston has just been diagnosed with pneumonia again and a fibrillating heart. They are worried he might not survive.

I want to crumple on the floor and cry. But everyone is staring at me, taking their cues from my behavior. I will myself to appear concerned but confident.

As a maid packs for me, I frantically pace around my office while aides phone the London airfields for an immediate flight, only to learn that they are all closed due to the thick fog that has settled over the city like a heavy blanket. Finally, one particularly tenacious aide informs me that if we can make it to RAF Lyneham in Wiltshire, the conditions at that site might permit our

471

departure. With Mary, Grace, and Jock in tow, we drive over four hours through the blackout and pea-soup fog to reach the airfield in Wiltshire. My heart thumping over Winston's condition, we board the plane.

After fifteen, then twenty, then twenty-five minutes without any movement, I begin to panic. What is going on? I worry that something has happened to Winston and that the terrible news is delaying our departure. Are they debating who is going to deliver the heartbreaking report to me? *No, no, no,* I think.

Finally, a beribboned officer steps onto the plane. After introducing himself, he says, "My deepest apologies, Mrs. Churchill, but this plane has a technical problem. We have been trying to find you another suitable aircraft here, but we only have an unheated Liberator bomber. We have checked, and no other airport is able to safely allow planes to depart."

I stand up and, without glancing at Mary, Grace, or Jock, say, "Then the unheated Liberator bomber it is."

The battle-hardened officer looks alarmed. "Mrs. Churchill, I'm not sure you understand the nature of the available plane. Its purpose is to fly and drop bombs, not carry passengers. Not only is there no comfortable, permanent seating, but there is no heat. It will be brutally cold."

"My husband, your prime minister, needs me. Please ready the aircraft for departure."

The staff switches our luggage and zips Jock, Grace, and me into flight suits — I've told Mary she needn't make this dangerous flight — and I almost laugh at the serious, bespectacled Grace in her flight suit, who insists on coming. But then I remember why we are taking this dangerous trip, and all humor leaves me. I step inside to find that the bomb racks had been removed and some kind soul has spread RAF rugs on the metal floor. Grace, Jock, and I settle into the makeshift seating as young soldiers pile blankets on us to protect us against the frigid temperatures. Temperatures that they themselves endure on a routine basis.

I am horribly nervous about Winston and, to a much lesser extent, this flight, and my legs are shaking. But I cannot afford to let this show. So after a few deep breaths, I reach into my luggage and pull out a backgammon board. "Care for a game?" I ask Jock.

Thirty games of backgammon, two thermoses of hot black coffee, and one stop in Gibraltar for refueling later, we touch down, and I step out of the bitterly cold airplane into the comparatively warm Tunisian afternoon. After a jarringly fast automobile ride, I reach General Eisenhower's white villa near ancient Carthage in Tunis, where Sarah, who had accompanied Winston on the latter leg of this trip, runs out to greet me.

Tears of relief are in her eyes. "We were so worried you wouldn't make it in time."

A sob catches in my throat. "Is he that bad?"

"He's been deteriorating and resisting every effort to make him well. You know how Papa is. I've been reading aloud to him from *Pride and Prejudice,* and the only thing he's said in four hours is a comparison of you to Elizabeth Bennet."

Tears streaming down my face, I follow Sarah and race to his side. But when I walk into his bedroom, I automatically step back. How could this diminished man, so sunken and gray, be my Winston? It has only been five weeks since I've seen him, but he is completely altered.

I am very nearly afraid to approach his bedside, and yet I do. When the heels of my shoes clatter on the hard bedroom floor, his eyes fly open, and I see the spark of my husband there in the blue depths. He croaks, "You came. You finally came."

I sink into the chair next to his bed, warm from the long hours Sarah has spent on it. I feel a strange mix of relief and fear course through me as I hold his hand and speak to him softly. He doesn't answer, but his breathing seems calmer, and once he's deeply asleep, the doctor whispers, "His color and his pulse are better than they've been for several days."

"This is an improvement?" I ask, incredulous. I have to choke back my tears at the state of my husband.

"Yes, one I attribute to your presence."

Lord Moran instructs me to take advantage of Winston's state to rest for a couple of hours, but within ninety minutes, Winston is awake, asking for me. Having determined to stay at his bedside constantly, I witness firsthand the overcooked dinner and breakfast he's served and immediately make alterations that I know will foster his health and energy. I insist on a new cook and discuss with him the sorts of clear soups and meats that will sustain Winston. Feeding this food to him myself, I ensure that he gets adequate nourishment and avoids stimulants, like his cigars and highly volatile work. Instead, I arrange for a steady stream of engaging but not taxing guests to visit with him for short periods, including his old crony Beaverbrook and Randolph. We hadn't seen Randolph for the better part of two years because of the strain about Pamela, and the tearful reunion between father and son conjures almost magical healing.

We celebrate a most unusual Christmas, with all of us, even Winston, attending services in a corrugated tin shed with stacks of ammunition. Just as the service draws to a close, I hear a fluttering of wings. A small white dove circles around and around near the ceiling, finally perching on a shelf just above the altar. A guardsman sitting behind me whispers rather loudly, "A dove means peace," and as soon as the service concludes, General Alexander rushes out to see if indeed Hitler has surrendered. When no such thing is reported, Winston announces, "Most likely, the minister released the dove himself to grant people a hopeful Christmas." From this wry remark, I know my husband is well on his way to recovery.

Soon afterward, we give General Eisenhower back his villa and depart to a villa at La Mamounia hotel in Marrakech for a period of convalescence. I serve as a barricade against all agitation, and in that capacity, I spend considerable time in the company of Winston's toughest military leaders, such as General Bernard Montgomery and Field Marshal Alan Brooke, the chief of the Imperial General Staff. Never allowing them to cow me, I instead develop a rather warm relationship with these otherwise intimidating men, who have no family to speak of in close proximity. I find them surprisingly desirous of companionship and increasingly candid about stressful matters, and I assist them as best I can with staffing matters and minor problems, always drawing a circle around Winston that I will not allow them to cross. When Winston's strength begins to show glimpses of itself, I arrange picnics in the Atlas foothills against a backdrop of ancient red buildings and pink and white oleander. I plan small, peaceful gatherings to stimulate his senses, but not overly so.

But I can forestall the war for only so long, and I begin to open the gate to more routine work, staffing the villa not only with the necessary domestic personnel but also, in addition to Jock and our own retinue, an army of secretaries and a naval officer. During Winston's long recuperation, the discontent with Winston I'd sensed simmering from Roosevelt and Stalin has come to a boil. I hear reports that Roosevelt plans to reach a favorable alignment with the perceived powerhouse of Russia, and it seems that Stalin no longer even pretends to tolerate Britain and its leader. They are moving ahead with decisions about critical missions; in fact, Winston just had a visit by Generals Eisenhower and Montgomery not only about his health as I'd hoped but about the massive assault plans made by Roosevelt and Stalin for the cross-Channel Operation Overlord. What choice does Britain have but to withstand this marginalization, dependent as we are on these countries for our survival in this war and beyond? But it saddens me beyond measure to think that our country, for so long the only one courageous enough to fight against the monstrous Hitler, must now take a secondary role.

Winston is in the process of becoming fully immersed in the developments about the alignment of America and Russia when General de Gaulle insists on visiting. De Gaulle, who had kept himself in check for a spell after our fateful dinner, has since treated Winston very badly, despite the fact that my husband has advocated for his leadership of the Free French. Roosevelt has resisted Winston's efforts to keep de Gaulle informed and has backed General Giraud instead of de Gaulle. With de Gaulle threatening to fly to Marrakech from Algiers, Winston must dive into the developments of war and the accompanying politics once again.

With a guest list of the British ambassador and the British consul general, I arrange a luncheon to "welcome" the general, whose behavior has been so impossibly poor that, at one point, Winston had to place him under house arrest. But I have a plan to neutralize this potentially disastrous occasion so that it does not lead to a devolution of Winston's health and a distraction from more critical issues. In order for this scheme to be successful, Winston must first maintain a cordial attitude toward de Gaulle during the luncheon, and I advise him so, extracting a promise from him.

We receive word that de Gaulle will arrive at approximately eleven o'clock. I arrange that Sarah and I will greet the general and his wife and that Sarah will lead Mrs. de Gaulle into the parlor while I take the general into the garden of our villa.

As de Gaulle and I stroll through the garden, I speak in French. I want there to be no confusion. "General de Gaulle, as you know, my husband has recently recovered from a serious bout of pneumonia."

"Of course, Madame Churchill. It was reported in the newspaper of every country in the free world," he answers perfunctorily.

"And you understand, of course, how critical his health and vitality are to the ongoing health and vitality of the free world you just mentioned."

"But of course." He begins to look slightly bored, which will suit my purposes well. I want to lull him into agreement.

"It seems we understand each other, as we always have." I pause.

"From our very first dinner," he answers with an absent smile and a brief nod.

"Then you will hopefully also understand that, in the past, you have acted in ways that have troubled my husband, even though he has staunchly defended you against not only the Nazis but the Americans as well."

He no longer looks bored. I can see that he is debating how to answer; he is torn between blaming my husband and his actions for his own misbehavior and acknowledging that, indeed, Winston has been his sole defender with the Americans, often at a cost to himself.

I take advantage of his hesitation. "The days ahead will be treacherous for us all, and not only in our fight against the Nazis. The health of my husband and the ease and stability of your relationship with him among the allies will be critical. Who knows

480

what might happen if that alliance breaks down? We must not risk it with unimportant misdeeds and accusations." I pause for effect. "General de Gaulle, please try to remember that we are your allies."

For once, de Gaulle is silent.

As the plates from the final luncheon course are cleared, the British ambassador tells a joke, and the chuckling does not subside until the dessert is served. The mood over the meal has been remarkably pleasant and relaxed, as everyone has remarked upon, except General de Gaulle and myself. We alone know why.

In the momentary silence, Winston speaks something that sounds like butchered French. As our guests chortle at this attempt, he says, "I decided that if I attempted French this afternoon, it might add a nice light touch to the occasion."

"If only it had been French, my dear," I say to more laughter.

"And here I thought I was doing rather well," Winston says with a rueful chuckle.

A huge burst of laughter overtakes every guest at the table, including de Gaulle himself. The general and I catch each other's eye, and he gives me a small nod of recognition and gratitude for the role I played today. I tuck away this rare, private acknowledgment of my involvement to bolster me for the long days ahead, where Winston will have to navigate the terrain of Roosevelt and Stalin as he navigates our country toward victory.

CHAPTER FORTY-FOUR

June 5–6, 1944
London, England

I am shaken awake by a troubled Winston. "I had the dream again, Clemmie," he whispers.

For a moment, I'm disoriented, but the pale light of dawn has begun to illuminate my bedroom in the Annexe, and I realize precisely where I am and exactly what the next twenty-four hours will bring. Suddenly, I am very awake and ready to help Winston in whatever way I can. In the coming hours, he will surely need it.

"Oh no." I pat the bed. "Crawl in."

I slide to the farthest edge of my bed to allow room for Winston. The bed groans with his weight, but I mask the sound with my shushing. I wrap my arms around him, and caressing his face, which is wet with tears, I ask, "Was it the same?"

"Exactly," he answers, then grows quiet.

483

He needn't describe the dream. He has had it frequently since the plans for Operation Overlord were finalized, and he's shared the nightmare in excruciating detail: wide beaches with sand dyed red with blood and crimson waves lapping the shore strewn with the bodies of dead soldiers. His recounting is so vivid that, some nights, I worry that I might have the dream myself. It is the embodiment of his deepest fear, and even though he would never say it, it harkens back to the horrible loss of life in the Dardanelles. He is terrified that history will repeat itself.

This day has loomed for years, ever since Roosevelt entered the war and the conferences between the American president and Winston began. Over those many meetings, they debated the strategy essential for the success of such a dangerous plan, a massive invasion of mainland Europe, and each man took turns fluctuating in enthusiasm for it, although no one ever doubted its necessity. Because of variability in resources and priorities, other missions took precedence, such as Operation Torch in northwest Africa, the Italian campaign, and support for Stalin's second front, but the concept of Operation Overlord never disappeared.

Once Roosevelt and Stalin became more

closely aligned — an inevitability that I'd worried about for months — the balance of power tipped in their favor, away from Winston, and my husband sensed Stalin and Roosevelt had already decided on this mass invasion of Normandy. This development did not surprise me, because I'd seen Roosevelt for the tactical game player and inveterate politician he is instead of the steadfastly loyal friend Winston believed him to be for too long. He offered Stalin and Roosevelt alternatives to the full-on invasion, which carried risks for enormous loss of life, as late as April, but Stalin insisted on this particular course, and Roosevelt agreed. What could Winston do? He told them we would proceed, and then he committed all his resources to the mission's success. Yet he desperately fears another Dardanelles.

In his despair over a bloodbath, he'd initially wanted to watch the D-Day landings from a destroyer near the beaches where the men would land. He'd first informed Admiral Ramsay, the commander of the landings, and then General Eisenhower, both of whom vehemently argued against his presence. But neither outright refusals on their parts nor pleas that his country needed him to stay in London swayed him

— until I organized a letter from the king. Only then did Winston agree to resist his nature to plunge into treacherous scenarios.

In approximately twenty-four hours, approximately one hundred fifty thousand American, British, Free French, and Canadian troops will land on the beaches of Normandy in the largest seaborne invasion in history, and Winston will not be there to watch. Even though I do not claim to have Winston's prescience, I know with utter certainty that this is the most critical moment yet in the future of the war. We are at the crux of it now, and we must show our mettle, whatever the outcome and whatever the cost.

I wrap Winston in my arms and whisper, "I know it seems impossible, but sleep if you can, Pug. Your country needs your full and alert attention in the morning."

Despite the decisive events secretly planned for the next dawn, the day proceeds as many other wartime days have proceeded. To call it familiar would be an insult to the word, but it follows a pattern to which I have become accustomed in this calamitous time. I spend the early morning answering the usual overflowing bag of letters from our citizens and forward their requests on to the requisite officials; I attend my regular committee meeting at Fulmer Chase Maternity Hospital for military wives; I visit air-raid shelters with Red Cross representatives, more important now than ever, as the Nazis have resumed their nightly bombing campaigns; I tour a bomb site and make lists of the victims' needs, unusually dire as the Nazis' new pilotless "buzz bombs" caused intense damage; and I speak to each of my daughters, taking care to check on Mary as she's alone, unlike the married Diana, and Sarah, who continues to see Gil, a situation not without its occasional discomforts. As I return to the Annexe, I see that Londoners are proceeding as normally as possible as well, walking purposefully through the streets and even stopping to chat with neighbors they pass. As if these were normal days.

How is Eleanor passing this surreal day? I wonder. Is she pretending at normalcy as well? Marveling at life progressing apace all around her, as I am? I cannot ask her; it would break all the security precautions around the secrecy of this day. Just as I can neither confide my worries in my sister, Nellie, nor share with her my hopes that we will avenge the death of her son Esmond.

Although Winston would like me to attend the meetings in the Map Room and elsewhere to assess the final details for the invasion — reviewing reports from meteorologists on critical weather and ocean conditions, checking on the status of the thousands of men in embarkation cages who are horribly sick on ocean waves, and plotting out the location of every one of the seven thousand vessels on his beloved maps — I cannot, except for the usual brief visit I make most days. The nation has known for some time that a mass invasion is imminent, and I can do nothing that might alert the populace and, through them, our enemies, to the precise date of the invasion. Winston's military commanders fear that a rushed visit to his offices will prompt concern; at least that's the excuse they offer for keeping me at bay. The day must appear as any other day, and I proceed as instructed. I have seen the plans displayed in the Map Room time and time again in any event. The exercise makes me feel like an actress in a woodenly acted and poorly scripted play, and I wonder if everyone I encounter sees through my ruse. Because all I can think about is Winston. How is my Pug faring?

Contrary to his military commanders' instructions, Winston and I do engage in one unusual activity, although no one else but us — and perhaps Mrs. Landemare — would notice. We dine alone. In the entire year, we have dined alone only three times. Tonight must be the fourth, as he needs my full attention and whatever comfort I can offer.

We are quiet at first, sipping on the clear soup that sustains him and the rare beef that doesn't but that he adores. He takes copious drinks from his wine, but I say nothing. If anyone deserves to anesthetize himself somewhat from the massive weight he carries upon his shoulders, he does. And I know it does nothing to dull his wits.

I break the uncommon silence. "I know this tension is unbearable, Pug. If I could lift it from you and carry it, even for the first night of the campaign, I would happily do so."

"Oh, Cat, I would never wish this burden upon you. It is your unsullied goodness that keeps me purposeful and strong."

"The decision is heavy, but it's the right one. I know it's colored with betrayals and fraught with uncertainties and apprehension — perhaps more than any other decision you've made in your entire life — but you are doing your duty to the people of this country. Just as you always have. Just as you must."

I share the same misgivings as Winston, but the die is cast, and the vessels have already set sail. The men are in place, ready to storm the beaches and perform acts of heroism and sacrifice never undertaken before. How can we betray them now by questioning our commitment to this course? I cannot allow him to fixate on such thoughts. He must have faith.

"But doing this duty may be doing them a great disservice," he answers.

"How? This campaign will begin the liberation of northwest Europe from the clutches of the Nazis. And that liberation will spread across Europe until we are free from the Nazis."

"But at what cost? I just cannot help but think that when the sun rises tomorrow morning" — he puffs on his cigar, and I realize that he plans on staying awake all night — "thousands of men may have been killed. As in my nightmare."

"And if you do not proceed with this mission and end this relentless war, how many tens of thousands *more* will die? Hundreds of thousands? What sort of nightmares will you have then?" I reach for his free hand and stare into his blue eyes. "My darling, everyone counts on you for the courage to continue."

He pauses for a long moment before answering but never averts his eyes. "I will stand watch and see how the mission unfolds. We are at the Rubicon."

I hold his gaze. "I will share your vigil with you."

"Will you really?"

"Tonight and every night."

CHAPTER FORTY-FIVE

May 12, 1945
London, England

My plane circles over the Northolt airfield over and over. A kind young officer offers me a drink in hopes of distracting me from the obvious, and I accept, but the drink does not make me oblivious. How could it? I distinctly heard the pilot receive a radio message that the Napier is delayed, and I know exactly who owns the Napier and what the message means. Winston is running late, and the pilot has been instructed to circle until the vehicle can race to meet my plane on the runway. Winston wants to make it seem as if he's been awaiting my arrival for hours.

I could be justifiably irritated by these circumstances. After all, I have been gone for nearly six weeks, and my arrival has been fixed for at least three days, with hourly updates. But I am too elated by the developments and too overjoyed to see my husband to suffer a silly fit of pique. I smile to myself, but my traveling companions, the stalwart Grace and Miss Mabel Johnson, the secretary to the Aid to Russia Fund, see it and return the grin. They undoubtedly believe I'm smiling at the relief and delight in finally returning home on the heels of such wondrous news, which is true. But I am also gratified by much more.

The plane finally makes its descent, and I slide my mirror out of my purse to straighten my hair and apply fresh lipstick. From my window, I see a flash of red as the wheels touch down, and I know it is Winston's car. No matter the lateness, he has arrived. Gathering my purse, I step off the plane from Russia.

When the gold-rimmed invitation arrived, I was quite astonished. I'd grown proud of the eight million pounds I raised for my Aid to Russia Fund, funded through voluntary salary deductions, door-to-door efforts, and events, even when Stalin and Roosevelt endeavored to take control over the war's direction. After all, I was doing it for the suffering people of Russia, not their leader. But I never thought I'd be singled out for my efforts, especially now that war victory was virtually assured. I usually watch and assess from the wings, unsung and often unnoticed.

Yet the Russian Red Cross wanted me to visit and inspect firsthand the excellent use they'd made of the funds I'd collected and the materials I'd sent over. The trip and accompanying tour throughout Moscow, Leningrad, and the countryside would take six to eight weeks, and I worried about leaving Winston for the long expanse, particularly because his mood had turned foul in the days after D-Day. Even though the casualties were far fewer than Winston had thought and Operation Overlord had indeed initiated the fall of the Nazis, the operation had yielded the terrible loss of thousands of men, and the mounting pressure to fell our enemy once and for all had soured his temper, not to mention the worry over his troubled relations with Roosevelt and Stalin. Even our jubilant November trip to Paris to celebrate its liberation at de Gaulle's invitation had provided only a brief respite from his mood. Did his temper stem from the awful loss of life and devastation to Europe due to the war, from concern over a lessening in his power as regards Stalin and Roosevelt, or from fears over the state of Europe in the postwar years and his place in a changing Britain? Winston was strangely silent on the subject of his humor.

"You must go, Clemmie. You could be the one positive force in Anglo-Russia relations and make some headway for us. Bridge the gap in our Russian relations and all that," Winston said when I expressed my reservations, although, of course, I did not attribute my hesitation to his mood. Since the February conference in Yalta, convened for the express purpose of discussing the postwar reorganization of Germany and Europe, Winston had grown increasingly suspicious of Stalin's intentions and the possible Soviet expansion into Eastern Europe. How could I decline the trip when Winston claimed it might do much good?

I accepted the invitation and ordered my uniforms for the journey, which designated my rank, vice president of County of London Branch, British Red Cross. When they arrived, the boxy fit was unflattering, so I had the uniforms tailored and paired them with the Red Cross berets. By the time I wore the uniform to my send-off tea with the queen, I almost felt like myself in the attire.

Although Winston expressed reservations about the trip when the departure date grew close, I proceeded, with Grace and Mabel joining me on the trip. When we stepped off the plane and onto the tarmac in Moscow on the first day of April after the multiday journey, I was overwhelmed with our welcome. Mr. and Mrs. Ivan Maisky, the former Russian ambassador and his wife; Paulina Molotov, the wife of the minister for foreign affairs; the British ambassador Sir Archibald Clark Kerr; and the American ambassador, our own Averell Harriman, were part of the large contingent greeting us. I was unexpectedly moved, as this was the first official reception held specifically for me and my contributions, and I had to hold back tears while I shook hands. Typically, everyone feted Winston.

I was immediately swept into a hectic itinerary of visits to hospitals, children's homes, factories that manufacture artificial limbs, ambulance stations, and portable hospital units. Every place our funds went, we toured, and for the first time, I comprehended the breadth and importance of the Aid to Russia Fund. Luncheons and dinners in my honor were interspersed with the touring, including one where I received the Soviet Red Cross Distinguished Service Medal, and we even attended the ballet, an exquisite version of *Swan Lake*.

Winston kept me apprised of the wartime

developments with constant cables and letters when they could be kept secure, as well as his horror over the concentration camps. We shared news and angst over the safety and location of Nellie's son Giles, who was still being held by the Nazis at Colditz Castle possibly for hostage value, and Winston's brother Jack, who was gravely ill. I prayed for their health and thanked God that at least, in this final hour of the war, we were not being troubled again by my awful Mitford cousins, some of whom had been pro-Nazi during the war and one of whom had actually married her husband at the home of Nazi leader Joseph Goebbels, with Hitler in attendance no less.

Winston's highest priority for my time in Russia was my meeting with Stalin. Ever since Winston expressed his displeasure at Russia's violation of the agreements made at the conference in Yalta, the terms about Poland and Romania specifically, Stalin had become ice cold toward my husband. Winston requested that I make a very particular statement to Stalin about his belief that an accord between Russia and English-speaking countries will be reached soon. I rehearsed the phrase over and over, even attempting it in Russian before jettisoning the effort and deciding that I would rely upon the interpreter. God knew I could not afford to misspeak in Russian and deliver the entirely wrong message.

The appointment with Stalin was set, but when the hour arrived, only I was permitted to enter his chamber, not Grace or Mabel. The long corridor from the guards' station to enormous double doors seemed interminable without their company, and when another set of guards granted me access, I entered a room that was no less vast than the corridors. At the far end of the impressive study, decorated in a neoclassical style, sat the dark-eyed Stalin behind his desk. Quite rudely, he did not glance up as he scribbled away, although he could hear me approach as my heels clattered and echoed in the vast space. Only when I stood directly before him did he look at me and, through an interpreter, say, "We thank you for the great work undertaken by the Aid to Russia Fund."

Nodding, I answered by offering my gratitude for his invitation and wonderful reception and handing him a gift. "From the Churchills."

As the Russian leader unwrapped the case containing a gold fountain pen, I said the exact words Winston urged me to say to Stalin.

When I was done speaking, he stared at me in complete silence for a long minute. My nerves started to overtake me, thinking about all the horrific rumors of torture at the Kremlin that we'd heard for years. I watched as he put the gold pen to one side of his desk and finally said, "I have my own writing utensil."

What did this vaguely ominous sentence mean? I surmised that relations between Moscow and London had deteriorated even further since I received my last missive from Winston, who, in any event, was severely limited in his reports because my mail was monitored. Fear began to set in. The Russians might be our Allies in these last days of the war, but they most certainly were not our friends. I did not respond, as I had no idea what to say, and I wondered what the future would hold for Britain and Russia.

"Thank you for your visit, Mrs. Churchill," Stalin finally said tersely, then he nodded to his guard, who promptly escorted me from the room.

His guards shepherded me out and delivered Grace, Mabel, and me directly into a waiting, well-equipped train that would take us across Russia to see firsthand the sites benefiting from our funds, beginning in Moscow and traveling to Leningrad. Although my interaction with Stalin had chilled me to the core, the cheers of the Russian people and their gratitude for the Aid to Russia Fund warmed me as we left the station. I could not make sense of the disparity between the two, other than Stalin's feelings toward my husband.

As our train made one of its many stops in locales both urban and rural over the next few weeks, we visited the devastated city of Stalingrad. We drove through a vast public square with a towering obelisk at its center, and I asked Mrs. Kislova, the interpreter assigned to us from the All-Union Society for Cultural Relations with Foreign Countries, about its significance, assuming that it was a historical treasure of some sort. "It is called the Brothers' Graves, and it marks a huge common grave for the thousands of citizens who died defending our city against the Nazis," she explained as we passed by houses that were no more than hovels that families had dug out of piles of rubble, and then she announced, "We are here."

Our planned visit for the afternoon was a children's home where, Mrs. Kislova had informed us, we would see mounds of equipment and supplies that our fund had financed. Grace, Mabel, and I stepped over debris to reach the imposing doors of the bullet-scarred hospital that, Mrs. Kislova told us, had been marked as a special target by the *Luftwaffe* bombers.

Her eyes wide, Grace, usually quiet, asked, "The Nazis intentionally targeted a children's hospital?"

Our interpreter gave us a matter-of-fact nod and answered, "To break our spirits."

When we entered the hall, children lined the halls of the foyer and wards. Wounded eight-year-old boys who'd fought with the partisans stood alongside scarred six-year-old girls who quaked at the sight of an unfamiliar face. Children without limbs, children with wracking coughs, children with oozing wounds, and children without eyes or ears. And that was the children who were capable of standing. Many more children lay in row after row of beds, most of them listless or unresponsive.

"Most of these children would not be alive without the aid you provided," Mrs. Kislova interpreted for the hospital warden. "Especially because most of their parents are dead."

Tears streaming down my cheeks, I stared directly at the worst casualties of war, for whom our supplies and medication could only stanch their unfathomable injuries.

Grace, Mabel, and I were still reeling from

our visit to the children's hospital when our train pulled into the next station, and I saw Mr. and Mrs. Molotov standing on the platform. What on earth were they doing here? Suddenly, my heart began beating wildly. Had something happened to Winston? Surely the British ambassador or Averell would have come if that was the case, I told myself.

Their aide, a Russian military officer, boarded our train first and had an animated conversation with our interpreter. They reached some kind of agreement, and then the Molotovs stepped onto train. Mrs. Kislova nodded deferentially to them as they passed, and I stood up and greeted them warmly as they entered my car. But Mr. Molotov's face was morose. "We come with bad news, Mrs. Churchill. President Roosevelt is dead," he said.

Roosevelt? Dead? It seemed incomprehensible, even though Winston had told me that he looked quite ill at the Yalta Conference with a grayness about his face and eyes. While I'd harbored misgivings about the American leader for some time, I was grateful for the role he played alongside us in this awful war, and I could not fathom the new world order without him. *How is Eleanor faring?* I wondered. More importantly for me, how was Winston?

I consoled Winston over a telephone call at our hotel later that day, and together, we scripted a letter for him to send to Stalin, which he hoped would also appear in the Russian newspapers. But nothing could dull the shock and distress he felt, I knew. No matter Roosevelt's recent machinations, Winston's loyalty had remained intact. He urged me to continue the tour, as every effort must be made to mend the British-Russian relationship, so we continued.

Not until we made our final return into Moscow did I feel a tug to return home once more, this time for more jubilant reasons. The British embassy sent over a representative to my hotel with the news that Mussolini had been captured and executed by anti-Fascists and that this was followed by the suicide of Hitler. When Germany finally surrendered on May 7, the tug to go home became a firm pull. Despite the fact that I couldn't make it back to London in time for Victory in Europe Day, or VE Day, a fact that upset me greatly, I made fixed plans to return to London and Winston.

In a surreal way, I did spend VE Day with Winston after all. On May 8, Grace, Mabel, and I gathered at the British embassy with the ambassador, his wife, Averell, and the diplomatic staff, and we heard my husband's voice broadcasting victory and freedom over the radio from London. Even though we were thousands of miles apart, even though I could not watch him make his victory statement to the House of Commons, even though I could not be there to see thousands cheer him on in Parliament Square, I felt my fingers link with his in celebration of our victory.

But as we walked out onto the Moscow streets afterward and I talked about the victory with the Russian diplomats and our interpreter, I began to understand how very divergent their views on the war and the armistice were from our own, and I marveled at how dissimilar the same event can appear to different people. *How distinct are the lenses through which we each perceive the world,* I thought. I prayed that the citizens we'd helped with the Aid to Russia Fund and the connections we'd made on this visit might serve as a bridge between Britain and Russia, if and when the differences in our perspectives divided us even further, as Winston was already predicting.

I take the final step off the plane and onto the tarmac, smiling back at Grace, who's been such a trusted secretary and friend these long years of the war. Winston waits for me on the edge of the runway, his arms brimming with several bouquets' worth of flowers and a wide, ebullient smile on his lips. Simultaneously, we walk forward until we meet in the middle, wrapping our arms around each other. The vibrant flowers are pressed within the folds of our embrace.

"Cat, how I've missed you," he whispers into my ear. Then he suddenly pulls back and looks me up and down. "You are still wearing your Red Cross uniform," he declares, as if I've forgotten.

I smile but do not comment. I'm delighted that he's noticed without me having to draw attention to my attire. I want him to view me in uniform as I've come to view myself in uniform. As one who's served her country well.

We separate reluctantly but link arms as we stroll toward Winston's red Napier. "We have peace, Pug. You made this happen," I say to him with a wide grin and a loud guffaw. My joy is unbridled at this news, no longer new, because I am in his presence; it almost hadn't seemed real until I could say the word aloud to him.

"No, Clemmie, we did this. It is *our*

peace," he replies with a squeeze of my hand.

The sun sets in swaths of shimmering gold against the sharp line of the horizon where sky meets land, and as it descends, I feel an unfamiliar tranquility descend upon me as well. All the strain and struggle that have comprised my life — my lonely and strange childhood, the wild swings of my unusual marriage, my struggle with motherhood, my compunction to constantly prove myself worthy, the tumult of two wars, even my pervasive sense of otherness — seem to fall away. In the vacuum of calm, I see with unexpected clarity that, without my unique hardships and failings, particularly with my children, I could not have become the Clementine who forged this path through politics and history, and without me, my husband could not have become the Winston who helped deliver peace to this broken world.

As we walk, I experience the most unusual sensation, as if we are passing into history at this very moment. Not later, when future generations have had their chance to dissect our actions and reconsider our decisions, but right now, as we stare out at the glow of the sunset on the landscape. When the successors to our time appraise Winston and this awful war, as they surely must, I know that they will see Winston's hand on the pen that scribes history. But, I wonder, will they see that my hand has also been on the pen all along?

AUTHOR'S NOTE

The ubiquitous cigar. The Homburg hat.
The pugnacious spirit. The famous
speeches. The V for victory sign. These
recognizable emblems of Winston Churchill
instantly evoke the famous British icon
credited with leading his country to victory
in World War II. I encountered the legendary statesman and his pervasive symbols
over and over again as I researched my novel
The Only Woman in the Room, which takes
place, in part, during World War II. But, as
often happens when I'm down the rabbit
hole of research, I began to wonder about
the women — in this case, one woman in
particular. Did Churchill undertake his
famous work alone? Where was his wife of
more than three decades during the fabled
events of World War II? What was she like?
These questions began to plague me, and I
became intrigued by the idea of Clementine
Churchill.

I took a short detour in my research about Hedy Lamarr to investigate Clementine Churchill. From the moment I dipped into her unusual background and read about the first time she met Winston, I was hooked by this bright, complicated, loyal, bold, and sometimes contentious woman. Her legacy was important yet largely unknown, and I knew I needed to tell my version of Clementine's story next.

As I followed her life and her relationship with Winston through the research, I realized that Winston wasn't alone during World War II — even though he's always pictured that way — but that Clementine was standing by his side all along, guiding him in his decision-making, influencing governmental leaders toward their shared goals, helping him navigate the tricky landscape of colleagues and staff, raising their children, and ensuring his well-being. I learned that she shared the burden of leadership not only during World War II, but in World War I as well, and she bolstered him all the years in between. *Lady Clementine* explores the tumultuous relationships and life of Clementine Churchill and hopefully brings out from the shadows into the light of modern day her potentially world-changing contributions.

But the more I learned about Clementine's personality and the role she played in her relationship with Winston, the more I came to see that she was iconic in her own right. A woman with a natural, keen interest in political issues — in particular, women's right to vote and the Liberal Party's social and humanitarian issues — she was stymied by her era's proscriptions on women's overt involvement in the political realm. When she married Winston, with whom she shared a passion for politics, she plunged into his political world in a manner that was unprecedented for its time. Carving out a unique role both behind the scenes and, to a limited extent, before the public, she rose up and claimed a political space that society told her she could not do. In asserting her own power — even if it derived from Winston — she wielded it for the good of the British people in wartime and for women in general. We may still be reaping the benefits of her labors today.

As Clementine assumed the mantle of leadership, she had to overcome her own hesitations and self-doubt to claim this opportunity and fulfill her long-held convictions about women's rights and social issues, thereby serving as an inspiration on many levels. In light of this, I can't help but wonder what more she might have ventured and accomplished had the strictures of her time been different. In an era more encouraging of women's ambitions, might Clementine Churchill have been a highly visible political participant rather than a largely invisible but otherwise mighty force? I'll leave that question to you now.

READING GROUP GUIDE

1. Winston Churchill is one of the most recognizable figures of modern history. What did you know about his personal life before you read *Lady Clementine?* Did you have any understanding of his wife and children in particular, and did the book challenge any preconceived ideas about his private life?
2. While Clementine's ancestral background was aristocratic, she grew up in relatively reduced financial circumstances, carrying the additional burdens of a peripatetic childhood and the uncertainty of her paternity. How did her unusual upbringing affect her behavior and opinions? How, in turn, did her belief system and background affect Winston, if at all?
3. *Lady Clementine* opens with Clem-

entine describing herself as being "set apart" from the rest of society. How did this feeling manifest throughout the novel, and did it change throughout her life? How did this sense of otherness impact her relationship with Winston?

4. Throughout the course of the book, Clementine is transformed from a bright but hesitant and sometimes self-doubting young bride into the formidable wife of the prime minister, with a power base of her own and an impressive list of initiatives. Did Clementine's metamorphosis surprise you, particularly given the historical limitations of women in the political realm? How did Clementine's relationship with Winston both further her growth and hinder it? What sacrifices did she have to make in order to become such an influential political wife?

5. While motherhood was different in the time period of the novel and the class in which the Churchills operated, Clementine struggled with it. How would you characterize Clementine as a mother? Did she evolve as a parent over the years? Do you

feel that she crossed the line of acceptability, even in the context of her time? How did her relationship with Winston impact her mothering? Compare and contrast modern motherhood with historical motherhood from this time, keeping in mind variations in class.

6. What drew Winston and Clementine together, and how did that change over the decades? How did Winston's political alliances impact their interactions? What goal united them when their political views weren't precisely aligned?

7. After she spends time with Eleanor Roosevelt, Clementine comes to a shocking realization about Winston's view of her identity, or at least the way he presents her identity to the Roosevelts. What is the importance of female relationships in Clementine's story and in the stories of other strong women?

8. Which, if any, of the characters in *Lady Clementine* do you find yourself relating to the most? Did you connect with Clementine?

9. What is the most surprising thing you learned about Clementine? Did

515

it relate to her parenting? Her marriage to Winston? Her relationship with Terence Philip on the *Rosauro?* The amount of time away from her family?

10. Please discuss the ways in which Clementine's life encompassed issues that were not only historic but modern as well.

11. Winston Churchill left an enormous mark on history, and he is credited with saving Britain during World War II — but you now know that Clementine was a deeply influential figure in Winston's professional and personal life behind the scenes. Do you think he would've been as successful if he didn't have Clementine supporting him? How would you characterize her legacy?

A CONVERSATION
WITH THE AUTHOR

While her husband is an enormously famous figure, Clementine Churchill is often relegated to the margins of history. How did you first hear of her, and what about her made you want to lend her story a voice?

During my time researching and writing books that — I hope — excavate important historical women from the shadows of the past and bring them out into the light of modern day, I feel as though I've developed an antenna for these women. As I was researching the onset of World War II for my novel *The Only Woman in the Room*, Winston Churchill, of course, figured prominently, and I couldn't help but wonder about his family, his wife in particular. While I do not profess to be a Winston Churchill expert, I did find it peculiar that I knew nothing about the spouse of one of the most recognizable men in history. Who was she?

What was she like? Where was she during all these world-changing events? So I went down the rabbit hole, as I often do when I'm intrigued, and I learned that Clementine Churchill was not only the quintessential woman behind the man, but also standing beside him — and often in front of him — helping him lead through some of the most critical moments in modern history. I knew hers was a story that deserved to be told.

Lady Clementine relies on a great deal of research, from the minutiae of British politics to the personal lives of historical figures. What did your research process look like for this book?

In some ways, my research for all my novels is quite similar. I begin by assembling and delving into any original source material that I can locate about the woman I'm writing about, filling in informational blanks with secondary source materials. Once I've finished amassing that data and created a timeline and broad outline, I'll cast my net wide, researching relevant details about the character's time period — from macro information such as political and military issues, cultural developments, and socioeconomic circumstances, to micro details such as attire, popular foods, and home decor. Unique aspects arise for each woman, of course, and I often find myself homing in on particular pieces of research. In Clementine's case, it was a collection of letters between Clementine and Winston spanning the course of their relationship (which encompassed much of their lives) assembled by their daughter Mary. Not only did these letters provide singular insight into Clementine's voice, but they also gave me an extraordinary look into the feelings they shared with each other, the way they spoke to each other and the topics about which they communicated.

This book is a piece of historical fiction, which of course means that while it's based heavily on historical figures and events, it necessitates a bit of artistic license. Were there any specific moments or characters that forced you to rely more on fiction than fact?

I approached this novel as I did my other historical fiction: I look at the research on the macro and micro aspects of my character's world as the architecture of my story — the foundation, the pillars, the roof. But in between the pillars and in the space between the foundation and the roof, there will always be gaps, unknowns from the research. And it is in those gaps that the fiction comes in to tell the story, using — I hope — a blend of the logic I developed over my decade as a lawyer, as well as my familiarity with the characters, time, and setting I've attained from the research. As just one example of this, on the night before D-Day, we know that Clementine spent part of that evening with Winston. But we do not know the precise conversations they shared or the comfort and advice she might have offered him, and we cannot know the exact impact those exchanges might have had on his decision-making and leadership on the critical day. Therein lies the fiction.

Like any relationship, Clementine and Winston's marriage changes with time. Theirs is especially strained, however, because of their growing political differences. Given this emotional complexity, was it difficult to write the evolution of their relationship?

Clementine and Winston had a particularly complex relationship because their bond not only filled emotional voids left in each other by their difficult upbringings, but it also fed their shared passion for politics and its underlying goals. In some ways, these two aspects of their relationship were intertwined. So when Winston's politics began to deviate from Clementine's, their relationship became difficult in some respects, and I had to really dig in to her psyche to envision how this would have affected her, given her feelings for her husband and their ongoing projects, as well as her somewhat fragile nerves. I imagined that, in order to carry them through challenging times, she focused upon those values that united them — the betterment of the lives of the English people and their safety in wartime — instead of the issues that divided them.

Clementine's inner conflict between her role as a mother and her career is something that can resonate with many contemporary women. Were you inspired by personal experience when you delved into this issue?

As a mother myself, I found researching and writing about Clementine's role as a mother particularly intriguing and eye-opening. I learned a tremendous amount not only about her very specific parenting experiences, but also about the mothering standards for women of her class in that era, which were quite different and much more hands-off than our own, and it made me reconsider various modern-day practices. This understanding provided a lens through which I could view Clementine's parenting decisions more fairly, because they were oftentimes very dissimilar to the choices mothers would likely make today. But no matter the distinctions between parenting practices of her day and ours, I believe Clementine's struggles over making the correct choices for her children — and living with the ramifications of poor selections — is something to which all mothers can relate, particularly those who juggle career demands as well.

As a writer of historical fiction, a large part of your job consists of creating deep inner lives for characters based on real people. Have you ever worried about misrepresenting someone or writing them inaccurately?
I always worry about my representation of the historical women about whom I write. I feel incredibly honored and privileged to tell their stories, along with a tremendous responsibility toward them. I try to keep that sense of responsibility at the forefront of my mind as I write my fictional interpretation of a piece of their histories — always

reminding myself that it is indeed fiction that I write.

Clementine was a deeply influential figure in Winston's professional and personal life. Do you think he would have been as successful if he hadn't had Clementine supporting him?

While no one can know for certain what Winston's legacy would have been without Clementine, I believe she was integral to his success. Historians can debate the impact her insights, intellect, and advice may have had on his political decision-making and leadership — particularly since the research isn't as robust as I might like in that arena — but there can be no doubt that she supported him enormously from an emotional perspective. That role alone was very likely critical to Winston's well-being, which ensured that he could fulfill the necessary leadership position in World War II. That said, I personally believe her professional and political impact was wide-ranging and key.

ACKNOWLEDGMENTS

The story *Lady Clementine* might have languished in the shadows — like countless narratives of other key historical women — without the support and dedication of so many people. I must begin, as always, with my wonderful agent, Laura Dail, whose fabulous advocacy and impeccable advice made this book — in all its forms — possible. I am incredibly fortunate to have the phenomenal folks at Sourcebooks helping to make *Lady Clementine* into the best version of itself and tirelessly championing its story, in particular my delightful and brilliant editor, Shana Drehs; Sourcebooks's inspiring leader, Dominique Raccah; not to mention the astonishing Todd Stocke, Valerie Pierce, Heidi Weiland, Kaitlyn Kennedy, Lizzie Lewandowski, Heather Hall, Michael Leali, Margaret Coffee, Beth Oleniczak, Tiffany Schultz, Ashlyn Keil, Adrienne Krogh, Will Riley, Danielle McNaughton, and Travis Hasenour. And my appreciation for all the marvelous booksellers and librarians and readers who have enjoyed and recommended *Lady Clementine,* as well as my other books, is boundless.

My extended family and friends have been key to my writing process, not to mention inspirational, especially my Sewickley crew, Illana Raia, Kelly Close, Laura Hudak, Daniel McKenna, Ponny Conomos Jahn, and my sistas. But it is Jim, Jack, and Ben — my boys — to and for whom I am endlessly grateful.

In terms of gratitude, I would be remiss not to mention the invaluable work undertaken by several writers, researchers, and family members to highlight Clementine Churchill's life and legacy. While there is an abundance of intriguing writing on Winston Churchill that touches on his wife, I highly recommend the following books for those who want to delve more deeply specifically into the nonfiction world of Clementine: (1) Mary Soames's *Winston and Clementine: The Personal Letters of the Churchills,* (2) Mary Soames's *Clementine Churchill: The Biography of a Marriage,* (3) Sonia Purnell's *Clementine: The Life of Mrs. Winston Churchill,* and (4) Jack Fishman's *My Darling Clementine: The Story of Lady Churchill.* And for those who relish an even deeper dive — one of a physically immersive nature — I recommend visits to Blenheim Palace, Chartwell, and the Churchill War Rooms, among many Churchillian locations in and around London, to get a sense of how the inimitable Clementine Churchill actually lived, and not just in my fictional worlds.

ABOUT THE AUTHOR

Marie Benedict is a lawyer with more than ten years' experience as a litigator at two of the country's premier law firms and Fortune 500 companies. She is a magna cum laude graduate of Boston College with a focus on history and a cum laude graduate of the Boston University School of Law. She is also the author of the *New York Times* bestseller *The Only Woman in the Room*, *Carnegie's Maid,* and *The Other Einstein.* She lives in Pittsburgh with her family.